AF553196

INTELLIGENT SYSTEMS AND NEURAL NETWORKS

INTELLIGENT SYSTEMS AND NEURAL NETWORKS

By

M. S. Chauhan

2016

SBS Publishers & Distributors Pvt. Ltd.
New Delhi

ISBN 13 : 9789380090764

First Published in 2016

Published by:

SBS PUBLISHERS & DISTRIBUTORS PVT. LTD.
2/9, Ground Floor, Ansari Road, Darya Ganj,
New Delhi - 110002,
INDIA
Tel: 0091.11.23289119 / 41563911
Email: mail@sbspublishers.com
www.sbspublishers.com

Preface

The integration of different learning and adaptation techniques to overcome individual limitations and to achieve synergetic effects through the hybridization or fusion of these techniques has, in recent years, contributed to a large number of new intelligent system designs. Computational intelligence is an innovative framework for constructing intelligent hybrid architectures involving Neural Networks (NN). Neural network is an artificial system. It is modeled after the way the human brain works through imitating how the brain's neurons are fired or activated. Several computing cells work in parallel to produce a result. This is usually seen as one of the possible ways artificial intelligence can work. Most neural networks can tolerate if one or more of the processing cells fail. This report is an introduction to Artificial Neural Networks. The various types of neural networks are explained and demonstrated, applications of neural networks like ANNs in medicine are described, and a detailed historical background is provided. Artificial neural networks (ANNs) are a family of statistical learning algorithms inspired by biological neural networks (the central nervous systems of animals, in particular the brain) and are used to estimate or approximate functions that can depend on a large number of inputs and are generally unknown. Artificial neural networks are generally presented as systems of interconnected "neurons" which can compute values from inputs, and are capable of machine learning as well as pattern recognition thanks to their adaptive nature.

Editor

Contents

Chapter 1

IMPROVED KOHONEN FEATURE MAP PROBABILISTIC ASSOCIATIVE MEMORY BASED ON WEIGHTS DISTRIBUTION

Shingo Noguchi[1] and Osana Yuko[1]

[1] Tokyo University of Technology, Japan

INTRODUCTION

Recently, neural networks are drawing much attention as a method to realize flexible information processing. Neural networks consider neuron groups of the brain in the creature, and imitate these neurons technologically. Neural networks have some features, especially one of the important features is that the networks can learn to acquire the ability of information processing.

In the field of neural network, many models have been proposed such as the Back Propagation algorithm [1], the Kohonen Feature Map (KFM) [2], the Hopfield network [3], and the Bidirectional Associative Memory [4]. In these models, the learning process and the recall process are divided, and therefore they need all information to learn in advance.

However, in the real world, it is very difficult to get all information to learn in advance, so we need the model whose learning process and recall process are not divided. As such model, Grossberg and Carpenter proposed the ART (Adaptive Resonance Theory) [5].

However, the ART is based on the local representation, and therefore it is not robust for damaged neurons in the Map Layer. While in the field of associative memories, some models have been proposed [6 - 8]. Since these models are based on the distributed representation, they have the robustness for damaged neurons. However, their storage capacities are small because their learning algorithm is based on the Hebbian learning.

On the other hand, the Kohonen Feature Map (KFM) associative memory [9] has been proposed. Although the KFM associative memory is based on the local representation as similar as the ART[5], it can learn new patterns successively [10], and its storage capacity is larger than that of models in refs.[6 - 8]. It can deal with auto and hetero associations and the associations for plural sequential patterns including common terms [11, 12]. Moreover, the KFM associative memory with area representation [13] has been proposed. In the model, the area representation [14] was introduced to the KFM associative memory, and it has robustness for damaged neurons. However, it can not deal with one-to-many associations, and associations of analog patterns. As the model which can deal with analog patterns and one-to-many associations, the Kohonen Feature Map Associative Memory with Refractoriness based on Area Representation [15] has been proposed. In the model, one-to-many associations are realized by refractoriness of neurons. Moreover, by improvement of the calculation of the internal states of the neurons in the Map Layer, it has enough robustness for damaged neurons when analog patterns are memorized. However, all these models can not realize probabilistic association for the training set including one-to-many relations.

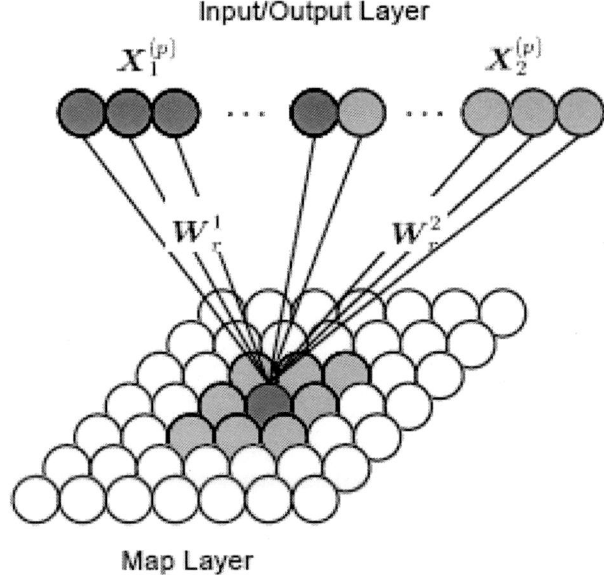

Figure 1. Structure of conventional KFMPAM-WD.

As the model which can realize probabilistic association for the training set including one-to-many relations, the Kohonen Feature Map Probabilistic Associative Memory based on Weights Distribution (KFMPAM-WD) [16] has been proposed. However, in this model, the weights are updated only in the area corresponding to the input pattern, so the learning considering the neighborhood is not carried out.

In this paper, we propose an Improved Kohonen Feature Map Probabilistic Associative Memory based on Weights Distribution (IKFMPAM-WD). This model is based on the conventional Kohonen Feature Map Probabilistic Associative Memory based on Weights Distribution [16]. The proposed model can realize probabilistic association for the training set including one-to-many relations. Moreover, this model has enough robustness for noisy input and damaged neurons. And, the learning considering the neighborhood can be realized.

KFM PROBABILISTIC ASSOCIATIVE MEMORY BASED ON WEIGHTS DISTRIBUTION

Here, we explain the conventional Kohonen Feature Map Probabilistic Associative Memory based on Weights Distribution (KFMPAM-WD)(16).

Structure

Figure 1 shows the structure of the conventional

KFMPAM-WD. As shown in Fig. 1, this model has two layers; (1) Input/Output Layer and (2) Map Layer, and the Input/Output Layer is divided into some parts.

Learning Process

In the learning algorithm of the conventional KFMPAM-WD, the connection weights are learned as follows:

1. The initial values of weights are chosen randomly.
2. The Euclidian distance between the learning vector $X^{(p)}$ and the connection weights vector Wi , $d(X^{(p)}, W_i)$ is calculated.
3. If $d(X^{(p)}, W_i)$ ^{t} is satisfied for all neurons, the input pattern X(p) is regarded as an unknown pattern. If the input pattern is regarded as a known pattern, go to (8).
4. The neuron which is the center of the learning area r is determined as follows:

$$r = \mathop{\mathrm{argmin}}_{\substack{i:D_{iz}+D_{zi}<d_{iz} \\ (for \forall z \in F)}} d\left(X^{(p)}, W_i\right)$$

where F is the set of the neurons whose connection weights are fixed. diz is the distance between the neuron i and the neuron z whose connection weights are fixed. In Eq.(1), Dij is the radius of the ellipse area whose center is the neuron i for the direction to the neuron j, and is given by

$$D_{ij} = \begin{cases} a_i, & (d^y_{ij} = 0) \\ b_i, & (d^x_{ij} = 0) \\ \sqrt{\dfrac{a_i^2 b_i^2}{b_i^2 + m_{ij}^2 a_i^2}(m_{ij}^2 + 1)}, & (\text{otherwise}) \end{cases}$$

where a_i is the long radius of the ellipse area whose center is the neuron i and b_i is the short radius of the ellipse area whose center is the neuron i. In the KFMPAM-WD, a_i and b_i can be set for each training pattern. m_{ij} is the slope of the line through the neurons i and j. In Eq.(1), the neuron whose Euclidian distance between its connection weights and the learning vector is minimum in the neurons which can be take areas without overlaps to the areas corresponding to the patterns which are already trained. In Eq.(1), a_i and b_i are used as the size of the area for the learning vector.

5. If $d(X^{(p)}, W_r) > t$ is satisfied, the connection weights of the neurons in the ellipse whose center is the neuron r are updated as follows:

$$W_i(t+1) = \begin{cases} W_i(t) + \alpha(t)(X^{(p)} - W_i(t)), & (d_{ri} \le D_{ri}) \\ W_i(t), & (\text{otherwise}) \end{cases}$$

where (t) is the learning rate and is given by

$$\alpha(t) = \frac{-\alpha_0 (t - T)}{T}.$$

Here, 0 is the initial value of (t) and T is the upper limit of the learning iterations.

6. (5) is iterated until d(X(p), Wr)≤ t is satisfied.
7. The connection weights of the neuron r Wr are fixed.
8. (2) (7) are iterated when a new pattern set is given.

Recall Process

In the recall process of the KFMPAM-WD, when the pattern X is given to the Input/Output Layer, the output of the neuron i in the Map Layer, x_i^{map} is calculated by

$$x_i^{map} = \begin{cases} 1, & (i = r) \\ 0, & (\text{otherwise}) \end{cases}$$

where r is selected randomly from the neurons which satisfy

$$\frac{1}{N^{in}} \sum_{k \in C} g(X_k - W_{ik}) > \theta^{map}$$

where θ^{map} is the threshold of the neuron in the Map Layer, and g(.) is given by

$$g(b) = \begin{cases} 1, & (|b| < \theta^d) \\ 0, & (\text{otherwise}). \end{cases}$$

In the KFMPAM-WD, one of the neurons whose connection weights are similar to the input pattern are selected randomly as the winner neuron. So, the probabilistic association can be realized based on the weights distribution.

When the binary pattern X is given to the Input/Output Layer, the output of the neuron k in the Input/Output Layer x_k^{io} is given by

$$x_k^{io} = W_{rk}.$$

IMPROVED KFM PROBABILISTIC ASSOCIATIVE MEMORY BASED ON WEIGHTS DISTRIBUTION

Here, we explain the proposed Improved Kohonen Feature Map

Probabilistic Associative Memory based on Weights Distribution (IKFMPAM-WD). The proposed model is based on the conventional Kohonen Feature Map Probabilistic Associative Memory based on Weights Distribution (KFMPAM-WD) [16] described in 2.

Structure

Figure 2 shows the structure of the proposed IKFMPAM-WD. As shown in Fig. 2, the proposed model has two layers; (1) Input/Output Layer and (2) Map Layer, and the Input/Output Layer is divided into some parts as similar as the conventional KFMPAM-WD.

Learning Process

In the learning algorithm of the proposed IKFMPAM-WD, the connection weights are learned as follows:

1. The initial values of weights are chosen randomly.
2. The Euclidian distance between the learning vector $X^{(p)}$ and the connection weights vector Wi , $d(X^{(p)}, W_i)$, is calculated.
3. If $d(X^{(p)}, W_i)$ θ^t is satisfied for all neurons, the input pattern $X^{(p)}$ is regarded as an unknown pattern. If the input pattern is regarded as a known pattern, go to (8).
4. The neuron which is the center of the learning area r is determined by Eq.(1). In Eq.(1), the neuron whose Euclid distance between its connection weights and the learning vector is minimum in the neurons which can be take areas without overlaps to the areas corresponding to the patterns which are already trained. In Eq.(1), ai and bi are used as the size of the area for the learning vector.
5. If $d(X^{(p)}, W_r)$ ^{t} is satisfied, the connection weights of the neurons in the ellipse whose center is the neuron r are updated as follows:

$$W_i(t+1) = \begin{cases} X^{(p)}, & (\theta_1^{learn} \leq H(\overline{d_{ri}})) \\ W_i(t) + H(\overline{d_{ri}})(X^{(p)} - W_i(t)), & (\theta_2^{learn} \leq H(\overline{d_{ri}}) < \theta_1^{learn} \\ & \text{and} H(\overline{d_{i^*i}}) < \theta_1^{learn}) \\ W_i(t), & (\text{otherwise}) \end{cases}$$

where θ_1^{learn} are thresholds. $H(\overline{d_{ri}})$ and $H(\overline{d_{i^*i}})$ are given by

Eq.(11) and these are semi-fixed function. Especially, $H(\overline{d_{ri}})$ behaves as the neighborhood function. Here, i* shows the nearest weight-fixed neuron from the neuron i.

$$H(\overline{d_{ij}}) = \frac{1}{1+\exp\left(\frac{\overline{d_{ij}}-D}{\varepsilon}\right)}$$

where $\overline{d_{ij}}$ shows the normalized radius of the ellipse area whose center is the neuron i for the direction to the neuron j, and is given by

$$\overline{d_{ij}} = \frac{d_{ij}}{D_{ij}}.$$

In Eq.(11), D (1 D) is the constant to decide the neighborhood area size and is the steepness parameter. If there is no weight-fixed neuron,

$$H(\overline{d_{i^*i}}) = 0$$

is used.

6. (5) is iterated until d(X(p), Wr)≤ t is satisfied.
7. The connection weights of the neuron r Wr are fixed.
8. (2) (7) are iterated when a new pattern set is given.

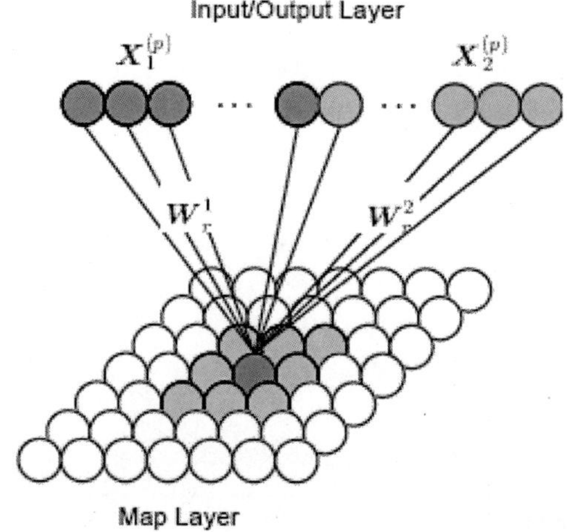

Figure 2. Structure of proposed IKFMPAM-WD.

Recall Process

The recall process of the proposed IKFMPAM-WD is same as that of the conventional KFMPAM-WD described in 2.3.

COMPUTER EXPERIMENT RESULTS

Here, we show the computer experiment results to demonstrate the effectiveness of the proposed IKFMPAM-WD.

Experimental Conditions

Table 1 shows the experimental conditions used in the experiments of 4.2 4.6.

Association Results

Binary Patterns

In this experiment, the binary patterns including one-to-many relations shown in Fig. 3 were memorized in the network composed of 800 neurons in the Input/Output Layer and 400 neurons in the Map Layer. Figure 4 shows a part of the association result when "crow" was given to the Input/Output Layer. As shown in Fig. 4, when "crow" was given to the network, "mouse" (t=1), "monkey" (t=2) and "lion" (t=4) were recalled. Figure 5 shows a part of the association result when "duck" was given to the Input/Output Layer. In this case, "dog" (t=251), "cat" (t=252) and "penguin" (t=255) were recalled. From these results, we can confirmed that the proposed model can recall binary patterns including one-to-many relations.

Table 1. Experimental Conditions.

Parameters for Learning		
Threshold for Learning	${}_{t}^{lear}n$	$1^{0-}4$
Neighborhood Area Size	D	3
Steepness Parameter in Neighborhood Function	ε	0.91
Threshold of Neighborhood Function (1)	${}_{1}^{lear}n$	0.9
Threshold of Neighborhood Function (2)	${}_{2}^{lear}n$	0.1
Parameters for Recall (Common)		
Threshold of Neurons in Map Layer	${}^{ma}p$	0.75
Threshold of Difference between Weight Vector and Input Vector	d	0.004
Parameter for Recall (Binary)		
Threshold of Neurons in Input/Output Layer	${}_{b}^{i}n$	0.5

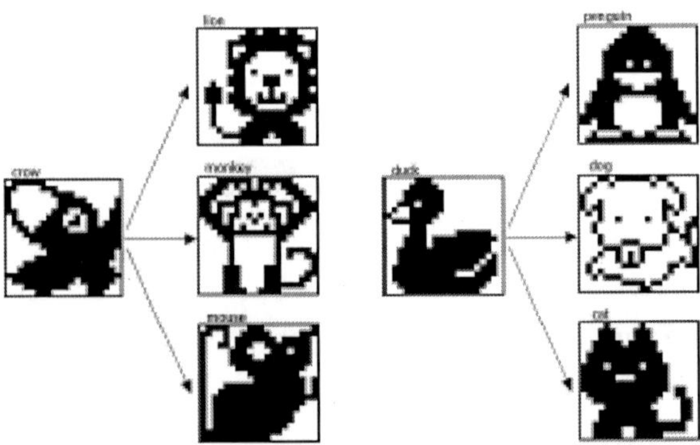

Figure 3. Training Patterns including One-to-Many Relations (Binary Pattern).

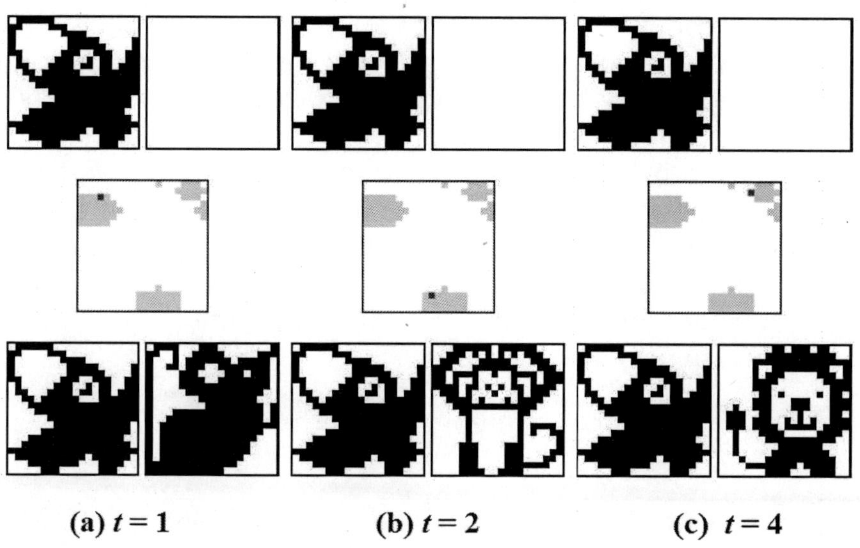

Figure 4. One-to-Many Associations for Binary Patterns (When "crow" was Given).

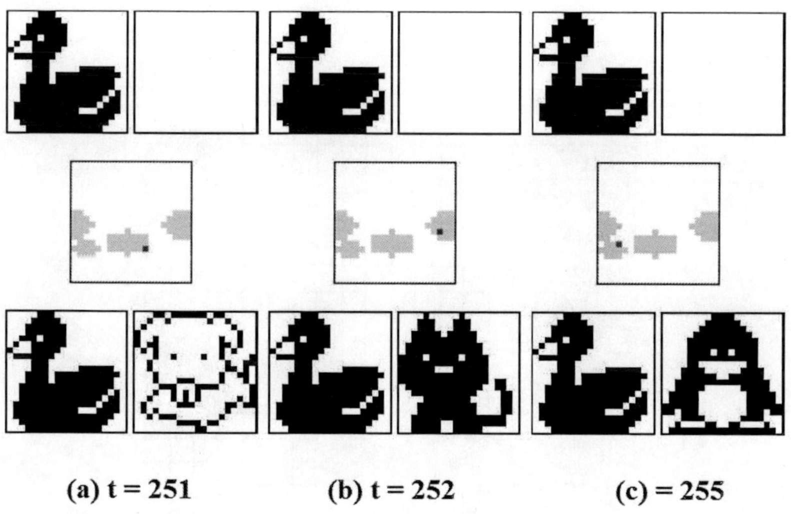

Figure 5. One-to-Many Associations for Binary Patterns (When "duck" was Given).

Figure 6 shows the Map Layer after the pattern pairs shown in Fig. 3 were memorized. In Fig. 6, red neurons show the center neuron in each area, blue neurons show the neurons in areas for the patterns including "crow", green neurons show the neurons in areas for the patterns including "duck". As shown in Fig. 6, the proposed model can learn each learning pattern with various size area. Moreover, since the connection weights are updated not only in the area but also in the neighborhood area in the proposed model, areas corresponding to the pattern pairs including "crow"/"duck" are arranged in near area each other.

Table 2. Area Size corresponding to Patterns in Fig. 3.

Learning Pattern	**Long Radius** $_a^i$	**Short Radius** $_b^i$
"crow"–"lion"	2.5	1.5
"crow"–"monkey"	3.5	2.0
"crow"–"mouse"	4.0	2.5
"duck"–"penguin"	2.5	1.5
"duck"–"dog"	3.5	2.0
"duck"–"cat"	4.0	2.5

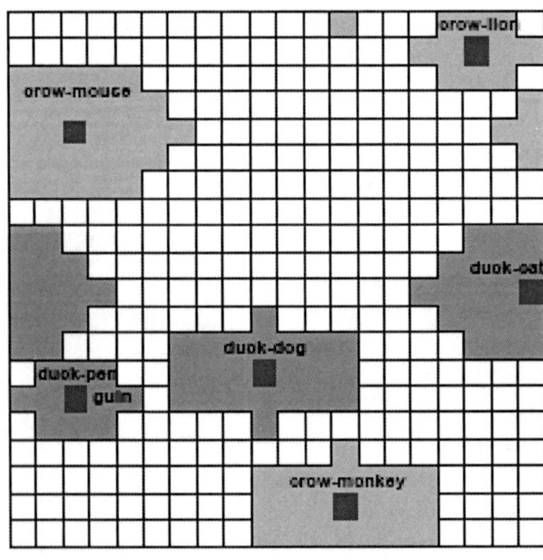

Figure 6. Area Representation for Learning Pattern in Fig. 3.

Table 3. Recall Times for Binary Pattern corresponding to "crow" and "duck".

Input Pattern	Output Pattern	Area Size	Recall Times
crow	lion	11 (1.0)	43 (1.0)
	monkey	23 (2.1)	87 (2.0)
	mouse	33 (3.0)	120 (2.8)
duck	penguin	11 (1.0)	39 (1.0)
	dog	23 (2.1)	79 (2.0)
	cat	33 (3.0)	132 (3.4)

Table 3 shows the recall times of each pattern in the trial of Fig. 4 (t=1250) and Fig. 5 (t=251 500). In this table, normalized values are also shown in ( ). From these results, we can confirmed that the proposed model can realize probabilistic associations based on the weight distributions.

Analog Patterns

In this experiment, the analog patterns including one-to-many relations shown in Fig. 7 were memorized in the network composed of 800 neurons in the Input/Output Layer and 400 neurons in the Map Layer. Figure 8 shows a part of the association result when "bear" was given to the Input/Output Layer. As shown in Fig. 8, when "bear" was given to the network, "lion" (t=1), "raccoon dog" (t=2) and "penguin" (t=3) were recalled. Figure 9 shows a part of the association result when "mouse" was given to the Input/Output Layer. In this case, "monkey" (t=251), "hen" (t=252) and "chick" (t=253) were recalled. From these results, we can confirmed that the proposed model can recall analog patterns including one-to-many relations.

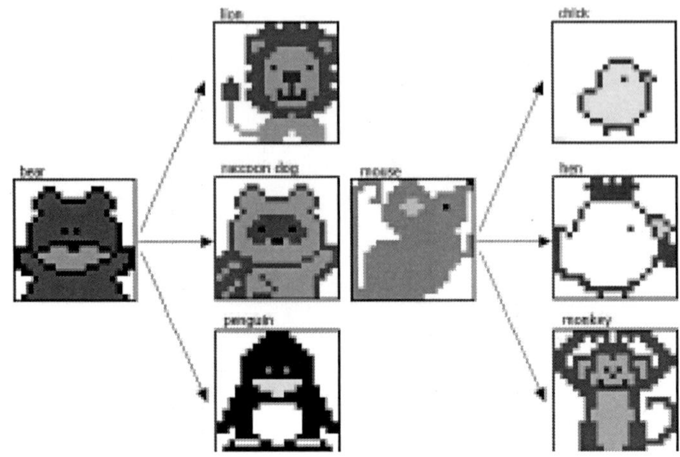

Figure 7. Training Patterns including One-to-Many Relations (Analog Pattern).

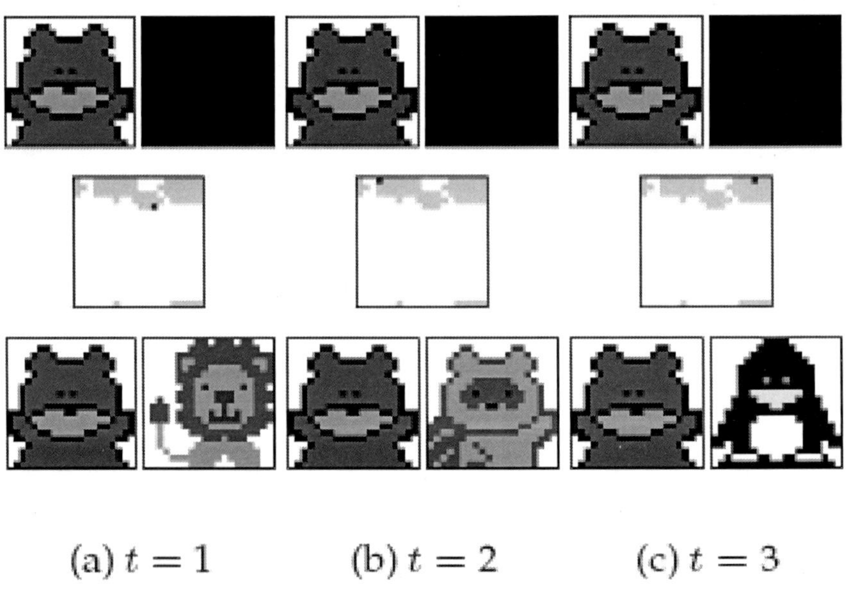

Figure 8. One-to-Many Associations for Analog Patterns (When "bear" was Given).

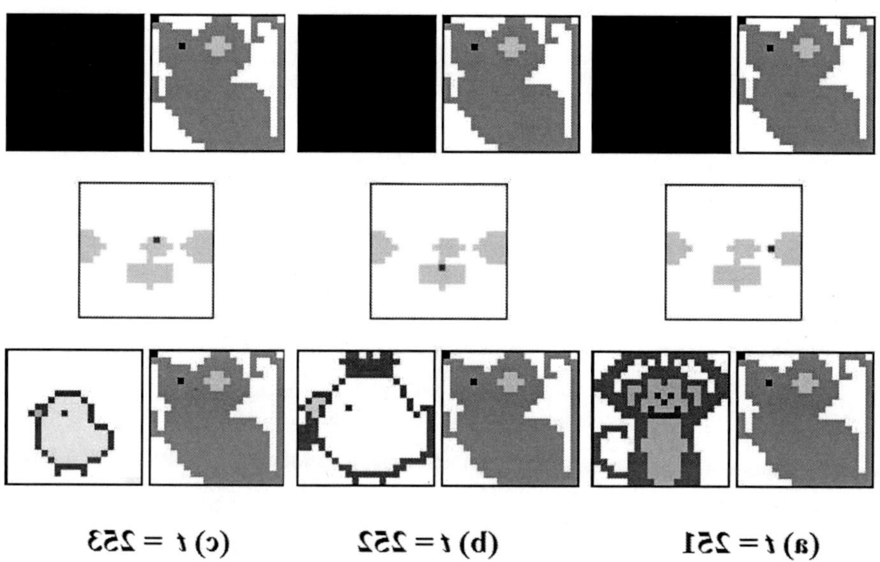

Figure 9. One-to-Many Associations for Analog Patterns (When "mouse" was Given).

Table 4. Area Size corresponding to Patterns in Fig. 7.

Learning Pattern	**Long Radius** ${}_a{}^i$	**Short Radius** ${}_b{}^i$
"bear"–"lion"	2.5	1.5
"bear"–"raccoon dog"	3.5	2.0
"bear"–"penguin"	4.0	2.5
"mouse"–"chick"	2.5	1.5
"mouse"–"hen"	3.5	2.0
"mouse"–"monkey"	4.0	2.5

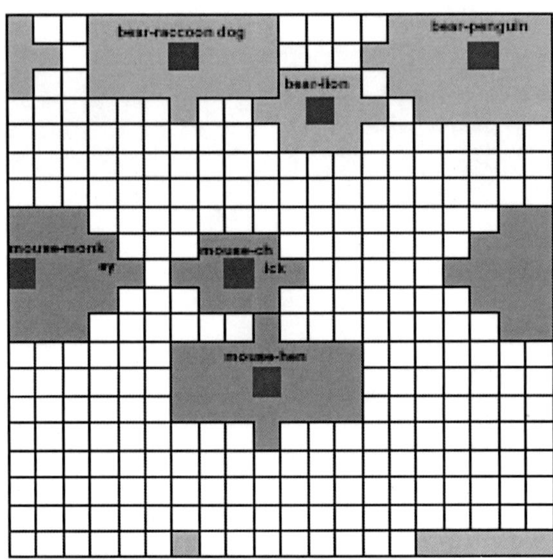

Figure 10. Area Representation for Learning Pattern in Fig. 7.

Table 5. Recall Times for Analog Pattern corresponding to "bear" and "mouse".

Input Pattern	Output Pattern	Area Size	Recall Times
bear	lion	11 (1.0)	40 (1.0)
	raccoon dog	23 (2.1)	90 (2.3)
	penguin	33 (3.0)	120 (3.0)
mouse	chick	11 (1.0)	38 (1.0)
	hen	23 (2.1)	94 (2.5)
	monkey	33 (3.0)	118 (3.1)

Figure 10 shows the Map Layer after the pattern pairs shown in Fig. 7 were memorized. In Fig. 10, red neurons show the center neuron in each area, blue neurons show the neurons in the areas for the patterns including "bear", green neurons show the neurons in the areas for the patterns including "mouse". As shown in Fig. 10, the proposed model can learn each learning pattern with various size area.

Table 5 shows the recall times of each pattern in the trial of Fig. 8 (t=1 250) and Fig. 9 (t=251 500). In this table, normalized values are also shown in ( ). From these results, we can confirmed that the proposed model can realize probabilistic associations based on the weight distributions.

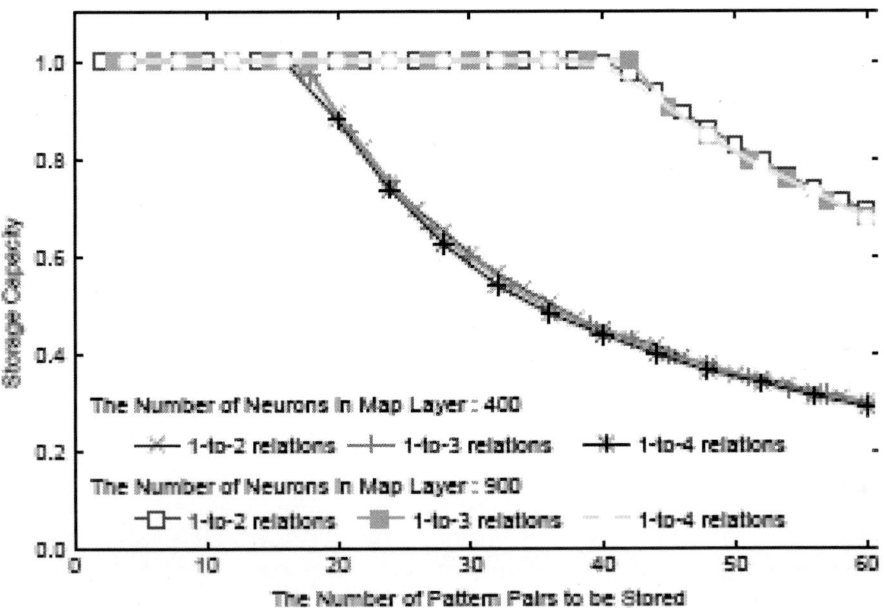

Figure 11. Storage Capacity of Proposed Model (Binary Patterns).

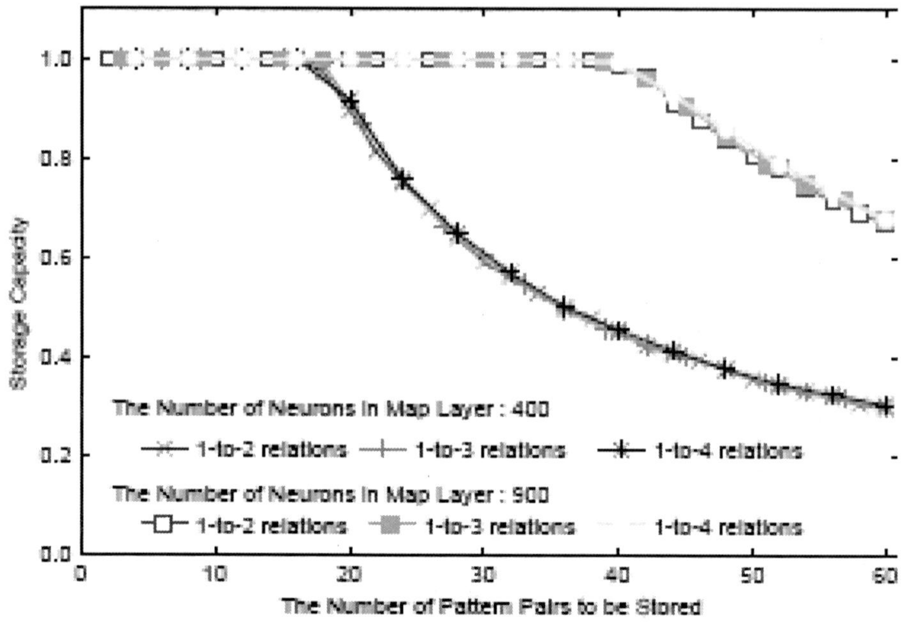

Figure 12. Storage Capacity of Proposed Model (Analog Patterns).

Storage Capacity

Here, we examined the storage capacity of the proposed model. Figures 11 and 12 show the storage capacity of the proposed model. In this experiment, we used the network composed of 800 neurons in the Input/Output Layer and 400/900 neurons in the Map Layer, and 1-to-P (P=2,3,4) random pattern pairs were memorized as the area (ai =2.5 and bi =1.5). Figures 11 and 12 show the average of 100 trials, and the storage capacities of the conventional model(16) are also shown for reference in Figs. 13 and 14. From these results, we can confirm that the storage capacity of the proposed model is almost same as that of the conventional model(16). As shown in Figs. 11 and 12, the storage capacity of the proposed model does not depend on binary or analog pattern. And it does not depend on P in one-to-P relations. It depends on the number of neurons in the Map Layer.

Robustness for Noisy Input

Association Result for Noisy Input

Figure 15 shows a part of the association result of the proposed model when the pattern "cat" with 20% noise was given during t=1 500. Figure 16 shows a part of the association result of the propsoed model when the pattern "crow" with 20% noise was given t=501 1000. As shown in these figures, the proposed model can recall correct patterns even when the noisy input was given.

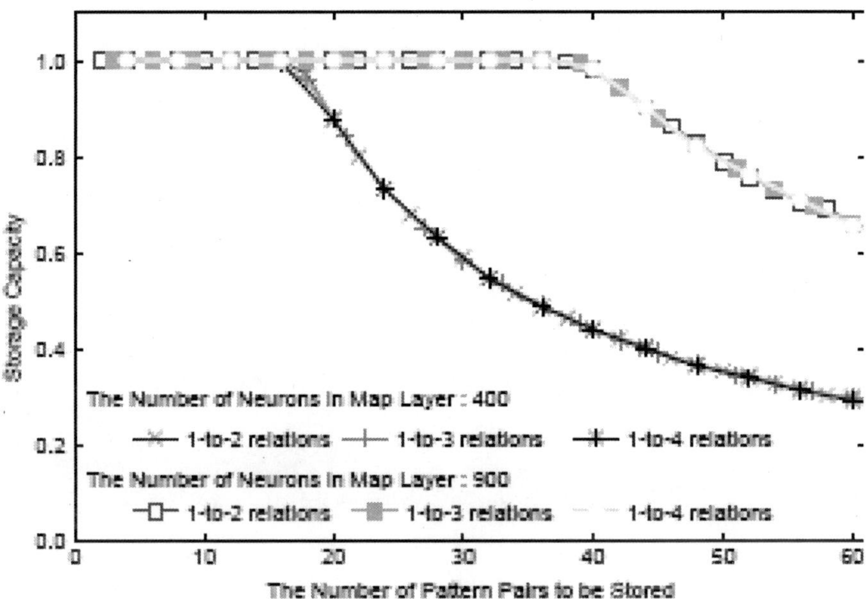

Figure 13. Storage Capacity of Conventional Model [16] (Binary Pattern.

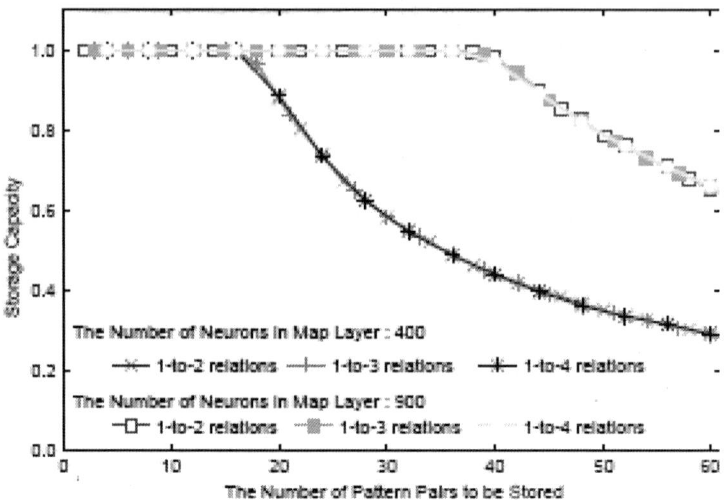

Figure 14. Storage Capacity of Conventional Model [16] (Analog Patterns).

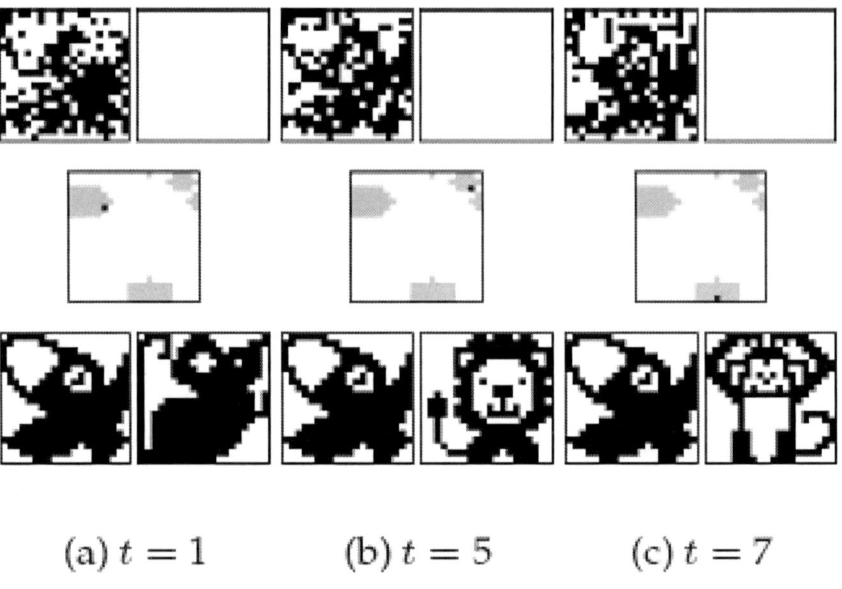

Figure 15. Association Result for Noisy Input (When "crow" was Given.).

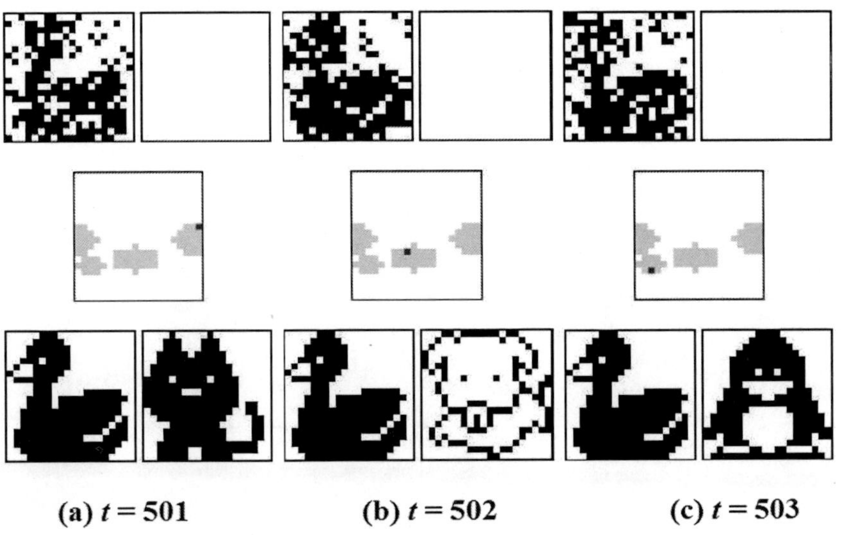

Figure 16. Association Result for Noisy Input (When "duck" was Given).

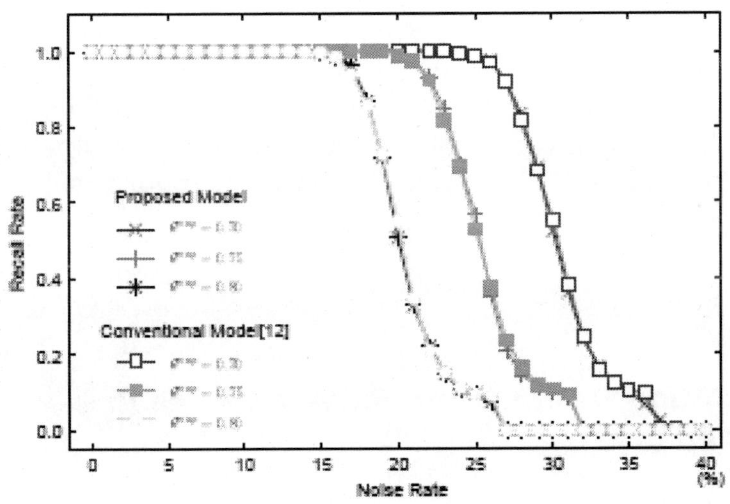

Figure 17. Robustness for Noisy Input (Binary Patterns).

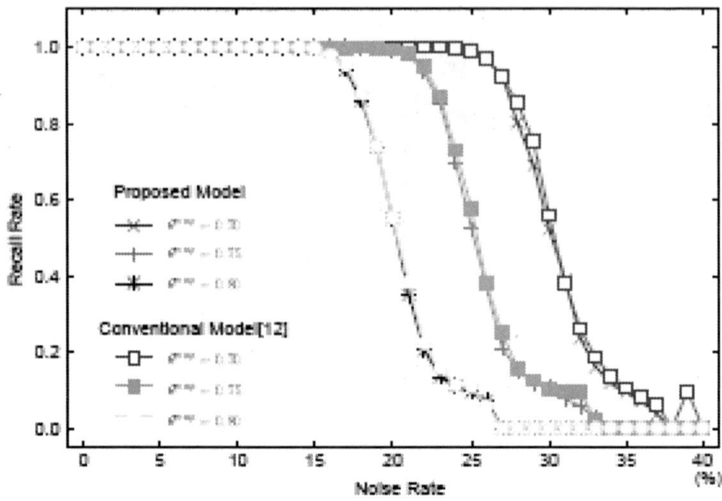

Figure 18. Robustness for Noisy Input (Analog Patterns).

Robustness for Noisy Input

Figures 17 and 18 show the robustness for noisy input of the proposed model. In this experiment, 10 randam patterns in one-to-one relations were memorized in the network composed of 800 neurons in the Input/Output Layer and 900 neurons in the Map Layer. Figures 17 and 18 are the average of 100 trials. As shown in these figures, the proposed model has robustness for noisy input as similar as the conventional model(16).

Robustness for Damaged Neurons

Association Result When Some Neurons in Map Layer are Damaged

Figure 19 shows a part of the association result of the proposed model when the pattern "bear" was given during t=1 500. Figure 20 shows a part of the association result of the proposed model when the pattern "mouse" was given t=501 1000. In these experiments, the network whose 20% of neurons in the Map Layer are damaged were used. As shown in these figures, the proposed model can recall correct patterns even when the some neurons in the Map Layer are damaged.

Robustness for Damaged Neurons

Figures 21 and 22 show the robustness when the winner neurons are damaged in the proposed model. In this experiment, 1 10 random patterns in one-to-one relations were memorized in the network composed of 800 neurons in the Input/Output Layer and 900 neurons in the Map Layer. Figures 21 and 22 are the average of 100 trials. As shown in these figures, the proposed model has robustness when the winner neurons are damaged as similar as the conventional model [16].

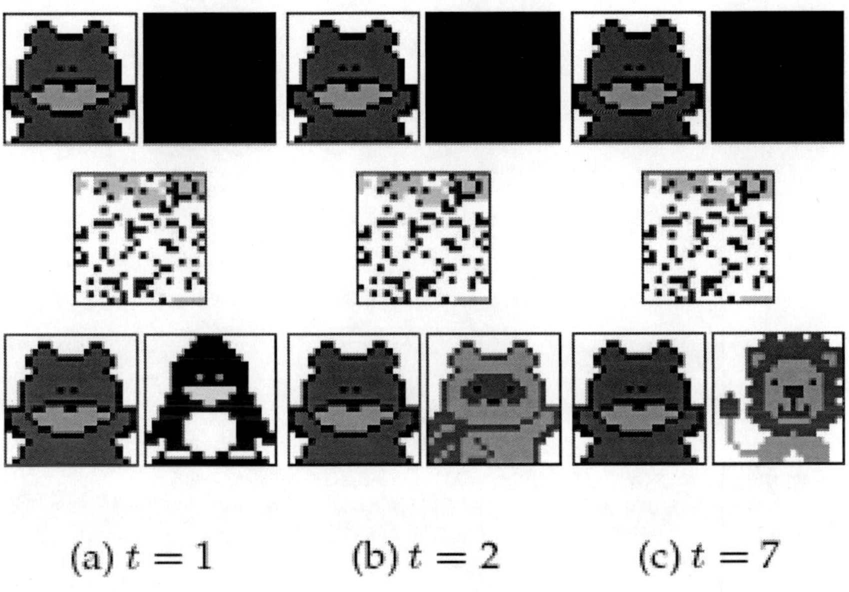

(a) $t = 1$ (b) $t = 2$ (c) $t = 7$

Figure 19. Association Result for Damaged Neurons (When "bear" was Given).

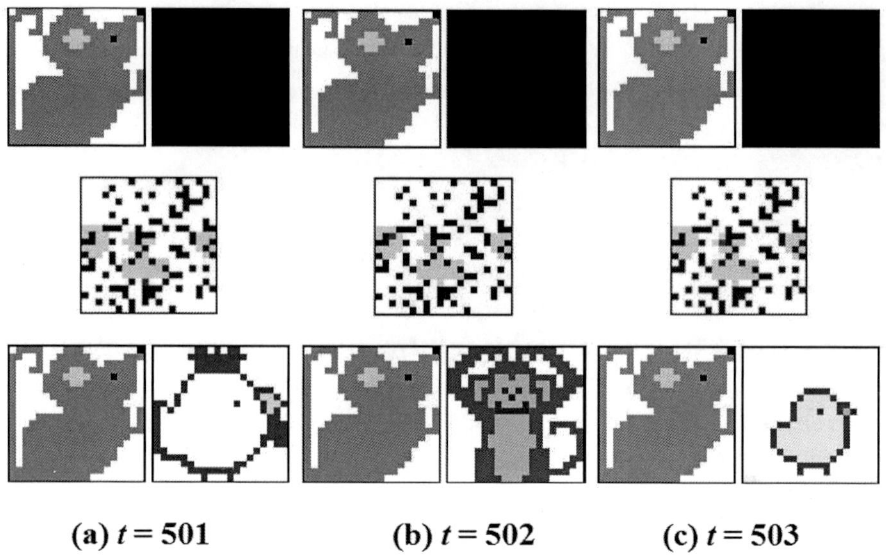

Figure 20. Association Result for Damaged Neurons (When "mouse" was Given).

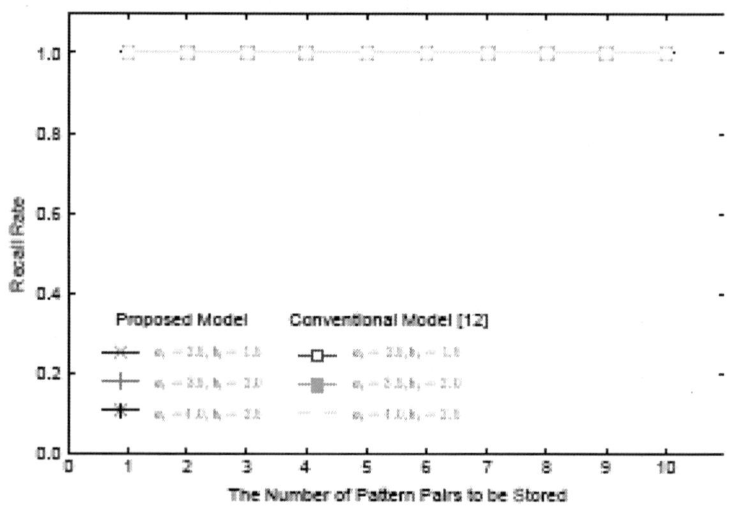

Figure 21. Robustness of Damaged Winner Neurons (Binary Patterns).

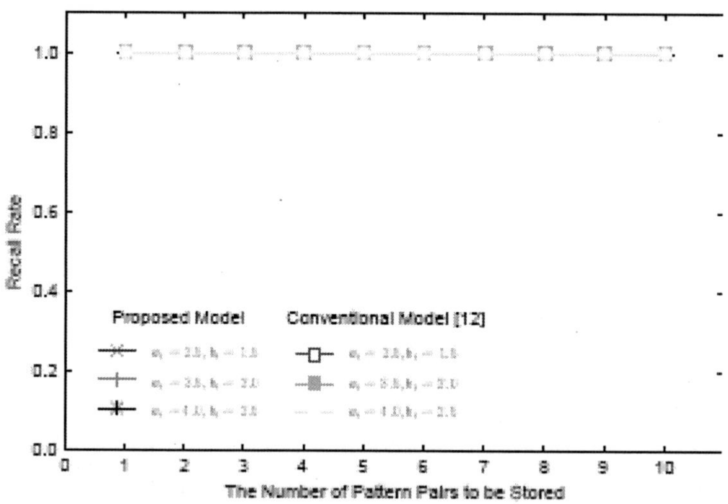

Figure 22. Robustness of Damaged Winner Neurons (Analog Patterns).

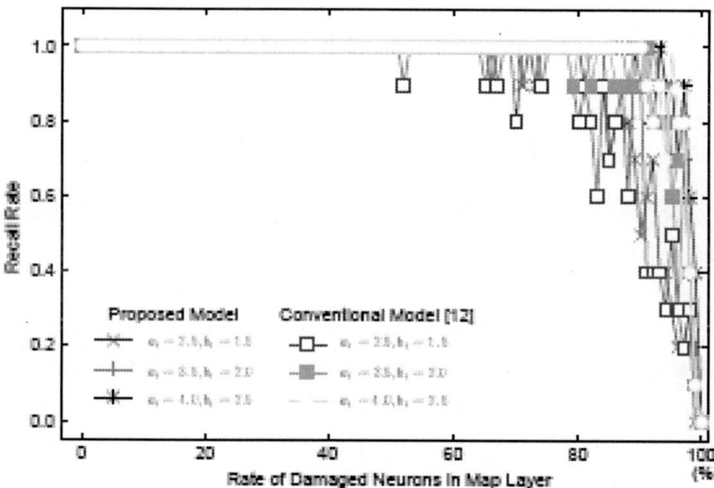

Figure 23: Robustness for Damaged Neurons (Binary Patterns).

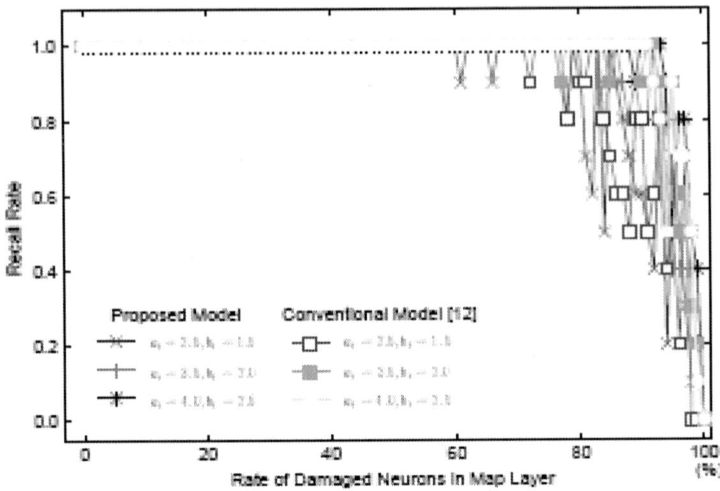

Figure 24. Robustness for Damaged Neurons (Analog Patterns).

Figures 23 and 24 show the robustness for damaged neurons in the proposed model. In this experiment, 10 random patterns in one-to-one relations were memorized in the network composed of 800 neurons in the Input/Output Layer and 900 neurons in the Map Layer. Figures 23 and 24 are the average of 100 trials. As shown in these figures, the proposed model has robustness for damaged neurons as similar as the conventional model [16].

Learning Speed

Here, we examined the learning speed of the proposed model. In this experiment, 10 random patterns were memorized in the network composed of 800 neurons in the Input/Output Layer and 900 neurons in the Map Layer. Table 6 shows the learning time of the proposed model and the conventional model(16). These results are average of 100 trials on the Personal Computer (Intel Pentium 4 (3.2GHz), FreeBSD 4.11, gcc 2.95.3). As shown in Table 6, the learning time of the proposed model is shorter than that of the conventional model.

CONCLUSIONS

In this paper, we have proposed the Improved Kohonen Feature Map

Probabilistic Associative Memory based on Weights Distribution. This model is based on the conventional Kohonen Feature Map Probabilistic Associative Memory based on Weights Distribution. The proposed model can realize probabilistic association for the training set including one-to-many relations. Moreover, this model has enough robustness for noisy input and damaged neurons. We carried out a series of computer experiments and confirmed the effectiveness of the proposed model.

Table 6. Learning Speed.

	Learning Time (seconds)
Proposed Model(Binary Patterns)	0.87
Proposed Model(Analog Patterns)	0.92
Conventional Model(16) (Binary Patterns)	1.01
Conventional Model(16) (Analog Patterns)	1.34

REFERENCES

1. D. E. Rumelhart, J. L. McClelland, the PDP Research Group Parallel Distributed Processing, Exploitations in the Microstructure of Cognition 11 Foundations, The MIT Press 1986
2. T. Kohonen, Self-Organizing Maps Springer 1994
3. J. J. Hopfield, Neural networks and physical systems with emergent collective computational abilities Proceedings of National Academy Sciences USA 79 2554 2558 1982
4. B. Kosko, Bidirectional associative memories IEEE Transactions on Neural Networks 18 1 49 60 1988
5. G. A. Carpenter, S. Grossberg, Pattern Recognition by Self-organizing Neural Networks The MIT Press 1995
6. M. Watanabe, K. Aihara, S. Kondo, Automatic learning in chaotic neural networks IEICE-A J78-A 6 686 691 1995 (in Japanese)
7. T. Arai, Y. Osana, Hetero chaotic associative memory for successive learning with give up function -- One-to-many associations --, Proceedings of IASTED Artificial Intelligence and Applications Innsbruck 2006
8. M. Ando, Y. Okuno, Y. Osana, Hetero chaotic associative memory for

successive learning with multi-winners competition Proceedings of IEEE and INNS International Joint Conference on Neural Networks Vancouver 2006

9. H. Ichiki, M. Hagiwara, M. Nakagawa, Kohonen feature maps as a supervised learning machine Proceedings of IEEE International Conference on Neural Networks 1944 1948 1993
10. T. Yamada, M. Hattori, M. Morisawa, H. Ito, Sequential learning for associative memory using Kohonen feature map Proceedings of IEEE and INNS International Joint Conference on Neural Networks 555 Washington D.C. 1999
11. M. Hattori, H. Arisumi, H. Ito, Sequential learning for SOM associative memory with map reconstruction Proceedings of International Conference on Artificial Neural Networks Vienna 2001
12. N. Sakurai, M. Hattori, H. Ito, SOM associative memory for temporal sequences Proceedings of IEEE and INNS International Joint Conference on Neural Networks 950 955 Honolulu 2002
13. H. Abe, Y. Osana, Kohonen feature map associative memory with area representation Proceedings of IASTED Artificial Intelligence and Applications Innsbruck 2006
14. N. Ikeda, M. Hagiwara, A proposal of novel knowledge representation (Area representation) and the implementation by neural network International Conference on Computational Intelligence and Neuroscience III 430 433 1997
15. T. Imabayashi, Y. Osana, Implementation of association of one-to-many associations and the analog pattern in Kohonen feature map associative memory with area representation Proceedings of IASTED Artificial Intelligence and Applications Innsbruck 2008
16. M. Koike, Y. Osana, Kohonen feature map probabilistic associative memory based on weights distribution Proceedings of IASTED Artificial Intelligence and Applications Innsbruck 2010

Chapter 2

USING ENSEMBLE OF NEURAL NETWORKS TO LEARN STOCHASTIC CONVECTION PARAMETERIZATIONS FOR CLIMATE AND NUMERICAL WEATHER PREDICTION MODELS FROM DATA SIMULATED BY A CLOUD RESOLVING MODEL

Vladimir M. Krasnopolsky,[1,2] Michael S. Fox-Rabinovitz,[2] and Alexei A. Belochitski[3,4]

[1]National Centers for Environmental Prediction, NOAA, College Park, MD 20740, USA

[2]Earth System Sciences Interdisciplinary Center, University of Maryland, College Park, MD 20740, USA

[3]Geophysical Fluid Dynamics Laboratory, NOAA, Princeton, NJ 08540, USA

[4]Brookhaven National Laboratory, Upton, NY 11973, USA

ABSTRACT

A novel approach based on the neural network (NN) ensemble technique is formulated and used for development of a NN stochastic convection parameterization for climate and numerical weather prediction (NWP) models. This fast parameterization is built based on learning from data simulated by a cloud-resolving model (CRM) initialized with and forced by the observed meteorological data available for 4-month boreal winter from November 1992 to February 1993. CRM-simulated data were averaged and processed to implicitly define a stochastic convection parameterization. This parameterization is learned from the data using an ensemble of NNs. The NN ensemble members are trained and tested. The inherent uncertainty of the stochastic convection parameterization derived following this approach is estimated. The newly developed NN convection parameterization has been tested in National Center of Atmospheric Research (NCAR) Community Atmospheric Model (CAM). It produced reasonable and promising decadal climate simulations for a large tropical Pacific region. The extent of the adaptive ability of the developed NN parameterization to the changes in the model environment is briefly discussed. This paper is devoted to a proof of concept and discusses methodology, initial results, and the major challenges of using the NN technique for developing convection parameterizations for climate and NWP models.

INTRODUCTION

Clouds and convection are among the most important and complex phenomena of the Earth's physical climate system. In spite of intense studies for centuries, clouds still provide an intellectual and computational challenge. Because of the vast range of time and space scales involved, researchers and models that they use typically focus on a particular component of a cloud system, with a narrow range of time and space scales, and prescribe features of the cloud that operate outside of that range. For example, microphysical models describing drop scale motions (e.g., drop coagulation) deal with the fine spatial and temporal scales (of order of millimeters (drop size) and seconds). For more detailed discussion of atmospheric moisture physics, see [1–4]. At the other end of the spectrum of representations of clouds is their representation in large-scale models, for example, in general circulation or global climate models (GCMs), which resolve atmospheric features with spatial scales of the order of 100 km, and temporal scales of the order of 10 minutes.

Numerical atmospheric and coupled atmospheric-oceanic-land models, or GCMs, used for climate and numerical weather predictions, are based on solving time-dependent 3-D geophysical fluid dynamics equations on the sphere. The governing equations of these complex models, based on conservation lows, can be written symbolically as

$$\frac{\partial \psi}{\partial t} + D(\psi, x) = P(\psi, x), \tag{1}$$

where ψ is a 3-D-prognostic or -dependent variable (e.g., temperature, wind, pressure, and moisture); D is model dynamics (the set of 3-D partial differential equations of motion, thermodynamics, etc., approximated with a spectral or grid-point numerical scheme); x is a 3-D-independent variable (e.g., latitude, longitude, and height); P is model physics (e.g., long and short-wave atmospheric radiation, turbulence, convection and large-scale precipitation processes, clouds, interactions with land and ocean processes, etc.) and chemistry (constituency transport, chemical reactions, etc.). While scientific problems using these models are among the most complex and computationally intensive applications in the history of scientific exploration, the models employ drastic simplifications in their treatment of many physical processes important in climate and weather.

Physical and other processes included in model physics, P, are so complicated that it is practically possible to include them into GCMs only as 1-D (in the vertical direction) simplified or parameterized versions (usually called parameterizations). Thus, the model physics is composed of parameterizations as $P = \sum_k P_k$. These parameterizations constitute the right hand side forcing for the model dynamics equations (1). From the mathematical point of view, each parameterization can be considered as a mapping, which is a relationship between two vectors:

$$\mathbf{Y} = P_k(\mathbf{X}), \tag{2}$$

where X is a vector consisting of profiles of atmospheric parameters describing the state of the atmosphere at a particular time at a particular location (a grid point) and Y is a vector of parameters providing an effective feedback to the atmosphere from the physical processes described by the parameterization P_k at the same location.

It is noteworthy that, after the very significant simplifications mentioned above and as it is formulated in (2), a parameterization does not depend on time and location explicitly. However, throughout model integration it is put in the environment, which changes in time and space when the parameterization is applied at different times and different horizontal locations (grid points) over the globe. The changes of the environment include temporal changes like diurnal, annual, other atmospheric and solar cycles, global climate changes, and spatial changes like the transition of the underlying surface from ocean to land and from one climate zone to another one (e.g., from the tropics to extra tropics). These internal changes constantly occurring throughout model integration reflect the actual external changes in the climate or weather system described by the model. In this paper, we investigate if our developed NN convection parameterization demonstrates the practically meaningful temporal and spatial generalization capability. The generalization capability allows the NN convection parameterization to adapt to changing atmospheric states produced throughout climate model simulations.

A GCM does not resolve multiple subgrid processes that occur on temporal and spatial scales much finer than the GCM resolution. However, subgrid processes and scales are the processes and scales of which physics represents and is defined on. Because of that both X and Y in (2) have significant uncertainties and are actually stochastic variables. X and Y in (2) are defined on a GCM grid, and their uncertainties are due to and represent the subgrid scale variability, which is not resolved by GCM.

Thus, the mapping (2), which establishes the relationship between two stochastic variables X and Y, is a stochastic mapping, and the parameterization P_k is a stochastic parameterization. Actually, the stochastic mapping is a family of mappings, each of which describes a relationship between two considered stochastic variables X and Y inside a range determined by the uncertainties of these variables with a probability determined by a joint probability distribution of these variables. The stochasticity of model physics parameterizations is a natural consequence of the finite model resolution, which leaves unresolved very important sub-grid scale processes [5]. Uncertainties of stochastic parameterization (2) carry important physical information about these sub-grid (unresolved on a GCM grid) physical processes and should be properly taken into account in GCMs.

Usually, parameterizations, P_k, are formulated using relevant first principles and observational data and are based on solving deterministic equations (like radiative transfer equations). They also contain some secondary empirical components based on traditional statistical techniques like regression. As the result, for widely used the state-of-the-art GCMs, all major components of model physics and chemistry, are based on solving deterministic first principle physical or chemical equations. Thus, in the process of development of such a physically based parameterization, the family of mappings that represents the stochastic parameterization (2) is collapsed to one member of the family, completely neglecting the stochastic nature of the parameterization. Therefore, a physically based parameterization represents only one arbitrarily selected member of the family of mappings that represents the stochastic parameterization (2).

In this study, we develop a stochastic convection parameterization based on the learning from data approach, using a neural network (NN) technique. If sufficient amount of observations related to atmospheric convection, cloudiness, and precipitation was available, we could have attempted to learn the parameterization directly from observations. Unfortunately, in reality the available observations are sparse in space and time and not sufficient for such developments. To alleviate the problem, we use data simulated by models that explicitly resolve processes at the smaller temporal and spatial scales; that is, these models have resolution of a couple of orders of magnitude higher than that of GCMs. These models are capable of representing and resolving processes that are relevant to many major features of cloud systems with the spatial scales of the order of several kilometers and temporal scales of seconds to minutes. These are so called cloud resolving models (CRM), which simulate component aspects and evolution of cloud systems much more realistically than large-scale models. We employ the CRM [6–8] initialized and forced by observational data to simulate a limited (but more expanded, in terms of the spatial and temporal resolution and the number of variables, than available observational data) amount of data (they are called "pseudo-observations"). Then we use a NN technique to develop a stochastic convection parameterization (2) by learning from the simulated pseudo-observations.

In our previous works, we successfully applied a NN technique to develop accurate and fast emulations of complex physically based parameterizations. Because of the complexity of the physical processes involved and the complexity of their mathematical and numerical representations, some of these parameterizations are the most time-consuming components of GCMs. We have developed NN emulations for the most time-consuming part of model physics: model radiation [9–13]. Because, as it was mentioned above, a physically based parameterization is represented by a single mapping, we successfully used a single NN to emulate a physically based parameterization. However, a single NN is not an adequate tool for emulating a stochastic mapping (2), which is actually a family of mappings. An adequate tool in this case is an ensemble of NNs, which can effectively emulate the stochastic mapping (2) [4].

In this study, we use the CRM developed and provided by Khairoutdinov and Randall [7]. We also use the GCM developed by the National Center for Atmospheric Research (NCAR) that is called the Community Atmospheric Model (CAM). Thus, in this study we (a) apply a NN ensemble technique to learn a NN stochastic convection parameterization from the pseudo-observations simulated by the CRM, (b) introduce this NN stochastic convection parameterization into the NCAR CAM, and (c) run climate simulations to test the validity of the new NN stochastic convection parameterization. In Section 2, we formulate our approach and describe details of the training set creation and NN training. In Section 3, the results of validation of the developed NN ensemble convection parameterization are described. Section 4 presents discussion of results and Section 5 contains conclusions.

FORMULATION OF THE APPROACH: DEVELOPMENT OF A NN ENSEMBLE CONVECTION PARAMETERIZATION FROM CRM DATA

In this study, we develop an ensemble of NNs which emulates the behavior of fine-scale CRM simulations at larger GCM scales in a variety of regimes and initial conditions. The resulting ensemble NN parameterization can be used as a novel, and computationally viable convection parameterization in GCMs. This approach has a realistic potential of producing a parameterization of a similar or better quality to the existing physically based parameterizations that are used in GCMs, effectively taking into account subgrid scale (in terms of a GCM) effects at a fraction of the computational cost of the existing approaches.

As we have shown in our previous works (e.g., [12]) any parameterization of model physics (2) can be emulated employing multilayer perceptron NNs using learning-from-data approach. This NN is an analytical approximation that uses a family of functions like

$$y_q = a_{q0} + \sum_{j=1}^{k} a_{qj} \cdot \phi\left(b_{j0} + \sum_{i=1}^{n} b_{ji} \cdot x_i\right); \quad q = 1, 2, \ldots, m, \tag{3}$$

where x_i and y_q are components of the input and output vectors X and Y, respectively, a and b are fitting parameters, and $\phi(b_{j0} + \sum_{i=1}^{n} b_{ji} \cdot x_i)$ is a "neuron." The activation function ϕ is usually a hyperbolic tangent, n and m are the numbers of inputs and outputs, respectively, and k is the number of neurons in (3). In the case of a stochastic parameterization, an ensemble of NNs (3) provides an adequate tool for representing a parameterization (2) [4].

Design and Development of NN Convection Parameterizations and Training Sets

Figure 1 summarizes the process of development of the NN parameterization. The CRM simulations use the TOGA-COARE (the international observational experiment in the tropics conducted for the 4-month period from November 1992 to February 1993) observational data for initialization and forcing and have the horizontal resolution ρ of 1 km, 64 or 96 vertical layers extending from the surface to ~30 km, and the time integration step of 5 s. We integrate the CRM over the domain of $256 \times 256\,\text{km}$.

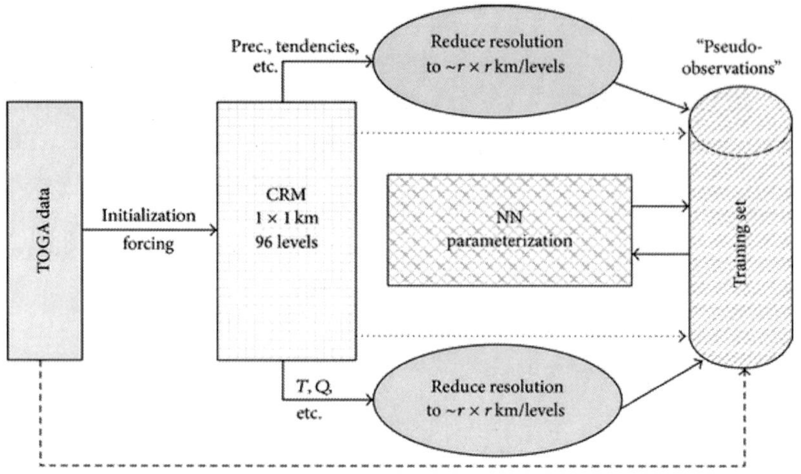

Figure 1. Development design of a NN convection parameterization. T, Q, and so forth refer to selected CRM-simulated fields used as inputs for NN parameterization; Prec., Tendencies, and so forth refer to selected CRM simulated variables used as NN outputs. The dotted and dashed lines indicate that observational and high-resolution simulated data can be added to the training data set if necessary.

The development of the NN parameterization is a multistep process. These steps are as follows.

1. CRM simulated data: the CRM has been run for the 4-month period (from November 1992 to February 1993 or for 120 days of the TOGA-COARE observational experiment), and the high 1 km resolution output of the model has been obtained. The CRM-simulated temperature, wind, humidity, and other data are in a good agreement with those of the TOGA-COARE observational data. Also, the CRM produces additional prognostic and diagnostic fields not observed in the TOGA-COARE experiment.
2. Reducing the horizontal resolution of the CRM simulated data: the CRM-simulated data are averaged in space and time. The data are averaged to a reduced horizontal resolution to r where $\rho < r \leq R,$, and ρ and R are the CRM and GCM resolutions correspondingly. Also the data are interpolated/averaged onto the number of vertical layers l=L, where L is the number of vertical layers in the GCM.

3. Projecting a CRM space of atmospheric states onto a GCM space of atmospheric states: the CRM has many variables that describe fine-scale processes not resolved by the GCM, for example, the condensed water in each CRM column. Such variables have no analogs in the GCM. From the point of view of a GCM "model reality" these variables are "hidden" variables responsible for sub-grid scale variability. The acknowledgement of this challenge requires development of the concept of uncertainty and "stochasticity"; it leads to recognition of a significant level of uncertainty in the pseudo-observations and of the stochasticity of the convection parameterization (2) learned from these data. The obtained set of "pseudo-observations" implicitly represents a stochastic convection parameterization with an uncertainty, which is an inherent feature of such a parameterization. Thus, only the variables that can be identified with the corresponding GCM variables or can be calculated from or converted to prognostic or diagnostic variables available in the GCM are selected to be included in the development set (called "pseudo-observations" in Figure 1; actually they are obtained from the averaged CRM simulated data). Only these variables are used as inputs and outputs of a NN convection parameterization. Thus, a subset of variables is selected from the reduced resolution CRM-simulated data created at the previous step (2), and this subset constitutes the NN development set. The dotted and dashed lines in Figure 1 show that, in principle, if it is found to be desirable, the high-resolution CRM-simulated data and/or even observed data can be added to the development set to enrich subgrid variability in the development data.
4. The developed "pseudo-observations" are separated into two sets, one set being used for training and another independent set for testing/validation. Then the NN parameterization is trained using the training set. Due to the inherent uncertainty of pseudo-observations, the parameterization represented by these data is a stochastic parameterization; it should be considered as a stochastic mapping. Thus, the NN parameterization is implemented as an ensemble of NNs.

All the aforementioned issues are discussed in detail in [4].

The validation procedure for the NN parameterization consists of two steps. First, the trained NN is applied to the test set and error statistics are calculated. Second, the tested NN parameterization is included into the GCM. This last step is the most important step of validation and of our approach.

NN Emulation of the Convection Parameterization and Estimation of Its Uncertainties

Data

The data set simulated for the NN development is limited by the length of the observational data set needed for forcing the CRM simulations (see Figure 1). The CRM was run for 120 days, using the TOGA-COARE forcing for the 256×256 km domain with 1 km resolution and 96 vertical layers (0–28 km). Then the simulated data were averaged at every hour of model integration to produce the simulation data set with an effective horizontal resolution of 256 km and 26 vertical levels. Finally, only variables that are available in the GCM (NCAR CAM) or can be calculated there have been selected. The final data set consists of 2,800 records of hourly mean data.

The simulation dataset was partitioned into two parts: a training set consisting of 2,240 records or 80% of data and a test set consisting of 560 records or 20% of data. Namely, first the 2,240 records are included in the training set and the last 560 records in the independent test set.

These two data sets have been used for the NN training and test/validation. As was noticed in the previous section, these data implicitly represent a stochastic parameterization and inherently contain an uncertainty, η, which is not a useless noise. However, in the process of learning the NN convection parameterization from pseudo-observations, from the point of view of a single NN trained using the data (both components X and Y of the data are stochastic variables), the situation is similar to the case when the data contain a significant level of noise.

Symbolically, the NN emulation of the stochastic parameterization (2) can be written as

$$Y = P_{\mathrm{NN}}(X) + \eta + \varepsilon, \tag{4}$$

where P_{NN} is a NN emulation of the mapping P_k (2) and ε is a NN approximation error. Thus, in the case of the stochastic parameterization, the NN emulation task is different from the task of emulating a deterministic radiation parameterization in the GCM [9–11]. For example, in the GCM the radiation parameterization, which is a closed analytical expression or a computer code (mapping) is usually considered as an "exact" source of radiation information (it is not considered as a stochastic parameterization with an uncertainty); thus, for the NN emulation approach the goal is to emulate it as accurate as possible. This can be done because, in this case, the simulated data can be produced using the given parameterization (mapping), and considered as accurate data (with no noise greater than the round off errors).

In the current work, the situation is different. We do not have an expression (or computer code) for the mapping (2) that we want to emulate with NN (3). We can only assume that it exists and, in this case, it is a stochastic mapping, which is represented by pseudo-observations. Because we derive pseudo-observation, using a rather complex data processing described in the previous section, from the data simulated by the CRM, the pseudo-observations include a significant level of uncertainty. The uncertainty and stochasticity are the essential conceptual features of the NN parameterization that we are going to learn from the pseudo-observations. In a sense, emulating stochastic parameterization is closer to the task of learning from noisy empirical data [14]. This important difference should be taken into account when the NN approximation is trained, the approximation error statistics are analyzed and interpreted, and the NN architecture is selected. For example, in the case of training, the usually used criterion of minimum of the root mean square error should be substituted by the requirement that the root mean square error should not exceed the uncertainty η or

$$\frac{1}{N}\sum_{i=1}^{N}[Y_i - P_{\mathrm{NN}}(X_i)]^2 < \eta^2, \tag{5}$$

where N is the number of records in the training set.

All NNs that satisfy the condition (5) are valid emulations of the stochastic parameterization (2). Actually, each of these NNs can be considered as an emulation of a member of the family of mappings that together represent the stochastic parameterization (2). Therefore, all NNs satisfying (5) together—the entire ensemble of NNs—represent the stochastic parameterization (2). It is clear now that any estimate of the magnitude of the uncertainty η is important for our approach. We will attempt to derive such an estimate in the next sections.

NN Architectures, NN Training, and Validation

Selecting an emulating NN architecture includes two different aspects and types of decisions: (i) the selection of inputs and outputs and their numbers (n and m in (3)), which, as we have already mentioned, are determined by the availability of the variables in the GCM, and (ii) the selection of the number of hidden neurons (k in (3)) in the emulating NN, which is determined by many factors (the length of the training set, the level of uncertainty in the data, the characteristics of conversions of the training and test errors, etc.).

Table 1 shows (in terms of inputs and outputs) the architecture we have experimented with here. The major inputs are the vertical profiles of the following model prognostic and diagnostic fields: T—a profile of temperature—and QV—a profile of water vapor concentration. We experimented also with additional inputs: time, latitude, and longitude to take into account the changes in the data environment where the NN is applied; however, because in this particular case we work with data from a relatively small area and over a relatively short period of time (120 days), explicit introduction of the time and location dependencies does not make any difference and does not complement the indirect dependence on the time and location introduced by inputs T and QV. These inputs themselves depend on time and location. The major outputs for NN architecture shown in Table 1 are the vertical profiles (or vectors) of the following model prognostic and diagnostic fields: Q1C (a profile of the "apparent heat source"), Q2 (a profile of the "apparent moist sink"), PREC (precipitation rates, a scalar), and CLD (a profile of cloudiness).

Table 1. NN architecture (inputs and outputs) investigated in the paper.

NN architecture	NN inputs		NN outputs			
In : out	*T*	QV	Q1C	Q2	PREC	CLD
36 : 55	18	18	18	18	1	18

T is temperature, QV is atmospheric moisture—vapor mixing ratio, Q1C: the "apparent heat source," Q2: the "apparent moist sink," PREC: precipitation rates, and CLD: cloudiness. Numbers in the table show the dimensionality of the corresponding input and output parameters. In : Out stand for NN inputs and outputs and show their corresponding numbers.

The numbers in Table 1 show how many vertical levels of the corresponding profile (26 levels maximum as in the NCAR CAM) have been included as inputs in the NN. Many profiles have zeros, or constants, or values that are almost constant (their standard deviations are very small) for the entire data set at some levels (usually for the upper model levels in the stratosphere). Zeros and constants should not be included in inputs or outputs because (1) they carry no information about input/output functional dependence and (2) if not removed they introduce additional noise in training. As for small values that are almost constant, these small signals may be in some cases not a noise but very important signals; however, taking into account the level of uncertainty in the problem, information that these small signals may provide is well below the level of uncertainty and is practically useless. Moreover, some of these variables were included in training and no improvement was observed. In general, if they are important, they should be normalized differently or weighted.

Next, the number of hidden neurons (HID) has to be selected. We varied HID, trained a corresponding NN, and tested it. Figures 2 and 3 show the results of these experiments for two output parameters, Q1C and PREC.

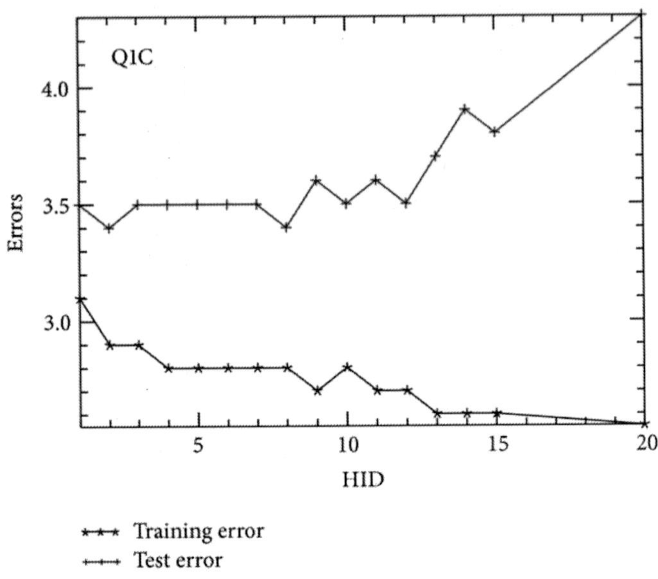

Figure 2. NN approximation errors on training (blue) and test (red) sets for Q1C. HID is the number of hidden neurons.

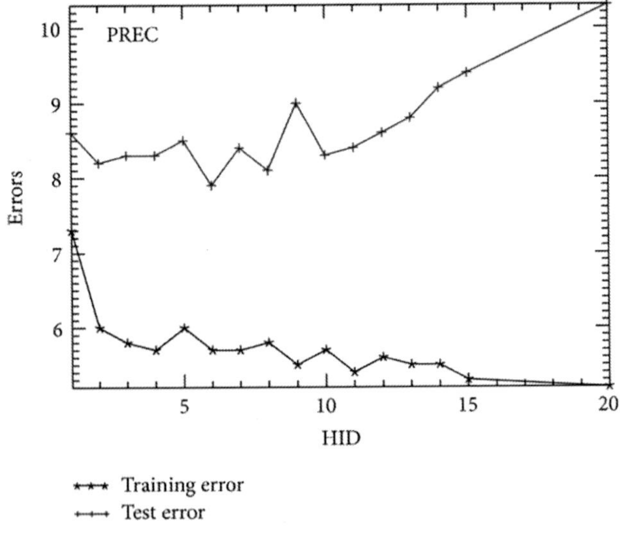

Figure 3. Same as in Figure 2 but for precipitation.

It is noteworthy that the NN training (a least square minimization) attempts to minimize the total $(\eta + \varepsilon)^2$, that is, the sum of the approximation error and the uncertainty. Because of very different statistical properties of these components, they can be considered as independent random variables and approximately separated as

$$(\eta + \varepsilon)^2 \approx \eta^2 + \varepsilon^2. \tag{6}$$

Thus, η can be roughly estimated using detailed information about the training and test statistics. This issue is discussed in more detail below.

Figures 2 and 3 demonstrate a situation that is usually observed when NN is trained using data with a significant level of noise. The training error, after a sharp initial drop, stays almost constant and then decreases slowly. The test error, after an initial drop, stabilizes and then increases. The interpretation of this behavior is well known. After the initial improvement of the approximation of the data due to an increasing flexibility of an approximating NN, a short interval of stability is reached (at HID ~3 to 7) when NN fits the signal inside the corridor of errors. Then with the increase of the flexibility of the approximating NN, it starts fitting the noise; that is, the overfitting occurs. The training error is slowly decreasing; however, the test error quickly increases. Table 2 shows the number of fitting parameters (NN weights) in NNs with different HID, which were used for Figures 2 and 3. Taking into account that the training set contains a limited number of records, 2240 records, it is not surprising that clearly pronounced overfitting is observed at HID>10 when the number of NN weights, N_C, becomes comparable with the number of data records.

Table 2. The number of fitting parameters (NN weights), N_C, at different values of HID = k (see (3)).

	HID					
	1	**2**	**5**	**10**	**15**	**20**
N_C	166	273	594	1129	1667	2199

Thus, we can conclude that, for a particular simulated data set used, HID=5 would be an acceptable choice for the number of hidden neurons in emulating NN. This value is inside of the intervals of stability of the training and test errors. Because for different NN outputs the interval of stability is slightly different, the choice of the optimal number of hidden neurons is hardly possible. The best solution of the problem, in our opinion, would be included in the NN ensemble members with various architectures (different numbers of hidden neurons and even with different inputs [4]).

The ensemble of ten NNs has been trained, and error statistics for seven of them that are significantly different are presented in Table 3. All NNs presented in Table 3 have the same number of inputs (36), outputs (55), and hidden neurons (5). They all have been initialized using the same initialization procedure [15] with different small random numbers. The ten different members of NN ensemble correspond to ten different local minima of the error function. Table 3 shows the comparison of NN ensemble member error statistics on the training set (Tr) and on the independent test set (Ts); both sets are described above in Section 2.2.1. For each NN output variable, three statistics were calculated (bias, RMSE, and correlation coefficient) by comparison of NN-generated output variables with the corresponding ones in the training or test set.

Table 3. NN ensemble member error statistics on training (Tr) and independent test (Ts) sets. CC is the correlation coefficient. HID = 5.

Data set	Ens. mem.	NN outputs											
		Q1C (K/day)			Q2 (K/day)			Prec (mm/day)			CLD (fractions)		
		Bias	RMSE	CC	Bias	RMSE	CC	Bias	RMSE	CC	Bias	RMSE	CC
Tr	2	$1 \cdot 10^{-3}$	2.8	0.75	$2 \cdot 10^{-2}$	4.0	0.63	$1 \cdot 10^{-2}$	6.0	0.85	$1 \cdot 10^{-4}$	0.07	0.91
	3	$2 \cdot 10^{-3}$	2.4	0.78	$2 \cdot 10^{-2}$	3.7	0.66	$1 \cdot 10^{-2}$	5.7	0.86	$2 \cdot 10^{-6}$	0.07	0.92
	4	$1 \cdot 10^{-3}$	2.3	0.81	$2 \cdot 10^{-3}$	3.7	0.68	$4 \cdot 10^{-3}$	5.2	0.89	$1 \cdot 10^{-4}$	0.07	0.92
	5	$2 \cdot 10^{-3}$	2.3	0.80	$1 \cdot 10^{-3}$	3.8	0.66	$2 \cdot 10^{-2}$	5.3	0.88	$3 \cdot 10^{-5}$	0.07	0.91
	6	$4 \cdot 10^{-4}$	2.3	0.80	$1 \cdot 10^{-3}$	3.8	0.64	$1 \cdot 10^{-3}$	5.3	0.88	$6 \cdot 10^{-5}$	0.08	0.89
	7	$2 \cdot 10^{-4}$	2.3	0.81	$3 \cdot 10^{-4}$	3.7	0.67	$7 \cdot 10^{-3}$	5.2	0.89	$5 \cdot 10^{-5}$	0.06	0.93
	9	$1 \cdot 10^{-3}$	3.1	0.73	$4 \cdot 10^{-3}$	4.0	0.64	$2 \cdot 10^{-2}$	5.8	0.86	$1 \cdot 10^{-4}$	0.07	0.90
Ts	2	−0.1	3.5	0.62	0.02	4.7	0.49	−1.1	8.5	0.68	0.03	0.11	0.81
	3	−0.6	3.5	0.62	−0.8	5.0	0.44	−5.1	10.6	0.66	0.01	0.11	0.81
	4	−0.5	3.0	0.70	−0.6	4.5	0.53	−4.0	8.8	0.73	0.00	0.09	0.86
	5	−0.1	2.9	0.71	−0.1	3.9	0.52	−1.8	7.8	0.74	0.01	0.08	0.87
	6	−0.3	2.9	0.70	−0.1	3.9	0.51	−2.6	8.0	0.74	0.01	0.08	0.88
	7	−0.4	2.9	0.73	−0.5	4.3	0.58	−3.3	7.9	0.77	0.00	0.07	0.92
	9	−0.7	3.8	0.65	−0.8	4.7	0.51	−4.1	8.6	0.76	0.01	0.10	0.84

The training errors (Tr) for all output parameters are significantly closer to each other for different NN ensemble members and less sensitive to the selection of HID (not shown in Table 3) inside the interval of stability (see Figures 2 and 3) than the test errors (Ts). Thus, the training errors can be considered as a rough estimate of the noise in the data, which is the inherent uncertainty η of the stochastic parameterization (2).

Following this assumption, we can approximately estimate the uncertainty η. For example, for Q1C the average training RMS error (calculated using Table 3) is about 2.4 K/day, which can be attributed to the uncertainty η. This estimate for the uncertainty for one of the model variable, which is introduced by taking into account sub-grid scale effects, is an important result per se. The quantitative information about the uncertainty is instrumental in evaluating the accuracy of the model forecast. Now, using (6) for the test error we can estimate the NN approximation error. For this example, the test error is 2.9 K/day and, following (6), only about 1.6 K/day of this error should be attributed to the NN approximation error. If we perform such a correction for all NN ensemble members presented in Table 3, we find out that, as in the aforementioned example, after the separation of the uncertainty (the training error), the NN approximation errors on the test set do not exceed (often they are smaller than) the uncertainty.

Figures 4, 5, and 6 illustrate performance of different members of the NN ensemble on the independent test set. Figure 4 demonstrates predictions of precipitation time series produced by different NN ensemble members in comparison with "pseudo-observations" (or "Data" in the figure legend). The NN ensemble members produce an envelope (with a rather measurable spread) which on average gives a very good prediction of precipitation on the test set. The spread of the envelope shows that there is still a measurable difference between NN ensemble members, and some of the members of the envelope (e.g.,) give results that are closer to the "pseudo-observations." The magnitude of the spread may serve as another measure of the uncertainty of the stochastic parameterization (2). It is in agreement with the measure we introduced above, with the magnitude of the training error for PREC shown in Table 3.

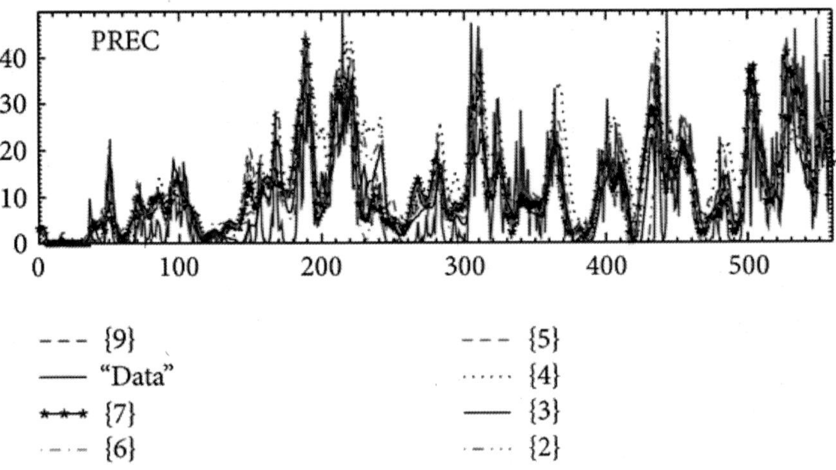

Figure 4. NN simulations of precipitation on the test set. Different curves presented in the figure represent seven significantly different members of the NN ensemble (see the numbers in parentheses) and verification data. The NN ensemble member {9} is shown by the thick-dashed red line.

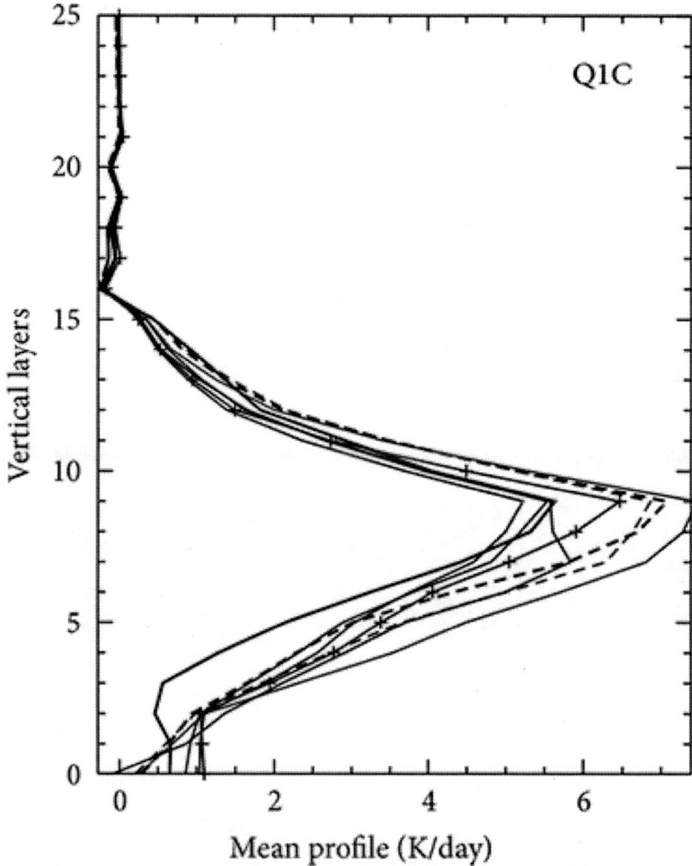

Figure 5. Q1C (the apparent heat source from convection) mean profiles on the test set produced by different NN ensemble members. The different curves presented in the figure correspond to different ensemble members; the thick solid line shows the verification data in the test set.

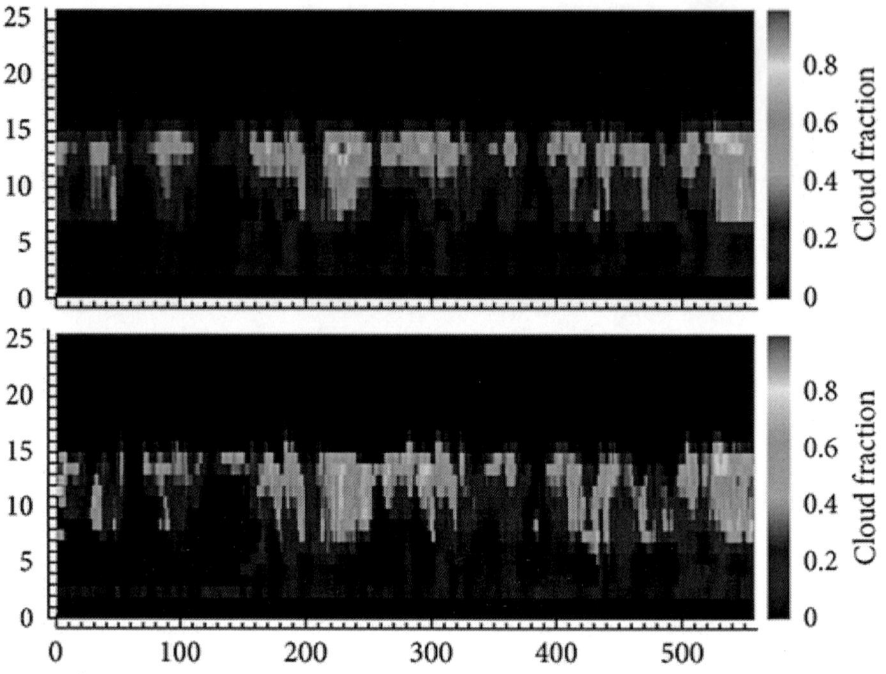

Figure 6. Hovmöller diagrams (the time evolution of vertical profiles) for the CLD profile time series: pseudo-observations, the upper panel and the NN ensemble mean, the lower panel. The -axis shows time in hours for the test/validation set.

Figure 5 depicts mean profiles for one of the outputs of the NN parameterization, Q1C. As in the case of precipitation, different members of the NN ensemble create an envelope with a significant spread for the mean profiles, and the magnitude of the spread is close to the training error for Q1C shown in Table 3. The differences between members inside the envelope are small as compared with the uncertainty; however, these differences are significant. They give estimates of the differences between members of the family of mappings representing the stochastic parameterization (2) and implicitly available in pseudo-observations.

Figure 6 shows the Hovmöller diagrams (the time evolution of vertical profiles) for the time series of cloudiness (CLD) profiles for the NN ensemble mean as compared with the verification data. The upper panel shows the time series of the pseudo-observation profiles, and the lower panel shows the time series of the profiles generated by NN ensemble. Each profile in the lower panel is the average of ten profiles generated by ten NN ensemble members. The patterns generated by the NN ensemble are a bit smoothed and diffused; they are not as sharp as the observed ones but are well recognizable. The NN ensemble mean represents the sequence of patterns well and without significant shifts.

As mentioned above, the NN errors on the raining set as well as the spread of the envelope created by different NN ensemble members represent the level of uncertainty in pseudo-observation data or the uncertainty of the stochastic parameterization (2). It means that, in the context of the current application (development of NN emulation for a stochastic convection parameterization (2)), selecting the best single emulating NN followed by the use of this "optimal" NN parameterization in the GCM is not the best approach.

All NNs presented here (as well as other NNs, for example, with different architectures, different number of neurons in the hidden layer evaluated in [4]) can be considered as valid emulations of the parameterization (2). These NNs should be considered as members of a NN ensemble realization of the stochastic parameterization (2) represented by a particular data set. The spread in the NN ensemble roughly reflects the skill (error) of the prediction that could be obtained using this NN ensemble.

VALIDATION OF THE STOCHASTIC NN CONVECTION PARAMETERIZATION IN NCAR CAM

We consider the results presented in this section mostly as a proof of concept for our NN approach to developing NN convection parameterizations. Keeping this in mind, we present the results from the standpoint of their general quality with a clear understanding that more precise quantitative climatological results could be expected in our future efforts.

The NN stochastic convection parameterization described in the previous sections has been implemented as the ensemble of NNs, which are trained on the averaged CRM simulated data "pseudo-observations". In this section, we discuss the results of introduction of the NN stochastic parameterization into the NCAR CAM. Here our goal is to verify whether the NN ensemble, emulating the stochastic convection parameterization (2), provides meaningful/realistic outputs when using the CAM inputs. We performed the validation of our NN parameterization in the following two experiments.

1. Over the TOGA-COARE location, the grid point (−2° S, 155° E) for the time period for which the TOGA-COARE data are available (the TOGA-COARE 4-month period from November 1992 to February 1993) we produced the grid-point time-mean profiles and time series.
2. Over the large tropical Pacific region (with the area size of $120^{\circ} \times 30^{\circ}$ and the following coordinates: 150° $E < lon < 90^{\circ}$ W; 15° S < lat < 15° N), we performed the parallel runs with the standard CAM and with the diagnostic CAM-NN run (see below) for the decadal (1990–2001) boreal winters, from November to February or NDJF, climate simulations. Throughout the CAM-NN run we applied at each grid point and at every time step the aforementioned ten NN ensemble members and calculated the ensemble mean for each NN output (Q1C, Q2, and CLD profiles, and for PREC).

Note that the parallel decadal climate simulations have been actually performed for 11 years, but the decadal means (actually 11 boreal winters or NDJF) used below for validation have not included the TOGA-COARE period (see above). The TOGA-COARE data for the 4-month period from November 1992 to February 1993 were used for initializing and forcing CRM simulations, that is, for creating simulated data, which was converted into pseudo-observations used for the NN ensemble training. The validation of the parallel runs has been done for the independent decade.

For simple/initial testing and validation of the NN stochastic convection parameterization (2) in the CAM, we introduced a diagnostic mode of integration. For the diagnostic mode of integration, at every time step, the NN convection parameterization is applied, all ten NN ensemble members are evaluated, and averages of their outputs are calculated and used as NN ensemble convection parameterization outputs. Hereafter this diagnostic run is called CAM-NN. These outputs have been accumulated and the averaged fields have been calculated and compared with those produced by the original CAM convection parameterization and NCEP reanalysis data [16, 17], which provides verification data for climate simulations. Note that reanalysis data (an integrated set of global observations) is produced (every 10 years or so) using a data assimilation system (DAS) which employs a GCM and observational data for past several decades, for example, from 1948 to 2010. A DAS is a complicated procedure, which involves nonlinear optimization in the space of very high dimensionality, combining or blending observational data with the GCM simulations to produce the best possible estimates of atmospheric states for a reanalysis period.

Validation of the NN Convection Parameterization Using the NCAR CAM for the TOGA-COARE Location and 4-Month Period from November 1992 to February 1993

At the first step of our validation, the outputs generated by the ensemble of ten NNs have been compared with CAM-simulated data for one grid point at the TOGA-COARE location (−2° S, 155° E) during the TOGA-COARE period, from November 1992 to February 1993. Thus, the CAM-simulated data were collocated in space and time with the averaged CRM simulated data.

We used the CAM-simulated T and QV as inputs for the NN ensemble trained on the averaged CRM-simulated data (pseudo-observations). The major NN outputs (CLD and PREC) obtained in this experiment have been compared with CAM CLD and PREC and with pseudo-observations. Figure 7 shows mean CLD profiles for the aforementioned experiment. The CAM-NN profile deviates from the pseudo-observation profile because the NN ensemble has been trained for pseudo-observation inputs, not for the CAM ones. It is also different from the CAM profile, which suggests that our stochastic NN convection parameterization effectively introduces in the CAM-NN run the convection and cloud physics, which is different from that of introduced in the parallel CAM run employing an existing CAM convection parameterization.

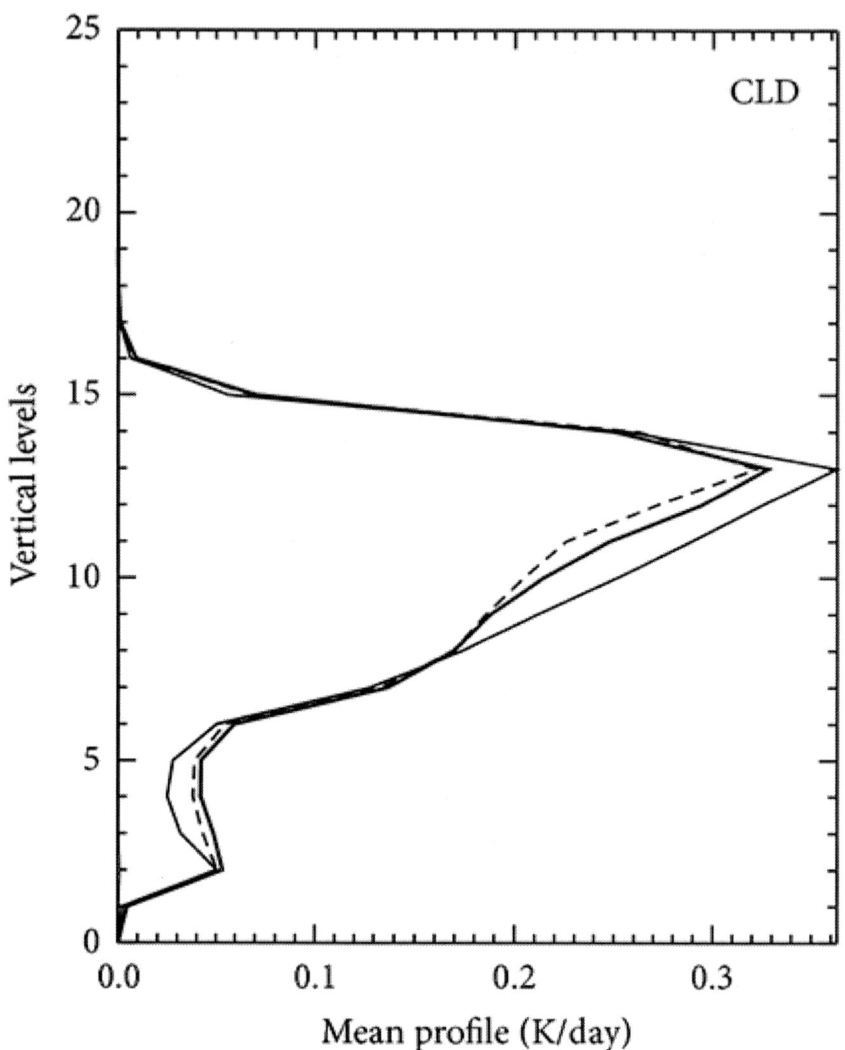

Figure 7. Three different mean cloud (CLD) profiles for the TOGA-COARE period: CAM-NN (thick solid), pseudo-observations (dashed), and CAM (solid).

Figure 8 shows the precipitation (PREC) time series produced by the original CAM run and the CAM-NN run using the NN ensemble mean. The scope, mean, and frequencies of the time series are quite similar for both models and look reasonable. Table 4 shows the bulk statistics for CLD and PREC variables for the CAM, CAM-NN runs and for pseudo-observations. Like in Figure 7 the statistics for the CAM-NN run are in between those of the CAM run and pseudo-observations; they are very reasonable and physically meaningful.

Table 4. Bulk statistics for CLD and PREC outputs for CAM, CAM-NN, and pseudo-observations (PO).

	Mean	Standard deviation	Min	Max
PREC in mm/day				
PO	9.22	11.24	0.	80.8
CAM-NN	8.50	8.14	0.	63.6
CAM	6.41	7.23	0.	43.5
CLD in fraction				
PO	0.072	0.154	0.	1.00
CAM-NN	0.104	0.240	0.	1.00
CAM	0.159	0.256	0.	1.00

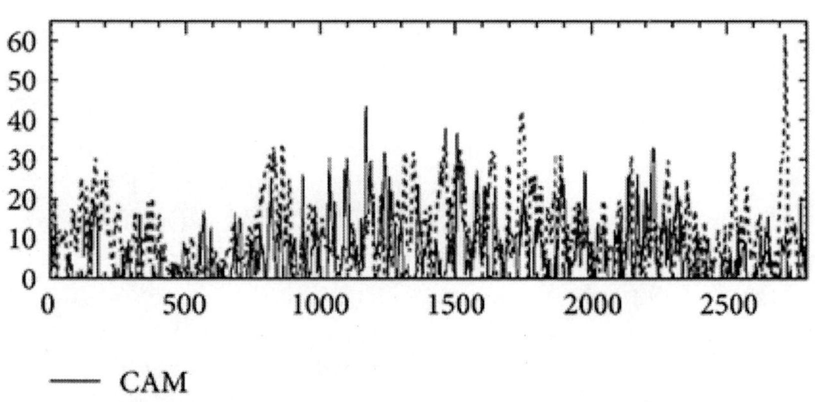

Figure 8. Precipitation (PREC, in mm/ day) time series: CAM (black solid) and CAM-NN (or NCAM) ensemble mean (red dashed).

Let us stress that we should not expect full similarity here between CAM-NN and CAM statistics, profiles, and time series. The CAM-NN results are generated by our NN convection parameterization learned from CRM cloud physics, which is different from the cloud physics implemented currently in the CAM. Full similarity of the CAM and CAM-NN results would mean that our NN convection parameterization is not different form the convection parameterization used in the CAM and has no value in terms of introducing new physics in the CAM. Even in this case, it may still be valuable in terms of higher computational performance providing also a possibility of using NN ensembles.

Evaluating the NN Convection Parameterization Generalization Ability in Parallel Decadal Climate Simulations for a Large Tropical Pacific Region

Encouraged by the aforementioned success of our NN parameterization in the CAM-NN, we extended our diagnostic tests beyond the TOGA-COARE location and beyond the time interval covered by the CRM simulated data to test the NN parameterization generalization ability and its ability to adapt to the changing data environment. Namely, we performed the parallel decadal CAM and CAM-NN simulations and analyzed their results over a large tropical Pacific region.

We would like to emphasize that the NN convection parameterization has been developed for the TOGA-COARE location, which is represented by just one grid point in the CAM and which is actually a small area in the Equatorial Pacific (marked by a star in the middle panel of Figure 11). Also the TOGA-COARE data have been produced only over a short 4-month period (from November 1992 to February 1993 or NDJF). To evaluate the NN convection parameterization generalization and adaptive ability, we applied the NN ensemble convection parameterization in the CAM-NN run for the entire large tropical Pacific region (with the area size of $120^{\circ} \times 30^{\circ}$ and the following coordinates: 150° E < lon < 90° W; 15° S < lat < 15° N) during the decadal (1990–2001, with the TOGA-COARE 4-month period from November 1992 to February 1993 excluded) run. This is a very hard test for the generalization and adaptive ability of the NNs trained over a single location and a short 4-month period.

As described above, the developed NN convection parameterization has been introduced into the CAM-NN and run in the aforementioned diagnostic mode, for which CAM inputs have been used for calculating NN convection outputs. Below we compare the parallel decadal CAM-NN and CAM simulations and validate them against the NCEP reanalysis. Because NN convection was trained using simulated data for the TOGA-COARE 4-month period (November 1992–February 1993), below we will analyze the decadal simulations for 4-month boreal winter seasons only.

The results of these decadal parallel climate simulations for the tropical Pacific region for decadal means of boreal winter (NDJF) distributions for total cloudiness (CLD) are shown in Figures 9, 10, and 11.

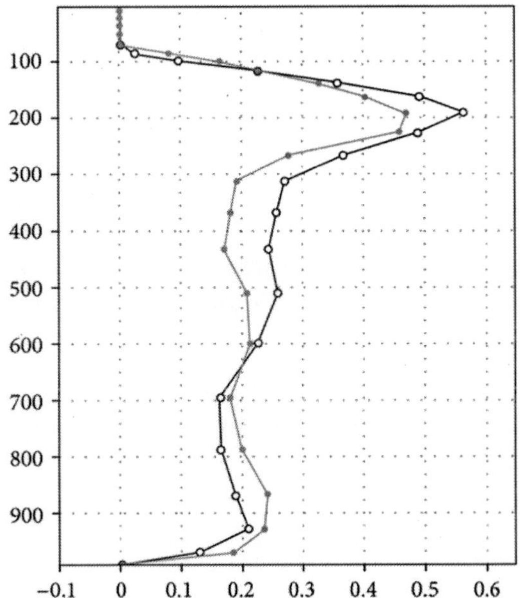

Figure 9. Vertical profiles of decadal boreal winter mean CLD for the TOGA-COARE location, in fractions, for the CAM-NN (open circles) and CAM (full circles) runs. Atmospheric pressure in hPa is the vertical coordinate.

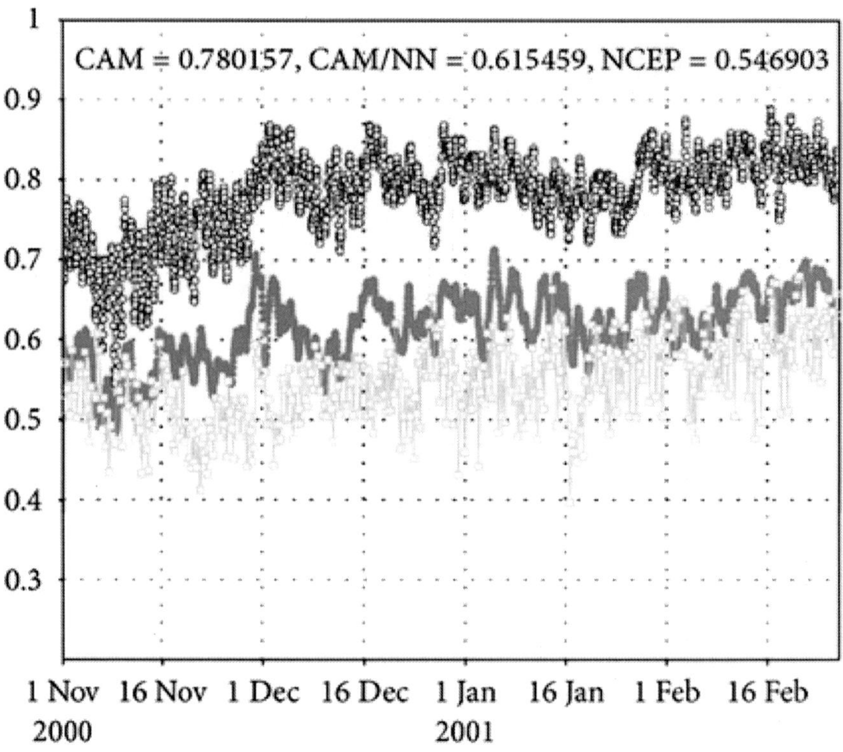

Figure 10. Time series of decadal boreal winter mean total cloudiness (CLD, in fractions) for the TOGA-COARE location for the CAM (black) and CAM-NN (green) runs, and for the NCEP reanalysis (yellow). Numbers in the figure show the mean values for the time series.

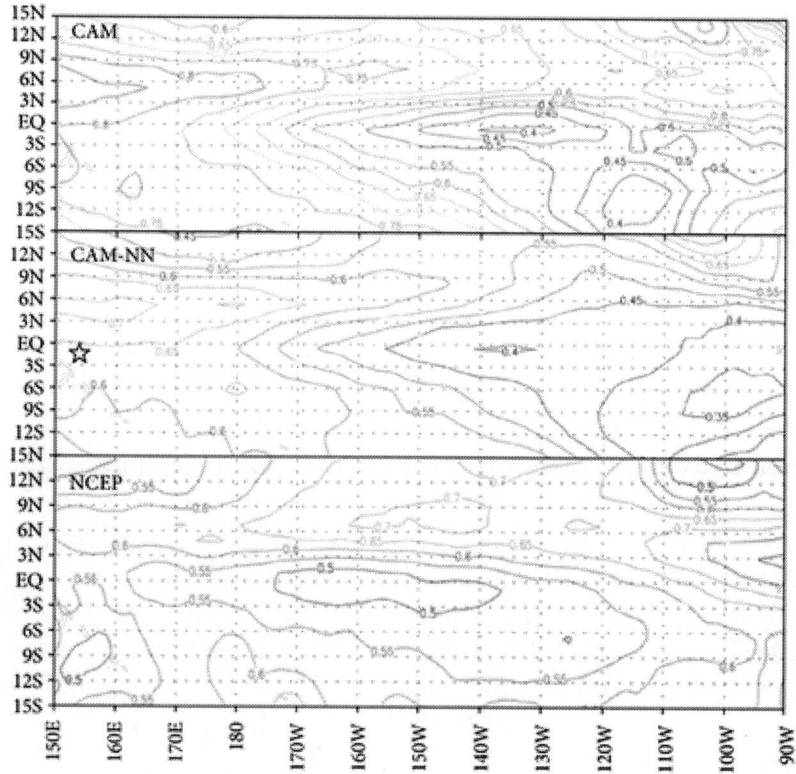

Figure 11. Decadal boreal winter mean cloudiness (CLD, in fractions) distribution for the CAM (upper panel) and CAM-NN (middle panel) runs over tropical Pacific region (with the area size of $120^\circ \times 30^\circ$ and the following coordinates: 150° E < lon < 90° W shown with the 10° interval; 15° S < lat < 15° N shown with the 3° interval). The lower panel shows the corresponding NCEP reanalysis decadal mean distribution. The TOGA-COARE location, for which the pseudo-observations were generated and the NN ensemble was trained, is shown by a star in the middle panel. The contour interval is 0.05°C.

The decadal mean CLD profiles for the TOGA-COARE location for the CAM-NN and CAM runs shown in Figure 9 are close to each other. Note that the decadal mean profiles are consistent with those shown for the CAM-NN and CAM runs in Figure 7 for the TOGA-COARE period. When comparing these two figures, the difference in the vertical coordinates should be taken into account. In Figure 7 the model vertical level number is used as the vertical coordinate, whereas in Figure 9 the atmospheric pressure in hPa is used. The conversion from one coordinate to another one is essentially nonlinear. The pressure of about 200 hPa corresponds to the vertical level number 13.

The frequencies and magnitudes of the decadal mean CLD time series for the CAM and CAM-NN runs presented in Figure 10 are similar and consistent. The time series for the CAM run show measurably higher magnitudes, with the mean of 0.78, compared to those of the time series for the CAM-NN run, with the mean of 0.61. The time series of the NCEP reanalysis show lower magnitudes, with the mean of 0.54, which are significantly closer to those of the time series for CAM-NN. Note that the CLD results presented in Figure 6 have shown a close agreement of the CRM-simulated (and grid-box averaged) data and the NN ensemble mean, at the TOGA-COARE location. In our view, the improvement of the CLD time series for the decadal CAM-NN run for a large tropical region can be attributed to both a good quality of the CRM-simulated data, which implicitly represent a better CRM cloud physics, and the positive impact from using the NN ensemble.

The horizontal distribution of total cloudiness for the large tropical Pacific Ocean region for the CAM-NN run versus the CAM control run and the NCEP reanalysis (Figure 11) have been produced and analyzed. For the region, the precipitation and cloudiness patterns for the parallel decadal CAM-NN and CAM simulations have been qualitatively and quantitatively compared.

The major result is that the regional CLD distributions for the decadal parallel runs presented in Figure 11 show a consistency and similarity, in terms of both the pattern and especially the magnitude, between the CAM-NN and CAM runs and, to some extent, with the NCEP reanalysis [17] used for validation. However, both the CAM and CAM-NN run patterns show some noticeable deviations from the NCEP reanalysis pattern. This is definitely the subject for the future improvements (see the future work outlined in Sections 4 and 5).

The CLD magnitudes for the CAM-NN run (Figure 11) are mostly closer to those of the NCEP reanalysis than the CLD magnitudes of the CAM run. However, such a positive feature should be mentioned cautiously because this is just an initial result. It is noteworthy that the CLD decadal time series for the TOGA-COARE location (Figure 10) and the CLD distribution for the tropical Pacific Ocean (Figure 11) are consistent in the sense that for both characteristics the CAM run shows measurably higher magnitudes compared to those of the CAM-NN run, the latter being closer to those of the NCEP reanalysis.

Similar results have been obtained for the decadal boreal winter precipitation distribution over the tropical Pacific Ocean region (see [4]).

DISCUSSION

At this initial stage of our development of the stochastic NN convection parameterizations, which is mostly the proof of concept, it seems reasonable to compare the CAM and CAM-NN runs mostly in terms of their general consistency between themselves and with the NCEP reanalysis. A detailed climatological analysis of regional and global simulations for all seasons will be done at the next stage of our development. It will be based on using extended more representative CRM simulations with broader spatial and temporal coverage for developing stochastic NN convection parameterizations for the CAM, which could be applied globally and for all seasons.

The CAM-NN results are generated by our NN convection parameterization learned from CRM cloud physics, which is different from the cloud physics currently implemented in the CAM convection parameterization. The CAM and CAM-NN results are consistent and quite similar, with some differences discussed above.

In our view, the results presented above in Sections 2 and 3 demonstrate a realistic potential of the presented NN ensemble approach for developing stochastic NN convection parameterizations. Our first attempt in this direction led to meaningful results despite the fact that for our development we used for the NN training a limited amount of data available over a small area in the tropical Pacific Ocean (the TOGA-COARE site) and during only four month (the TOGA-COARE period from November 1992 to February 1993). We obtained physically meaningful results not only over this particular location and time interval, but our decadal climate simulation for cloudiness and precipitations over this location and over the extended large tropical Pacific Ocean region look meaningful even without introduction in NNs an explicit time and location dependencies. These results demonstrate: (1) a very good generalization ability of the NN ensemble in this application and (2) a good ability of the NN ensemble to adapt to a changing data environment using implicit dependencies of NN inputs on time and location without introducing these dependencies explicitly.

These two issues are extremely important for future development of this approach. Our final goal is to develop a global NN convection parameterization, which can be used in the CAM and other global GCMs. To achieve this goal, a representative global data set of pseudo-observations is required. However, data for initialization and forcing CRM are available only over a few sites (TOGA-COARE, ARM, etc.); thus, CRM simulations initialized and driven by a limited amount of observations are not representative in terms of different global geographical locations and different weather conditions. Hopefully, the aforementioned data could be augmented by data simulated by the CRM, which is initialized and driven not only by observations but also by GCM-simulated data. In principle, the CRM could be run in such a way at each GCM grid point for a long period of time and supply a representative global set of pseudo-observations. However, since the CRM runs are very time consuming, this scenario is not practically feasible. In this context, good generalization and adaptation abilities of the stochastic NN convection parameterization demonstrated in this study become crucial; they will hopefully allow us to reduce the number of locations for generating pseudo-observations to a manageable and computationally affordable number of grid points.

It is noteworthy that the NN ensemble convection parameterization is very fast, contrary to any alternative approaches that have been developed to introduce new cloud and convective physics in GCMs (see [4], for details). These alternative approaches are very time consuming and barely affordable for climate simulations and weather prediction.

CONCLUSIONS

In this paper we introduce a novel approach to development of NN convection parameterizations based on applying the NN ensemble technique. This approach has been conceptually formulated and developed. Several very important notions are introduced which constitute the conceptual skeleton of the approach:

1. pseudo-observations which are the result of averaging and projecting of high-dimensional and high-resolution CRM-simulated data. The pseudo-observations contain the uncertainty which is a result of averaging and projection of the original CRM simulated data,
2. stochastic mapping/parameterization that is implicitly defined by pseudo-observations with uncertainties,
3. NN ensemble emulation that is an adequate tool for emulating stochastic mappings/parameterizations,
4. adaptation to temporal and spatial change in the environment, in which the NN ensemble parameterization performs through implicit time and location dependencies of NN inputs.

Our future plans include the following:

1. running CRM simulations initialized and forced by GCM-simulated data and by reanalysis data to generate a more representative data set that will include a broader range of convection regimes, longer time periods, more locations, and more diverse weather conditions,
2. using the representative global data set produced in this way to train a global NN convection parameterization,
3. testing the NN convection parameterization trained using these new data in the CAM in diagnostic and prognostic modes,
4. introducing tools allowing the NN parameterization to adapt to changes in the environment by: (1) using time and location as additional inputs in the NN parameterization and (2) using dynamically adjustable NN parameterization based on approaches developed in [18]. The approaches use various procedures to recognize new atmospheric states emerged due to the changes in the environment. These states are used for an online adjustment of the NN parameters.

ACKNOWLEDGMENTS

The authors would like to thank Prof. Marat Khairoutdinov (SUNY) for providing the CRM (SAM), Dr. Peter Blossy for providing simulated data and consultations on SAM, and Dr. Philip J. Rasch (DOE PNNL) for multiple and fruitful discussions: MMAB Contribution no. 293.

REFERENCES

1. L. J. Donner and P. J. Rasch, "Cumulus initialization in a global model for numerical weather prediction," Monthly Weather Review, vol. 117, pp. 2654–2671, 1989.
2. P. J. Rasch, J. Feichter, K. Law et al., "A comparison of scavenging and deposition processes in global models: results from the WCRP Cambridge workshop of 1995," Tellus B, vol. 52, no. 4, pp. 1025–1056, 2000. View at Scopus
3. P. J. Rasch, M. J. Stevens, L. Ricciardulli et al., "A characterization of tropical transient activity in the CAM3 atmospheric hydrologic cycle," Journal of Climate, vol. 19, no. 11, pp. 2222–2242, 2006. View at Publisher · View at Google Scholar · View at Scopus
4. V. Krasnopolsky, M. Fox-Rabinovitz, A. Belochitski, P. Rasch, P. Blossey, and Y. Kogan, "Development of neural network convection parameterizations for climate and NWP models using Cloud Resolving Model simulations," NCEP Office Note 469, 2011, http://www.emc.ncep.noaa.gov/officenotes/newernotes/on469.pdf.
5. T. N. Palmer and P. D. Williams, "Introduction. Stochastic physics and climate modeling," Philosophical Transactions of the Royal Society A, vol. 366, pp. 2421–2427, 2008. View at Publisher · View at Google Scholar
6. M. F. Khairoutdinov and D. A. Randall, "A cloud resolving model as a cloud parameterization in the NCAR community climate system model: preliminary results," Geophysical Research Letters, vol. 28, no. 18, pp. 3617–3620, 2001. View at Publisher · View at Google Scholar · View at Scopus
7. M. F. Khairoutdinov and D. A. Randall, "Cloud resolving modeling of the ARM summer 1997 IOP: model formulation, results, uncertainties, and sensitivities," Journal of the Atmospheric Sciences, vol. 60, no. 4, pp. 607–625, 2003. View at Scopus
8. F. Guichard, J. C. Petch, J. L. Redelsperger et al., "Modelling the diurnal cycle of deep precipitating convection over land with cloud-resolving models and single-column models," Quarterly Journal of the Royal Meteorological Society, vol. 130, no. 604, pp. 3139–3172, 2004. View at Publisher · View at Google Scholar · View at Scopus
9. V. M. Krasnopolsky, M. S. Fox-Rabinovitz, and D. V. Chalikov, "New approach to calculation of atmospheric model physics: accurate and fast neural network emulation of longwave radiation in a climate model," Monthly Weather Review, vol. 133, no. 5, pp. 1370–1383, 2005. View at

Publisher · View at Google Scholar · View at Scopus

10. V. M. Krasnopolsky, M. S. Fox-Rabinovitz, and A. A. Belochitski, "Decadal climate simulations using accurate and fast neural network emulation of full, long- and short wave, radiation," Monthly Weather Review, vol. 136, pp. 3683–3695, 2008. View at Publisher · View at Google Scholar
11. V. M. Krasnopolsky, M. S. Fox-Rabinovitz, Y. T. Hou, S. J. Lord, and A. A. Belochitski, "Accurate and fast neural network emulations of model radiation for the NCEP coupled climate forecast system: climate simulations and seasonal predictions," Monthly Weather Review, vol. 138, no. 5, pp. 1822–1842, 2010. View at Publisher · View at Google Scholar · View at Scopus
12. V. M. Krasnopolsky, "Neural network emulations for complex multidimensional geophysical mappings: applications of neural network techniques to atmospheric and oceanic satellite retrievals and numerical modeling," Reviews of Geophysics, vol. 45, Article ID RG3009, 2007. View at Publisher · View at Google Scholar
13. V. Krasnopolsky, "Neural network applications to developing hybrid atmospheric and oceanic numerical models," in Artificial Intelligence Methods in the Environmental Sciences, S. E. Haupt, A. Pasini, and C. Marzban, Eds., pp. 217–234, Springer, 2009.
14. V. Krasnopolsky, "Neural network applications to solve forward and inverse problems in atmospheric and oceanic satellite remote sensing," in Artificial Intelligence Methods in the Environmental Sciences, S. E. Haupt, A. Pasini, and C. Marzban, Eds., pp. 191–205, Springer, 2009.
15. D. Nguyen and B. Widrow, "Improving the learning speed of 2-layer neural networks by choosing initial values of the adaptive weights," in Proceedings of the International Joint Conference on Neural Networks (IJCNN '90), vol. 3, pp. 21–26, San Diego, Calif, USA, June 1990. View at Scopus
16. E. Kalnay, M. Kanamitsu, R. Kistler, et al., "The NCEP/NCAR 40-year reanalysis project," Bulletin of the American Meteorological Society, vol. 77, pp. 437–471, 1996.
17. S. Saha, S. Moorthi, H.-L. Pan, et al., "The NCEP climate forecast system reanalysis," Bulletin of the American Meteorological Society, vol. 91, pp. 1015–1057, 2010. View at Publisher · View at Google Scholar
18. V. M. Krasnopolsky, M. S. Fox-Rabinovitz, H. L. Tolman, and A. A. Belochitski, "Neural network approach for robust and fast calculation of physical processes in numerical environmental models: compound parameterization with a quality control of larger errors," Neural Networks, vol. 21, no. 2-3, pp. 535–543, 2008. View at Publisher · View at Google Scholar · View at Scopus

Chapter 3

A UNIFIED FRAMEWORK FOR GPS CODE AND CARRIER-PHASE MULTIPATH MITIGATION USING SUPPORT VECTOR REGRESSION

Quoc-Huy Phan,[1] Su-Lim Tan,[2] Ian McLoughlin,[3] and Duc-Lung Vu[1]

[1]University of Information Technology, Km 20, Ha Noi Highway, Linh Trung Ward, Thu Duc, HCMC 70000, Vietnam

[2]Singapore Institute of Technology, 25 North Bridge Road, Singapore 179104

[3]School of Information Science and Technology, University of Science and Technology of China, No. 443 Huangshan Road, Hefei, Anhui 230027, China

ABSTRACT

Multipath mitigation is a long-standing problem in global positioning system (GPS) research and is essential for improving the accuracy and precision of positioning solutions. In this work, we consider multipath error estimation as a regression problem and propose a unified framework for both code and carrier-phase multipath mitigation for ground fixed GPS stations. We use the kernel support vector machine to predict multipath errors, since it is known to potentially offer better-performance traditional models, such as neural networks. The predicted multipath error is then used to correct GPS measurements. We empirically show that the proposed method can reduce the code multipath error standard deviation up to 79% on average, which significantly outperforms other approaches in the literature. A comparative analysis of reduction of double-differential carrier-phase multipath error reveals that a 57% reduction is also achieved. Furthermore, by simulation, we also show that this method is robust to coexisting signals of phenomena (e.g., seismic signals) we wish to preserve.

INTRODUCTION

Multipath is defined as one or more indirect replicas of the line-of-sight (LOS) signal from satellites arriving at a receiver's antenna from a satellite. It normally occurs due to reflection from objects in the vicinity of the receiver and constitutes a major error source that contaminates receivers' measurements, resulting in performance degradation of GPS positioning solutions. The errors induced by multipath are typically up to 15 meters for C/A code [1] and a few centimeters for carrier-phase measurements [2]. Multipath mitigation is hence important for a variety of applications which utilize this data, such as ionospheric monitoring [3], geodesy [4, 5], and navigation [6].

On the one hand, multipath mitigation is a very challenging task. As multipath is site-dependent, differencing measurements among multiple short-baseline receivers (DGPS) are unlikely to help. Furthermore, aggressively removing multipath error may harm wanted coexisting information and perturbations such as seismic signals induced by an earthquake, as their frequency spectra likely overlap with that of the contaminating multipath error.

Various mitigation approaches have been proposed in the literature, classified into either frequency-domain or time-domain processing. The former is based on spectral analysis of multipath error in the frequency domain using fast fourier transform (FFT) [7], or wavelet decomposition [8, 9]. However, they unintentionally rule out other coexisting signals. To overcome this issue, signal-to-noise (SNR) measurements [10, 11] can be used as alternative for analysis. Unfortunately, this suffers from unavailability and inconsistency in units from different types of receivers. Time-domain methods range from the popular carrier smoothing filter (CSF) [12, 13], band-pass finite impulse response (FIR) filter [14, 15] to stacking [16–18]. These methods also tend to filter out coexisting signals of interest and require high-rate data to boost their performance [16].

In previous works [19, 20], we propose a regression model, which integrates kernel support vector regression (SVR) with geometrical features to deal with the code multipath error prediction on ground fixed GPS stations. To the best of the authors' knowledge, this is the first work using machine learning to address GPS multipath error estimation. This paper extends our previous work to define a unified framework for both code and carrier-phase multipath mitigation. The contribution of this paper is threefold: (1) deriving geometric models for code and carrier-phase multipath errors, (2) formulating multipath error estimation as a regression problem with geometrical features, and (3) unifying the framework for code and carrier-phase multipath estimation using support vector regression.

The rest of this paper is organized as follows. Section 2 briefly reviews the mathematical models of GPS measurements and derives the geometrical models of multipath errors. By posing multipath estimation as a nonlinear regression problem, Section 3 defines the framework for multipath mitigation. Experimental results and discussions for code and carrier-phase multipath mitigation will be presented in Sections 4 and 5, respectively. The conclusion will follow in Section 6.

GPS MEASUREMENTS AND CODE MULTIPATH EXTRACTION

In this section, we briefly review the GPS measurement data as generated by GPS receivers. Following this, geometrical models will be derived for both code and carrier-phase multipath errors.

GPS Measurements

The code measurement ρ_1 and carrier-phase measurement ϕ_1 for channel L1 are given as in (1) and (2), respectively [13, 21]. The measurements for L2 are similar,

$$\rho_1 = r + c(\delta_u - \delta_s) + I_1 + T + M_1^{\rho} + \varepsilon_1^{\rho}, \quad (1)$$

$$\phi_1\lambda_1 = r + c(\delta_u - \delta_s) - I_1 + T + N_1\lambda_1 + M_1^{\phi} + \varepsilon_1^{\phi}, \quad (2)$$

where r represents the true range from a satellite to a receiver, δ is clock bias, the subscripts and refer to the user (receiver) and the satellite, respectively, c is the speed of light, T, I, M^{ρ}, ε^{ρ}, M_1^{ϕ}, and ε_1^{ϕ} denote tropospheric delay, ionospheric delay, code multipath error, random receiver noise on code, carrier-phase multipath error, and random receiver noise on carrier-phase, respectively, and the symbols λ_1 denote wavelengths of L1. The term N_1 is the ambiguous integer of L1. The opposite signs of the ionospheric delays in (1) and (2) are due to the fact that the ionosphere affects code and carrier measurements equally but in opposite directions when the signals travel through the dispersive ionospheric layer in the atmosphere [2].

Geometrical Model of Code Multipath

Ideally, in a multipath-free environment, only one direct signal is received by the antenna from each satellite. However, no environment is completely multipath-free in practice. A receiver antenna receives one or more replicas of the direct signal reflected from objects near the LOS path, particularly those in the vicinity of the receiver. As a result, the receiver will track a composite signal that is a combination of the direct path and the multipath replicas.

For clarity, let us consider the simplified case of one multipath signal. Let A_d and A_m denote the amplitudes of the direct signal and the multipath signal, respectively, δ the path delay, ψ the multipath relative phase in radians, $\alpha = A_m/A_d \leq 1$ the ratio of the multipath and direct amplitudes, and θ and μ the azimuth and elevation angles, respectively. The position of any reflecting object is described as a planar surface tilted relative to the local level with a tilt angle γ at a distance *h* from the antenna centre as illustrated in Figure 1.

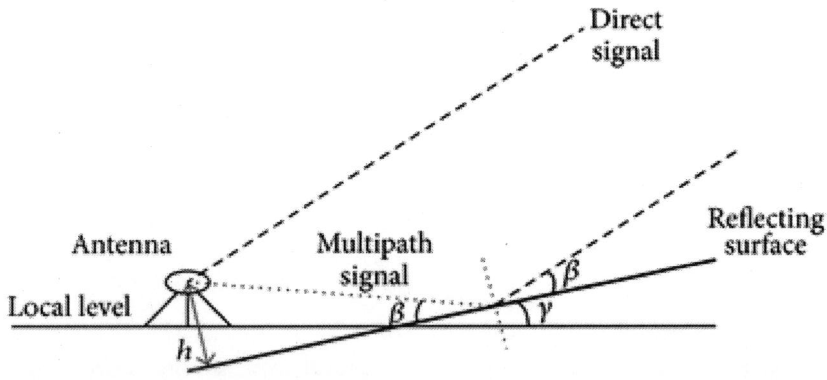

Figure 1. The direct signal and one multipath signal with simplified geometry.

Let β denote the reflection angle relative to the reflecting surface; the induced code multipath error is given as [16]:

$$M^{\rho} = \frac{\alpha\delta\cos\psi}{1+\alpha\cos\psi}. \tag{3}$$

In order to obtain the geometrical model, we need to relate multipath error with geometrical parameters, that is, azimuth and elevation angles. Assuming that the satellite, antenna, and normal vector to the reflecting surface are coplanar, multipath reflections fall into two categories: forward-scatter and backscatter [22] as in Figure 2.

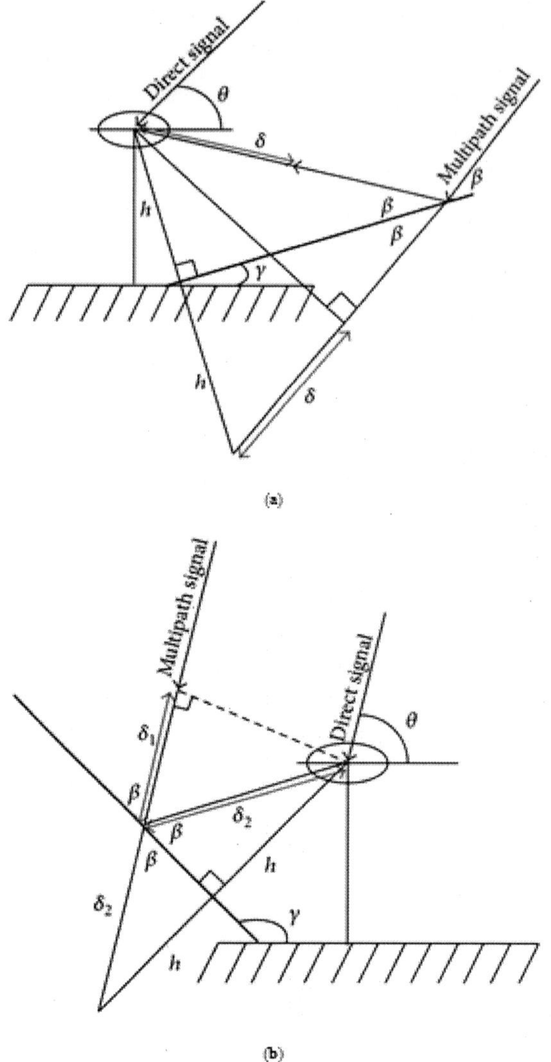

Figure 2. Multipath reflections: (a) forward-scatter and (b) backscatter.

In both forward-scatter and backscatter scenarios, it is easily to obtain

$$\delta = 2h \sin \beta, \tag{4}$$

$$\psi = \frac{2\pi}{\lambda}\delta = \frac{2\pi}{\lambda}2h \sin \beta. \tag{5}$$

Furthermore, using the convention of angles measured anticlockwise over the interval $[0^{\circ}180^{\circ}]$, $\beta + \gamma = \theta$ for forward-scatter whereas $\beta + \theta = \gamma$ for backscatter. To generalize,

$$\beta = |\theta - \gamma|. \tag{6}$$

Substituting (4), (5), and (6) into (3), the code multipath equations corresponding to one reflecting signal can be rewritten as

$$M^{\rho} = \frac{\alpha 2h \sin(|\theta - \gamma|) \cos((4\pi h/\lambda) \sin(|\theta - \gamma|))}{1 + \alpha \cos((4\pi h/\lambda) \sin(|\theta - \gamma|))}. \tag{7}$$

In the general case of *m* reflecting signals, the total code multipath is the sum of the individual code multipath:

$$M^{\rho} = \frac{\sum_{i=1}^{m} \alpha_i 2h_i \sin(|\theta - \gamma_i|) \cos((4\pi h_i/\lambda) \sin(|\theta - \gamma_i|))}{1 + \sum_{i=1}^{m} \alpha_i \cos((4\pi h_i/\lambda) \sin(|\theta - \gamma_i|))}. \tag{8}$$

Geometrical Model of Carrier-Phase Multipath

The effect of multipath on carrier-phase measurement can be demonstrated by the phasor diagram in Figure 3. Additionally, let A_c denote the amplitude of the composite signal which is the combination of the multipath signal and the direct signal. ϕ_d, ϕ_c, and ψ are the direct signal's phase, the composite signal's phase and the multipath relative phase with respect to the direct signal, respectively. δ_{ϕ} denotes the phase error due to multipath.

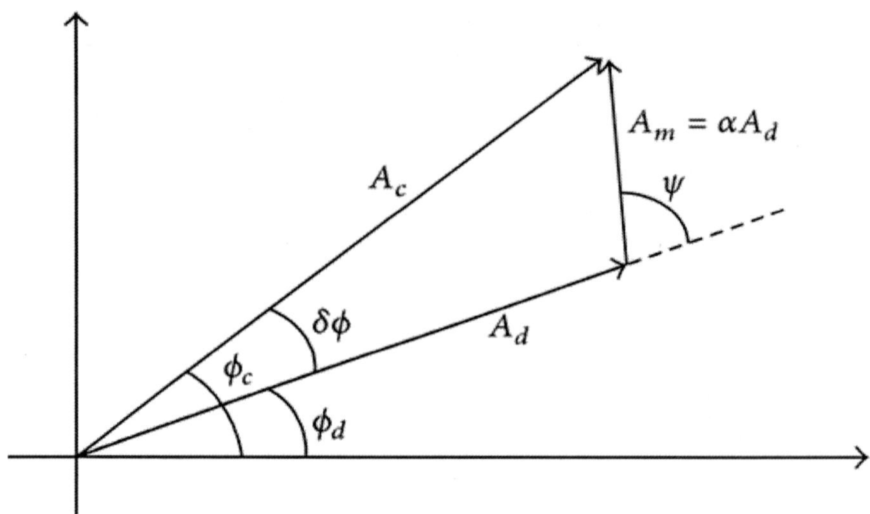

Figure 3. Effect of multipath to carrier-phase measurement.

The phase error due to multipath is easily derived in terms of multipath parameters as follows:

$$\tan(\delta\phi) = \frac{A_m \sin(\psi + \phi_0)}{A_d + A_m \cos(\psi + \phi_0)} = \frac{\alpha \sin(\psi + \phi_0)}{1 + \alpha \cos(\psi + \phi_0)}, \tag{9}$$

where ϕ_0 is a possible phase offset at time 0. Therefore,

$$\delta\phi = \arctan\left(\frac{\alpha \sin(\psi + \phi_0)}{1 + \alpha \cos(\psi + \phi_0)}\right). \tag{10}$$

Substituting (5) into (10), we obtain the phase error caused by one multipath signal:

$$\delta\phi = \arctan\left(\frac{\alpha \sin((4\pi h/\lambda)\sin(|\theta - \gamma|) + \phi_0)}{1 + \alpha \cos((4\pi h/\lambda)\sin(|\theta - \gamma|) + \phi_0)}\right). \tag{11}$$

In general case of m multipath signals,

$$\delta\phi = \arctan\left(\frac{\sum_{i=1}^{m} \alpha \sin\left((4\pi h_i/\lambda)\sin\left(|\theta - \gamma_i|\right) + \phi_0^i\right)}{1 + \sum_{i=1}^{m} \alpha \cos\left((4\pi h_i/\lambda)\sin\left(|\theta - \gamma_i|\right) + \phi_0^i\right)}\right). \tag{12}$$

MULTIPATH MITIGATION FRAMEWORK USING NON-LINEAR SUPPORT VECTOR REGRESSION

In this section, we will define the unified framework for code and carrier-phase multipath mitigation followed by the formulation to solve multipath estimation as nonlinear regression using support vector regression algorithm.

Multipath Mitigation Framework

Under assumption that the multipath environment around a ground fixed receiver is held fixed, then quantities α_i, h_i, γ_i in in (8) and (12) will remain constant. As a result, code multipath error M^ρ and carrier-phase multipath error $\delta\phi$ are complicated functions of satellite-relative elevation angle and azimuth angle θ in the general case which characterizes the geometry of the satellite with respect to the receiver. Give these functions, in order to compute multipath errors, it is necessary to somehow evaluate the functions in (8) and (12) given as an azimuth/elevation pair. Viewed as a regression problem, these functions will be approximated by learning from the historical multipath data and satellite orbital information. Specifically, estimating code and carrier-phase multipath errors is a 2-dimensional regression setting:

$$\text{multipath} = f\,(\text{azimuth}, \text{elevation})\,. \tag{13}$$

The rationale behind this approach is the observation that a fixed receiver experiences highly sidereal day-to-day correlation of satellite-receiver geometry and multipath error. It is well known that the GPS satellite orbits were selected to have a period of half a sidereal day (23 hours 56 minutes 4 seconds) with a daily repeating ground track [23, 24]. Because of this, satellite visibility from any point on earth is the same from day to day, with the satellites appearing in their positions approximately 4 minutes or 236 seconds earlier each day due to the time difference between the sidereal and solar day. Furthermore, for a fixed station, its surroundings and the antenna usually do not change significantly across consecutive days. Therefore, GPS multipath signals are expected to largely repeat over the same time period. Our proposed approach leverages this observation with a regression approach to approximate the function of the repeatable multipath error.

Code and carrier-phase multipath errors can be estimated independently, but the procedure for training the estimators is the same. Satellite-specific multipath estimator will be trained using ε-SVR [25], a well-known support vector regression algorithm. After being trained, the code and carrier-phase multipath estimators will be used to provide estimate of multipath errors. Afterwards, these estimates will be used to correct code and carrier-phase measurements to achieve multipath mitigation.

Nonlinear Regression for Multipath Estimation

Among various kinds of regression models, SVRs [25, 26] are well known to have more potential advantages than traditional models, such as neural networks [27]. They are based on the strong statistical learning theory and have been shown to be less prone to overfitting as well as being independent of the dimensionality of the input space. We employ ε-SVR [25], which is most commonly used for regression problem. In the hard margin loss setting for ε-SVR, the estimate has at most ε deviation from the actual target for all training data, meaning that one does not care about errors as long as they are less than , but will not accept any deviation larger than this. Nevertheless, owing to noise in data, we usually use soft margin loss setting to allow for some errors by introducing slack variables in the formulation of ε-SVR.

We denote input vector as $x \in \mathbb{R}^n$ and denote a value of multipath error as $y \in \mathbb{R}$. Given the multipath model in (8) and (12), our goal is to learn a function $f : \mathbb{R}^n \mapsto \mathbb{R}$ mapping from an observation vector to an estimate of multipath error $\hat{y}$. Formally, this can be accomplished by first choosing a set of training samples $\{(x_1, y_1), \ldots, (x_N, y_N)\} \in \mathbb{R}^n \times \mathbb{R}$. Due to noise in the training data, it is unlikely that $f(x_i)$ will be equal to $L(f(x), y)$ for all , so a loss function must also be chosen to quantify the penalty for $f(x_i)$ differing from y_i. The estimator f can be found by minimizing the total loss over the training data.

For each satellite, the multipath estimator is trained using ε-SVR [25]. We denote the regression function $f(x) = \langle w, \varphi(x)\rangle + b$, where ω is the weight vector in the kernel feature space, $b \in \mathbb{R}$ is a bias term, $\langle \cdot, \cdot \rangle$ denotes the dot product, and φ is the kernel feature map of data point x. The ε-insensitive loss function given by (14) is chosen so that the function $f(x)$ is found to have at most deviation from the targets y_i for all training samples:

$$L(f(x), y) = \begin{cases} 0, & \text{if } |f(x) - y| < \varepsilon, \\ |f(x) - y| - \varepsilon, & \text{otherwise,} \end{cases} \tag{14}$$

$f(x)$ can be solved through the following optimization problem [25]:

$$\begin{aligned} &\text{minimize} \quad \frac{1}{2}\|w\|^2 + C\sum_{i=1}^{N}(\xi_i + \xi_i^*) \\ &\qquad\qquad y_i - \langle w, \varphi(x_i)\rangle - b \le \varepsilon + \xi_i \\ &\text{subject to} \quad \langle w, \varphi(x_i)\rangle + b - y_i \le \varepsilon + \xi_i^* \\ &\qquad\qquad \xi_i, \xi_i^* > 0, \quad i = 1, \ldots, N, \end{aligned} \tag{15}$$

where ε is the parameter of the ε-insensitive loss function that controls the accuracy of the regressor. The constant $C > 0$ adjusts the tradeoff between the regression error and the regularization on *f*. $\xi = \{\xi_1, \ldots, \xi_N\} \in \mathbb{R}^N$ and $\xi^* = \{\xi_1^*, \ldots, \xi_N^*\} \in \mathbb{R}^N$ are slack variables allowing errors around the regression function. After solving the optimization problem, the form of the estimator is

$$\begin{aligned} f(x) &= \sum_{i=1}^{N_{SV}} \omega_i \langle \varphi(x), \varphi(p_i) \rangle + b \\ &= \sum_{i=1}^{N_{SV}} \omega_i \kappa(x, p_i) + b, \end{aligned} \tag{16}$$

where $\omega_1, \ldots, \omega_{N_{SV}}$ are scalar coefficients, $p_1, \ldots, p_{N_{SV}}$ are support vectors, and $\kappa : \mathbb{R}^n \times \mathbb{R}^n \mapsto \mathbb{R}$ is a kernel function. *f(x)* depends only on the training samples having nonzero coefficients (support vectors) through the representation of the kernel function *k*. The Gaussian kernel given by (17) is reasonably chosen due to its ability to handle nonlinearity:

$$\kappa(x_i, x_j) = \exp\left(-\eta \|x_i - x_j\|^2\right), \tag{17}$$

where η is kernel bandwidth. Solving the regression problem by ε-SVR, learning from training data, code multipath error can be estimated for each visible satellite.

EXPERIMENT I: CODE MULTIPATH MITIGATION

In this section, we will describe experiments conducted to train multipath estimators and subsequently use them for multipath mitigation. We demonstrate that our approach outperforms state-of-the-art results in code multipath mitigation in terms of standard deviation. The advantages of the exploited methods will be also discussed.

Experimental Data Set

The data set used for evaluation was recorded at a sampling rate of 0.1 Hz from a GPS monitoring station equipped with a Trimble NetRS receiver on the rooftop of the N2 building in Nanyang Technological University (NTU) campus (Singapore) during five consecutive days: from the day of year (Day) 306 to 310 of 2010. The nominal position of the observation site is (−1507932.6167, 6195587.6757, 148897.9990) in the earth-centered, earth-fixed (ECEF) Cartesian coordinate system [13]. Rooftops are usually bad multipath environments since there are often many vents and other reflective objects within the GPS antenna field of view. In the photographs shown in Figure 4, it can be seen that the observation site is surrounded by many buildings and reflectors which make multipath potentially more severe. During the evaluation period there were 31 visible satellites ranging from PRN 2 to PRN 32 observed at this site.

Figure 4. The observation site on the rooftop of N2 building (NTU campus).

To illustrate the repeatability of GPS satellite geometries, Figure 5 plots the geometries of 4 visible satellites with respect to the observation site during 4 consecutive days from Day 306 to Day 309. For the sake of simplicity and clarity, only 4 of 31 in-view satellites whose full arcs completely fall in each day period are plotted. As seen from these plots, the footprints of the day-to-day repeated geometries of the satellites are obviously exposed.

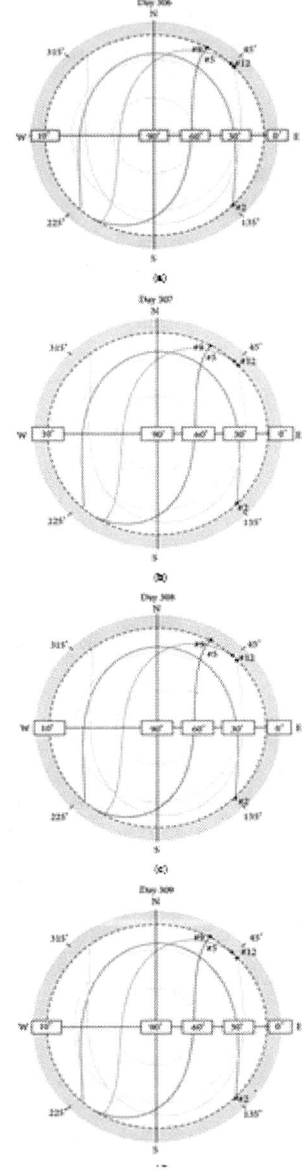

Figure 5. Geometry footprints of 4 satellites PRN 02, 05, 09, and 12 in 4 consecutive sidereal days.

Likewise, in order to illustrate the day-to-day repeatability of code multipath error, Figures 6(a) and 6(b) plotted the code multipath sequences extracted from the recorded data set during four observation days from Day 306 to Day 309. The code multipath error can be extracted in batch mode from code measurements using code-minus-carrier (CmC) combination on a whole arc [9, 13]. The correlation is more clearly revealed after we smoothed the sequences with a CSF [9] having a 50-second window to largely remove high-frequency noise. The original multipath sequences are plotted in blue and CSF-smoothed multipath sequences are plotted in red. Day-to-day correlation of the two multipath sequences is numerically evaluated by their normalized cross-correlation. Pair-wise normalized cross-correlation values of the multipath sequences are tabulated in Table 1 for PRN 12 with blue and red values representing the original and smoothed multipath sequences, respectively. The day-to-day correlation is around 89% between two consecutive days and slowly degrades with time. This is understandable since cumulative environmental changes become noticeable as the time span increases.

Table 1. Normalized cross-correlation of PRN 12's multipath sequences for original data shown in blue and for CSF-smoothed data shown in red

	Day 306	Day 307	Day 308	Day 309
Day 306	N/A	0.6668	0.5215	0.5215
Day 307	0.9055	N/A	0.6513	0.5254
Day 308	0.8775	0.8988	N/A	0.6260
Day 309	0.8649	0.8630	0.8851	N/A

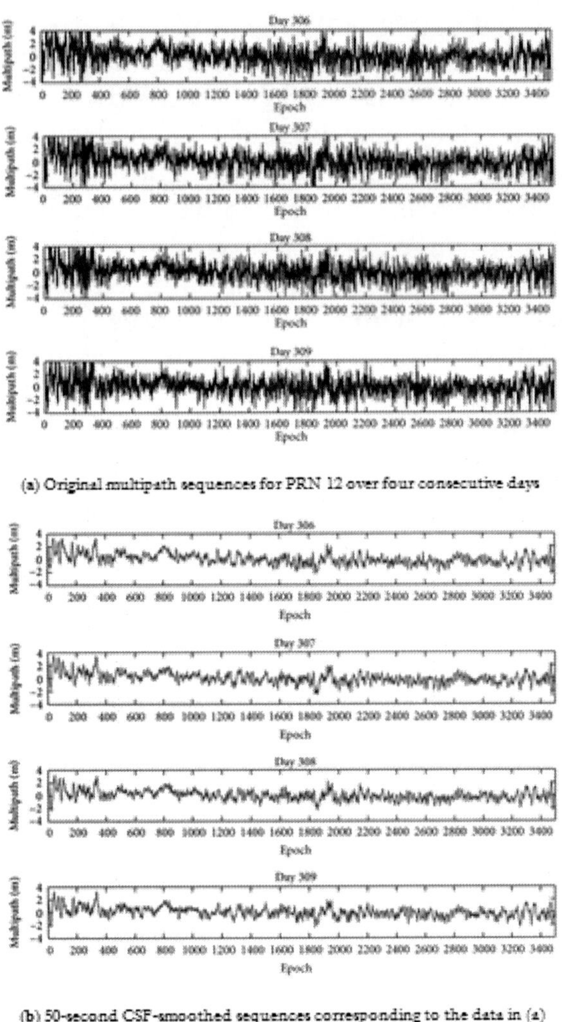

(a) Original multipath sequences for PRN 12 over four consecutive days

(b) 50-second CSF-smoothed sequences corresponding to the data in (a)

Figure 6. Multipath sequences of PRN 12 in four sidereal days from Day 306 to Day 309 of 2010.

Training Code Multipath Estimators

For each satellite, the training data is prepared using 4-day data from Day 306 to Day 309 extracted from the experimental data set, which we have found to be redundant enough to capture distribution of multipath sequences. Azimuth and elevation angles of the satellites in degrees with respect to the receiver, which are inputs for training, are computed from the broadcast navigation data [13]. For the desired multipath outputs, after being detached from observation data, the CmC sequences containing multipath errors are filtered with CSF to remove high-frequency noise. The effect of this smoothing on the multipath error is negligible as long as the smoothing window is shorter than the highest rate multipath. The smoothing window is set to 50 seconds (equivalent to 5 epochs) which is only a fraction of the shortest anticipated multipath fading period of 200 seconds [9, 28]. Thus, the receiver noise was significantly reduced without removing the multipath which was to be quantified. This smoothing operation helps to clearly expose multipath patterns and, as a result, to enhance the estimators' generalization.

Scaling is applied to the training data before use. Azimuth angles, elevation angles, and code multipath values are scaled to the range [-1; + 1]. The main advantage of scaling is not only to avoid numerical difficulties during the calculation but also to prevent domination of values in greater numeric ranges over those in smaller numeric ranges.

The libSVM package (http://www.csie.ntu.edu.tw/~cjlin/libsvm), which implements ε-SVR, was used to find the support vectors and coefficients of each satellite-specific code multipath estimator. ε, the kernel parameter and the penalty parameter of the error term , must be chosen as a priori. It is not known beforehand which parameter values are best for a given problem; consequently, some kind of model selection (parameter search) must be done. For and , grid search and cross-validation were applied for parameter search. Following the recommended libSVM approach, a coarse grid search was firstly performed on exponentially growing sequences of $\eta = 2^{-15}, 2^{-13}, \ldots, 2^{3}$ and $C = 2^{-5}, 2^{-3}, \ldots, 2^{15}$ followed by cross-validation for each pair of with a fixed . The result with the best 6-fold cross-validation accuracy was picked. With this strategy, better region on the grid can be identified and finer grid-search across those regions. was searched separately in the range (0.005–0.1) with step size of 0.005 after the best pair has been chosen.

Learning from the training data set, the support vectors and coefficients in (16) are found for multipath estimation of each satellite.

Each separately trained estimator should estimate multipath error when presented with a new observation of azimuth/elevation angles thereafter.

Experimental Results

In order to evaluate the performance of code multipath estimators, the proper multipath correction is directly applied to code measurements for Day 310. Note that the inputs must be scaled as they were during the training phase, and the estimated multipath values subsequently need to be descaled.

For the sake of demonstration, Figure 7 presents pseudorange multipath errors and responses of the multipath estimator corresponding to PRN 12 in the Day. As observed, standard deviation of the multipath sequence is significantly reduced after being corrected with the responses of the SVR estimator.

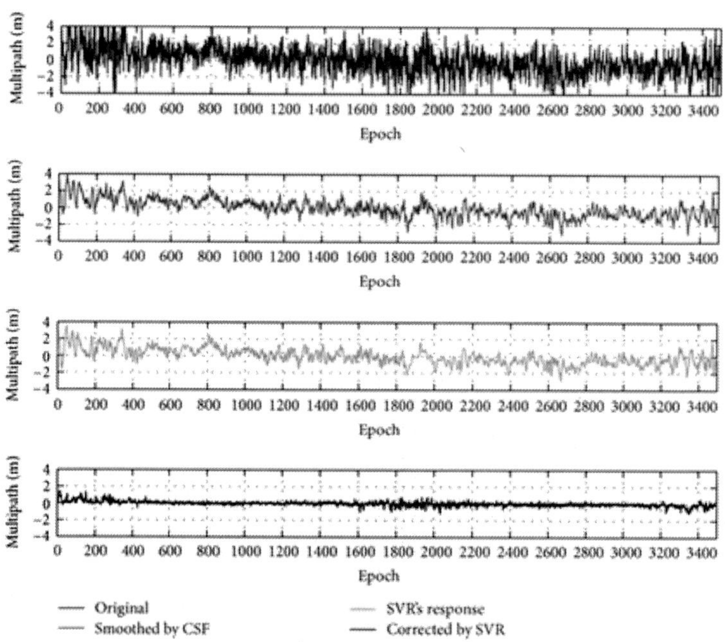

Figure 7. Original pseudorange multipath, CSF-smoothed pseudorange multipath, SVR-estimator response, and SVR-corrected pseudorange multipath of PRN 12 of the orbital plane B in Day 310 of 2010.

Performance of all multipath estimators corresponding to the visible satellites is tabulated in Table 2 where multipath reduction is measured in terms of the reduced standard deviation of multipath errors.

Table 2. Standard deviation (m) of noise before and after correction applied with CSF and SVR estimators

PRN	Original	CSF corrected	SVR corrected
02	1.4927	0.9992 (33.06%)	0.3671 (75.41%)
03	1.1479	0.6741 (41.28%)	0.2478 (78.41%)
04	1.4009	0.8913 (36.38%)	0.2201 (84.29%)
05	1.2474	0.7722 (38.10%)	0.2325 (81.36%)
06	1.3194	0.6957 (47.28%)	0.2946 (77.67%)
07	1.2561	0.8768 (30.20%)	0.2711 (78.42%)
08	1.2806	0.8680 (32.22%)	0.2409 (81.19%)
09	1.3406	0.7955 (40.66%)	0.3599 (73.15%)
10	1.2084	0.7954 (34.18%)	0.2193 (81.85%)
11	1.4290	0.9993 (30.07%)	0.2995 (79.04%)
12	1.4813	0.9943 (32.87%)	0.2509 (83.06%)
13	1.5451	0.9960 (35.54%)	0.4969 (67.84%)
14	1.4514	0.8575 (40.92%)	0.2880 (80.16%)
15	1.3496	0.9539 (29.32%)	0.3034 (77.52%)
16	1.2200	0.7730 (36.64%)	0.3902 (68.01%)
17	1.4946	0.9515 (36.34%)	0.2763 (81.51%)
18	1.7889	1.1555 (35.40%)	0.3425 (80.85%)
19	1.1336	0.6832 (39.73%)	0.2506 (77.90%)
20	1.3501	0.8263 (38.80%)	0.2020 (85.04%)
21	1.1886	0.7329 (38.34%)	0.3492 (70.62%)
22	1.2568	0.8065 (35.83%)	0.3058 (75.67%)
23	1.2730	0.8483 (33.36%)	0.3378 (73.47%)
24	1.4779	0.9000 (39.11%)	0.1706 (88.46%)
25	1.4986	0.9260 (38.21%)	0.2914 (80.55%)
26	1.4292	0.9721 (31.99%)	0.2940 (79.43%)
27	1.9437	1.1705 (39.78%)	0.2504 (87.12%)
28	1.2519	0.8063 (35.59%)	0.2662 (78.74%)
29	1.6434	1.0105 (38.51%)	0.5116 (68.87%)
30	1.3446	0.8137 (39.48%)	0.1207 (91.02%)
31	1.3725	0.8317 (39.40%)	0.2569 (81.28%)
32	1.3985	0.8607 (38.46%)	0.2675 (80.87%)
Average reduction		36.68%	78.99%

The percentages of reduction range from 68% to 91%. On average, calibrating the data with CSF followed by the SVR estimators gains improvement from 36.68% to 78.99%. With the assumption about unchanged surroundings of this approach, performance of the multipath estimators would depend upon how fast the reflecting surfaces along the propagation direction change. The environmental changes are expected to be different for different propagation directions of the GPS satellites. Therefore, the variation in performance of the estimators as seen in Table 2 is expected.

The goodness of the corrections can also be illustrated in the positional domain. Figure 8 shows the variation of the solved positions from the nominal position of the receiver. Weighted least mean square single-point positioning [13] with broadcast navigation data was applied to the data of Day 310. The measurements were only multipath corrected while other noises and biases (e.g., atmosphere delays, etc.) were not calibrated. The plot reveals noticeably higher centralization of the solution on the data corrected with SVR estimators over those obtained from the original data and the 50-second CSF-smoothed data. The reduction of standard deviation of coordinate time series North, East, and Up is tabulated separately in Table 3.

Table 3. Standard deviation (m) of coordinate time series

	Original	CSF corrected	SVR corrected
North	0.9136	0.7223 (20.94%)	0.5902 (35.40%)
East	1.2180	0.9997 (17.92%)	0.9033 (25.94%)
Up	2.6069	2.1715 (16.70%)	1.9496 (25.21%)

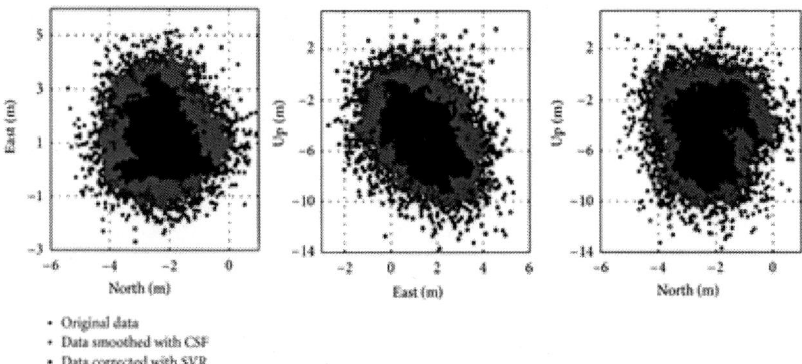

Figure 8. Positioning solution on original data, CSF-smoothed data, and SVR-corrected data of Day 310 of 2010.

DISCUSSIONS

For comparison, Table 4 tabulates numerical performance of different methods in terms of percentage of reduced multipath error. The performance of CSF is reported with a 100-second smoothing window [13]. The performance range of the frequency analysis method using fast fourier transform (FFT) [7] is reported with block sizes of 256 and 512, respectively, whilst the block size of the frequency analysis method using wavelet analysis [9] is 100 seconds. In particular, the performance of the FIR filter method [14] is unreliable as only one satellite (PRN 9) was used for analysis. It is clear that SVR estimators significantly outperform the other reported methods. The state-of-the-art performance of SVR estimators on pseudorange multipath reduction emphasizes the efficiency of the proposed method. However, as the accumulative environmental changes become more and more severe over time, the performance of the estimators would temporally degrade. Therefore, the multipath estimators need to be equipped with adaptability, which has not been addressed so far.

Table 4. Performance comparison of code multipath mitigation methods

CSF [13]	58%
FIR Filter [14]	75%
FFT [7]	50%–70%
Wavelet [9]	55%–65%
SVR estimator	68%–91%

Unlike the multipath stacking-based approaches [16, 17, 29], modeling multipath errors as functions of continuous variables (i.e., azimuth and elevation angles) does not experience the difficulty in the determination of the time-shifting period. In addition, the interpolation ability of the trained estimators makes them applicable for different data rates provided that training data is adequate to capture the underlying distribution of multipath errors. Furthermore, with the nature of sparsity, the multipath estimators just count on a subset of training data, being simpler while requiring less storage. All of these imply better scalability.

Another distinct advantage of the proposed approach is that it is able to preserve other signals of studied phenomena such as deformation caused by earthquakes. This is achieved by training the models with data on normal days without displacement before using them to correct data on the subsequent days where a phenomenon occurs. For the purpose of demonstration, we simulated an earthquake-like event by adding the signal given in (18) to PRN 12's pseudorange measurements for Day 310:

$$e(t) = 2\cos\left(\frac{\pi}{10}t + \pi\right) + \cos\left(\frac{\pi}{15}t\right). \tag{18}$$

Since signals of phenomena are usually low frequency [14, 23], the frequencies of the simulated event were chosen to exhibit diminishing effects of CSF, which is a low-pass filter [9, 12]. The PRN 12's pseudorange multipath sequence was smoothed by CSF with a

50-second smoothing window and then corrected by the trained PRN 12's SVR estimator. As shown in Figure 9, the corrected multipath sequence aligns very well with the event signal; that is, the event signal is not affected significantly.

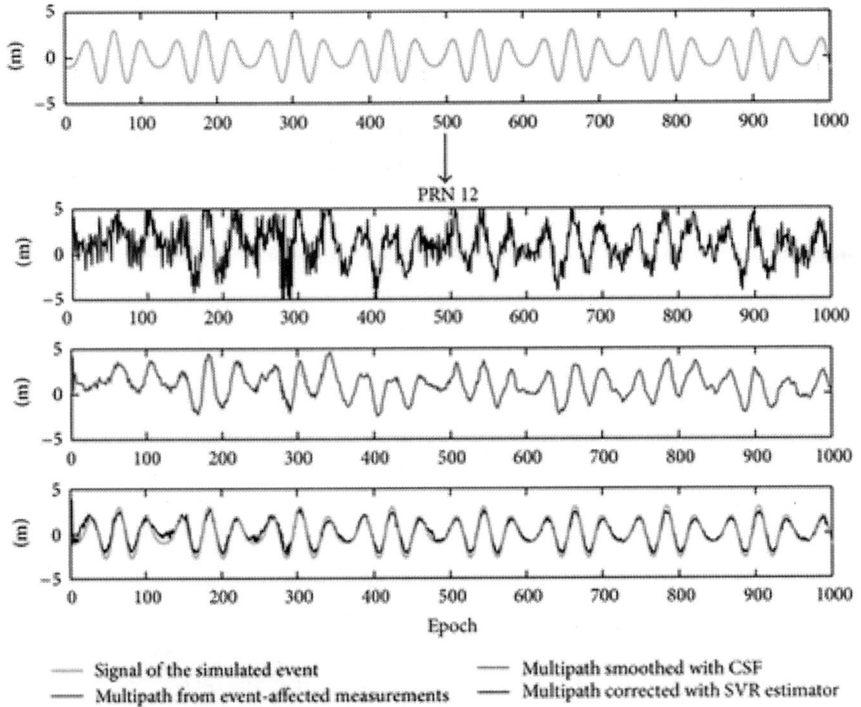

Figure 9. Simulation of event signal added to pseudorange measurements of PRN 12. It can be seen that the event signal is indeed left intact from correction of the PRN 12's SVR estimator.

Although carrier-phase multipath error is more sensitive to environmental variation, it also saw correlation on a sidereal daily basis [15, 29]. Therefore, the proposed method could be extended to apply to carrier-phase multipath mitigation.

EXPERIMENT 2: CARRIER-PHASE MULTIPATH MITIGATION

Double-Differential Carrier-Phase Multipath

Unlike code multipath error, carrier-phase multipath error cannot be isolated using combinations of code and carrier-phase measurements of one receiver alone. In order to do that, double differential (DD) combination of two short-baseline receivers (<10 km) is used. In practice, high-precision applications rely on this combination for relative positioning. The DD combination of two satellites a and b observed at two receivers A and B is given by

$$\phi_{AB}^{ab} = \Delta T^{ab} - \Delta I^{ab} + \Delta M^{\phi,ab} + \lambda \Delta N^{ab} + \Delta \varepsilon^{\phi,ab}. \tag{19}$$

In (19), clock error terms are eliminated through the differencing process. Furthermore, for a short baseline, atmospheric effects are approximately equal, leading to $\Delta T^{ab} \approx 0$ and $\Delta M^{ab} \approx 0$.

The integer ambiguity term ΔN^{ab} can be computed by debiasing over the entire DD sequence as long as there are no cycle slips. The multipath effect, hence, is dominant in the DD measurements which can now be written as

$$\phi_{AB}^{ab} = \Delta M^{\phi,ab} + \Delta \varepsilon^{\phi,ab}. \tag{20}$$

The DD multipath error is the composition of four multipath errors of the four carrier-phase components. Denote θ_j^i and φ_j^i the elevation and azimuth angles of the satellite i with respect to the receiver j, DD multipath error actually depends on eight geometrical variables:

$$\Delta M^{\phi,ab} = f_{\phi}\left(\theta_{A}^{a}, \varphi_{A}^{a}, \theta_{B}^{a}, \varphi_{B}^{a}, \theta_{A}^{b}, \varphi_{A}^{b}, \theta_{B}^{b}, \varphi_{B}^{b}\right). \tag{21}$$

Fortunately, at each epoch, eight variable parameters can be calculated given the orbital information of the satellites broadcast to the receivers and nominal positions of the receivers which are known beforehand. Therefore, the DD multipath function f_{ϕ} can be learned from historical data.

Experimental Data Set

In this experiment, two short-baseline stations from the IGS monitoring network were chosen. Their continuous 1-second data during two consecutive days (Day 050 and 051 of 2011) were downloaded from IGS data archive (http://igscb.jpl.nasa.gov/components/prods.html). The stations named KIR0 and KIRU whose corresponding geodetic coordinates are (21.0602°, 67.8776°, 497.9000 m) and (20.9684, 67.8573, 391.1000 m) (20.9684°, 67.8573°, 391.1000 m) in (longitude, latitude, and height) triplet or equivalent to (2242.624 km, 5516.729 km, 2277.795 km) and (2245.915 km, 5519.218 km, 2268.268 km) in ECEF coordinate system. They are located in Kiruna, Sweden, with a separation distance of approximately 10 km. Figure 10 shows photographs of the locations and surroundings of the two stations. As seen in Figure 10, the stations' vicinity is covered by snow; therefore, the multipath environment is expected to change quickly even in a short time span as the weather changes. If so, the performance of the multipath estimator would degrade.

(a)

(b)

Figure 10. IGS observation stations: (a) KIRU and (b) KIR0.

The station KIRU is selected as the reference station. With predetermined nominal positions of the stations, the geometrical parameters of the satellites with respect to the stations can be computed easily at every epoch given the broadcast navigation data. In order to extract DD multipath as described earlier, a satellite with high elevation is usually selected as a reference to form the DD combination [1, 13]. The pair of satellites PRN 8 and PRN 18 with the longest DD sequences are thus selected for analysis. PRN 8, with higher elevation peak, is used as the reference satellite. Their geometries with respect to the two stations are illustrated in Figure 11.

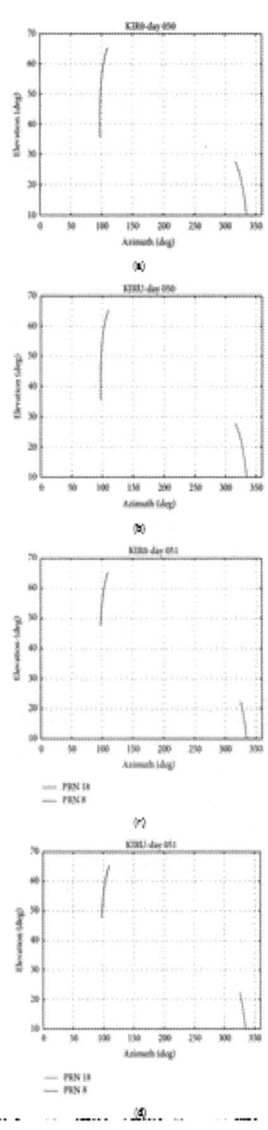

Figure 11. Geometries of PRN 8 and PRN 18 with respect to KIR0 and KIRU in Day 050 and Day 051.

Training Multipath Estimator

In order to train a DD multipath estimator for the satellite pair, the steps that have been done previously for code multipath estimation will again be performed. The geometrical data and multipath errors in Day 050 are scaled to before feeding to the training program. The libSVM package that implements -SVR algorithm is employed to train the multipath estimators. The values of , the Gaussian kernel parameter , and the penalty parameter of the error term are again chosen using grid search and cross-validation with the same strategy as described previously for code multipath mitigation.

Learning from the training data set, the support vectors and coefficients of the DD multipath estimator are found. Finally, the multipath estimator should estimate DD multipath error when presented with a new observation of azimuth/elevation angles thereafter. The estimated multipath error will be used to correct carrier-phase DD of the satellite pair in the successive days.

Experimental Results

In order to demonstrate the ability of the proposed method, the trained estimator is used to estimate the carrier-phase multipath error of the following Day 051. From top to bottom, Figure 12 shows the original multipath sequence, the response of the trained estimator, and the corrected multipath sequence with the response. The standard deviations of the original multipath sequence and the corrected multipath sequence are 2.15 cm and 0.92 cm, respectively. In other words, the multipath error has been reduced by 57.2% using the trained multipath estimator. Although only two data sets for one satellite pair have been presented here, this preliminary result provides a strong indication that the proposed technique can be applied to the carrier-phase multipath mitigation problem.

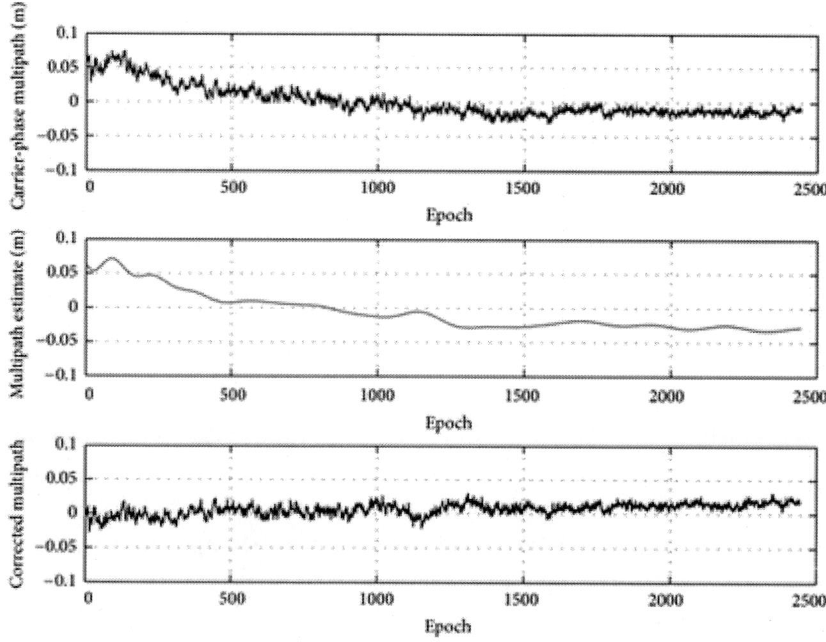

Figure 12. Original carrier-phase multipath (blue), response of the trained multipath estimator (red), and corrected carrier-phase multipath (black) sequences of the satellite pair PRN 18–PRN 8.

DISCUSSION

As expected, the response of the multipath estimator can capture the dominant trend of the multipath sequence which is the dominant component of the multipath error [8, 9]. However, the result of the proposed method when applied to carrier-phase multipath mitigation seems to be lower than what was achieved for code multipath mitigation. It is explainable as there is no equivalent smoothing algorithm like CSF to smooth the multipath sequence to attenuate high-frequency noise during training and correction. Although it is unwise to conclude firmly since the experimental result is only for one pair of satellites, for the sake of comparison, the proposed method outperforms the FIR filter method (39.8%–56.1%) [15], and the frequency-domain processing methods relying on analysis of SNR measurements (20%) [10, 22]. It provides a motivation for further exploration of the proposed method on the carrier-phase multipath mitigation problem.

However, this result is incomparable to that of the direct frequency-domain processing methods using wavelets such as those of Elhabiby et al. [8], which can reduce carrier-phase DD multipath up to 84%. It is because these methods can attenuate both errors from low to high frequencies to achieve better mitigation effects at the cost of filtering out other signals if their frequency content overlaps with multipath's frequency content. Although it has not been proven and more comprehensive experiments need to be conducted in future work, the proposed method should share similar advantages of code multipath estimators that it, intuitively, does not affect other phenomena signals. This could be fulfilled if data without displacement is used for training before estimating multipath error for data with displacement. Therefore, for applications where additional important signals such as seismic signals exist, the proposed method is promising.

As carrier-phase multipath is much more sensitive to environmental changes than pseudorange multipath, the data training over a short time span is more suitable for training SVR estimators under the constant environment assumption. It leads to higher data rates being required for training in order to retain data density. However, it does not strictly require high-rate data (≥1 Hz) as stacking-based approaches do [17, 29]; only data rates that can capture the underlying distribution of the multipath error are required. Fortunately, the proposed method is also scalable with data rate due to its inherent sparsity. In other words, only a subset of training data which are support vectors are kept and involved in the computation. However, if the number of support vectors is significantly large, computational complexity may still be a concern for real-time operation. This issue needs further exploration.

CONCLUSION

This paper has presented a unified framework based on nonlinear support vector regression to address the GPS code and carrier-phase multipath mitigation problems for ground fixed GPS stations. Based on analysis of the geometry of multipath signal reflections, geometrical models of multipath errors are developed. More specifically, multipath errors corresponding to a satellite are mathematically formulated as functions of the satellite's geometry with respect to a receiver, which is parameterized by azimuth and elevation angles. As a result, the problem of multipath error estimation amounts to regression problem where the multipath functions are approximated by learning from training data using -SVM algorithm. Finally, the trained multipath estimators are employed to correct measurements for successive days. The proposed method demonstrates good performance and is scalable to data rate. Furthermore, the multipath estimators do not affect the simulated signal of phenomena.

ACKNOWLEDGMENT

This work was done while Q.-H. Phan was a graduate research student at School of Computer Engineering, Nanyang Technological University, Singapore.

REFERENCES

1. B. Hoffmann-Wellenhof, H. Lichtenegger, and J. Collins, GPS: Theory and Practice, Springer, Wien, Austria, 2001.
2. A. Leick, GPS Satellite Surveying, 3rdJohn Wiley & Sons, New York, NY, USA, 2004.
3. G. J. Bishop, D. S. Coco, P. H. Kappler, and E. A. Holland, "Studies and performance of a new technique for mitigation of pseudorange multipath effects in GPS ground stations," in Proceedings of the 1994 National Technical Meeting of The Institute of Navigation, pp. 231–242, San Diego, Calif, USA, January 1994. View at Scopus
4. N. Kubo and A. Yasuda, "How multipath error influences on ambiguity resolution," in Proceedings of the 16th International Technical Meeting of the Satellite Division of The Institute of Navigation (ION GPS/GNSS '03), pp. 2142–2150, Portland, Ore, USA, 2003.
5. Y. Zhang, ,High performance differential global positioning system for long baseline application [Ph.D. thesis], Ohio University, 2005.
6. B. Parkinson and P. Enge, "Differential GPS," in Global Positioning System, B. Parkinson, J. Spilker, P. Axelrad, and P. Enge, Eds., vol. 2, pp. 3–49, American Institute of Aeronautics and Astronautics, Washington, DC, USA, 1996.

7. Y. Zhang and C. Bartone, "Multipath mitigation in the frequency domain," in Proceedings of the IEEE/ION Position Location and Navigation Symposium (PLANS '04), pp. 486–495, Athens, Ga, USA, April 2004. View at Scopus
8. M. Elhabiby, A. El-Ghazouly, and N. El-Sheimy, "A new wavelet-based multipath mitigation technique," in Proceedings of the 21st International Technical Meeting of the Satellite Division of the Institute of Navigation (ION GNSS '08), pp. 625–631, Savannah, Ga, USA, September 2008. View at Scopus
9. Y. Zhang and C. Bartone, "Real-time multipath mitigation with WaveSmooth™ technique using wavelets," in Proceedings of the 17th International Technical Meeting of the Satellite Division of the Institute of Navigation (ION GNSS '04), pp. 1181–1194, Long Beach, Calif, USA, September 2004. View at Scopus
10. A. Bilich, K. M. Larson, and P. Axelrad, "Modeling GPS phase multipath with SNR: case study from the Salar de Uyuni, Boliva," Journal of Geophysical Research B, vol. 113, no. 4, Article ID B04401, 2008. View at Publisher · View at Google Scholar · View at Scopus
11. C. Rost and L. Wanninger, "Carrier phase multipath mitigation based on GNSS signal quality measurements," Journal of Applied Geodesy, vol. 3, no. 2, pp. 81–87, 2009. View at Publisher · View at Google Scholar
12. P. Y. Hwang, G. A. McGraw, and J. R. Bader, "Enhanced Differential GPS carrier-smoothed code processing using dual-frequency measurements," Navigation, vol. 46, no. 2, pp. 127–137, 1999. View at Scopus
13. P. Misra and P. Enge, Global Positioning System: Signals, Measurements, and Performance, IGanga-Jamuna Press, Lincoln, Mass, USA, 2nd edition, 2006.
14. L. Ge, S. Han, and C. Rizos, "Multipath mitigation of continuous GPS measurements using an adaptive filter," GPS Solutions, vol. 4, pp. 19–30, 2000. View at Scopus
15. H. Liu, X. Li, L. Ge, C. Rizos, and F. Wang, "Variable length LMS adaptive filter for carrier phase multipath mitigation," GPS Solutions, vol. 15, no. 1, pp. 29–38, 2011. View at Publisher · View at Google Scholar · View at Scopus
16. P. Axelrad, K. Larson, and B. Jones, "Use of the correct satellite repeat period to characterize and reduce site-specific multipath errors," in Proceedings of the 18th International Technical Meeting of the Satellite Division of The Institute of Navigation (ION GNSS '05), pp. 2638–2648, Long Beach, Calif, USA, September 2005. View at Scopus
17. K. M. Larson, A. Bilich, and P. Axelrad, "Improving the precision of high-rate GPS," Journal of Geophysical Research, vol. 112, no. B5, 2007. View at Publisher · View at Google Scholar
18. P. Zhong, X. Ding, L. Yuan, Y. Xu, K. Kwok, and Y. Chen, "Sidereal filtering based on single differences for mitigating GPS multipath effects on short baselines," Journal of Geodesy, vol. 84, no. 2, pp. 145–158, 2010. View at Publisher · View at Google Scholar · View at Scopus

19. Q. H. Phan and S. L. Tan, "Mitigation of GPS periodic multipath using nonlinear regression," in Proceedings of 19th European Signal Processing Conference (EUSIPCO '11), pp. 1795–1799, Barcelona, Spain, 2011.
20. Q. H. Phan, S. L. Tan, and I. McLoughlin, "GPS multipath mitigation: a nonlinear regression approach," GPS Solutions, 2012. View at Publisher · View at Google Scholar
21. B. Parkinson, "Introduction and heritage of NAVSTAR, the Global Positioning System," in Global Positioning System, B. Parkinson, J. Spilker, P. Axelrad, and P. Enge, Eds., vol. 1, pp. 3–28, American Institute of Aeronautics and Astronautics, Washington, DC, USA, 1996.
22. A. Bilich and K. M. Larson, "Mapping the GPS multipath environment using the signal-to-noise ratio (SNR)," Radio Science, vol. 42, no. 6, 2007. View at Publisher · View at Google Scholar · View at Scopus
23. Y. Bock, R. M. Nikolaidis, P. J. de Jonge, and M. Bevis, "Instantaneous geodetic positioning at medium distances with the Global Positioning System," Journal of Geophysical Research B, vol. 105, no. 12, pp. 28223–28253, 2000. View at Scopus
24. J. F. Genrich and Y. Bock, "Rapid resolution of crustal motion at short ranges with the Global Positioning System," Journal of Geophysical Research, vol. 97, no. 3, pp. 3261–3269, 1992. View at Scopus
25. A. J. Smola and B. Schölkopf, "A tutorial on support vector regression," Statistics and Computing, vol. 14, no. 3, pp. 199–222, 2004. View at Publisher · View at Google Scholar · View at Scopus
26. V. Vapnik, The Nature of Statistical Learning Theory, Springer, New York, NY, USA, 1995.
27. C. M. Bishop, Neural Networks for Pattern Recognition, Oxford University Press, Oxford, UK, 1996.
28. J. Dickman, C. Bartone, Y. Zhang, and B. Thornburg, "Characterization and performance of a prototype wideband airport pseudolite multipath limiting antenna for the local area augmentation system," in Proceedings of the 2003 National Technical Meeting of The Institute of Navigation, pp. 783–793, Anaheim, Calif, USA, 2003.
29. K. Choi, A. Bilich, K. M. Larson, and P. Axelrad, "Modified sidereal filtering: implications for high-rate GPS positioning," Geophysical Research Letters, vol. 31, no. 22, pp. 1–4, 2004. View at Publisher · View at Google Scholar · View at Scopus

Chapter 4

FUZZIFIED DATA BASED NEURAL NETWORK MODELING FOR HEALTH ASSESSMENT OF MULTISTOREY SHEAR BUILDINGS

Deepti Moyi Sahoo and S. Chakraverty

Department of Mathematics, National Institute of Technology Rourkela, Rourkela, Odisha 769 008, India

ABSTRACT

The present study intends to propose identification methodologies for multistorey shear buildings using the powerful technique of Artificial Neural Network (ANN) models which can handle fuzzified data. Identification with crisp data is known, and also neural network method has already been used by various researchers for this case. Here, the input and output data may be in fuzzified form. This is because in general we may not get the corresponding input and output values exactly (in crisp form), but we have only the uncertain information of the data. This uncertain data is assumed in terms of fuzzy number, and the corresponding problem of system identification is investigated.

INTRODUCTION

System identification methods in structural dynamics, in general, solve inverse vibration problems to identify properties of a structure from measured data. The rapid progress in the field of computer science and computational mathematics during recent decades has led to an increasing use of process computers and models to analyze, supervise, and control technical processes. The use of computers and efficient mathematical tools allows identification of the process dynamics by evaluating the input and output signals of the system. The result of such a process identification is usually a mathematical model by which the dynamic behavior can be estimated or predicted. The system identification problem has been nicely explained in a recent paper [1]. The same statements from [1] are reproduced below for the benefit of the readers.

The study of structures dynamic behavior may be categorized into two distinct activities: analytical and/or numerical modeling (e.g., finite element models) and vibration tests (e.g., experimental modal models). Due to different limitations and assumptions, each approach has its advantages and shortcomings. Therefore, in order to determine the dynamic properties of the structure, reconciliation processes including model correlation and/or model updating should be performed. Model updating can be defined as the adjustment of an existing analytical/numerical model in the light of measured vibration test. After adjustment, the updated model is expected to represent the dynamic behavior of the structure more accurately as proposed by Friswell et al. [2]. With the recent advances in computing technology for data acquisition, signal processing, and analysis, the parameters of structural models may be updated from the measured responses under excitation of the structure. This procedure is achieved using system identification techniques as an inverse problem. The inverse problem may be defined as determination of the internal structure of a physical system from the system's measured behavior, or estimation of an unknown input that gives rise to a measured output signal according to Tanaka and Bui [3].

Comprehensive literature surveys have been provided on the subject of model updating of the structural systems by Alvin et al. [4], and Time series methods for fault detection and identification in vibrating structures were presented by Fassois and Sakellariou [5]. Shear buildings are among the most widely studied structural systems. Previous works on model updating of shear buildings rely mostly on using modal parameter identification and physical or structural parameter identification to drive the corresponding update procedures. As regards the publications, Marsi et al. [6] gave various methodologies for different types of problems in system identification. Various techniques for improving structural dynamic models were reviewed in a review paper by Ibanez [7], and studies made by Datta et al. [8] related to system identification of buildings done until that date were also surveyed. Some of the related publications may be mentioned as those of Loh and Tou [9] and Yuan et al. [10].

It is known that, the systems which may be modeled as linear, the identification problem often turns in to a non-linear optimization problem. This requires an intelligent iterative scheme to have the required solution. There exists various online and offline methods, namely, the Gauss-Newton, Kalman filtering and probabilistic methods such as maximum likelihood estimation, and so forth. However, the identification problem for a large number of parameters, following two basic difficulties are faced often:(i) objective function surface may have multiple maxima and minima, and the convergence to the correct parameters is possible only if the initial guess is considered as close to the parameters to be identified;(ii)inverse problem in general gives non-unique parameter estimates. To overcome these difficulties, researchers have developed various identification methodologies for the said problem by using powerful technique of Artificial Neural Network (ANN). Chen [11] presented a neural network based method for determining the modal parameters of structures from field measurement. Using the observed dynamic responses, he trained the neural network based on back-propagation technique. He then directly identified the modal parameters of the structure using the weight matrices of the neural network. In particular, Huang et al. [12] presented a novel procedure for identifying the dynamic characteristics of a building using a back-propagation neural network technique. Another novel neural network based approach has been presented by Kao and Hung [13] for detecting structural damage. A decentralized stiffness identification method with neural networks for a multi degree of freedom structure has been developed by Wu et al. [14]. Localized damage detection and parametric identification method with direct use of earthquake responses for large-scale infrastructures has also been proposed by Xu et al. [15]. A neural network based strategy by Xu et al. [16] was developed for direct identification of structural parameters from the time domain dynamic responses of an object structure without any Eigen value analysis.

System identification on the other hand tries to identify structural matrices of mass, damping and stiffness directly. Among various methodologies in this regard Chakraverty [17], Perry et al. [18], Wang [19], Yoshitomi and Takewaki [20], and Lu and Tu [21] developed different techniques to handle the system identification problems. Yuan et al. [10] developed a methodology that identifies the mass and stiffness matrices of a shear building from the first two orders of structural mode measurement. Koh et al. [22] proposed several Ga-based sub structural identification methods, which work by solving parts of the structure at a time to improve the convergence of mass and stiffness estimates particularly for large systems. Chakraverty [17] proposed procedures to refine the methods of Yuan et al. [10] to identify the structural mass and stiffness matrices of shear buildings from the modal test data. The refinement was obtained using Holzer criteria. Tang et al. [23] utilized a differential evolution (DE) strategy for parameter estimation of the structural systems with limited output data, noise polluted signals, and no prior knowledge of mass, damping, or stiffness matrices. Recent works on model updating of multistory shear buildings for simultaneous identification of mass, stiffness, and damping matrices using two different soft-computing methods have been developed by Khanmirza et al. [1]. It may be seen from above that Artificial Neural Networks (ANNs) provide a fundamentally different approach to system identification. They have been successfully applied for identification and control of dynamics systems in various fields of engineering because of excellent learning capacity and high tolerance to partially inaccurate data.

It is revealed from the above literature review that various authors developed different identification methodologies using ANN. They supposed that the data obtained are in exact or crisp form. But in actual practice the experimental data obtained from equipments are with errors that may be due to human or equipment error, thereby giving uncertain form of the data. Although one may also use probabilistic methods to handle such problems. Then, the probabilistic method requires huge quantity of data which may not be easy or feasible. Thus in this paper, a minimum number of data are taken in fuzzified form to have the essence of the uncertainty. Accordingly, in this paper, identification methodologies for multistory shear buildings have been proposed using the powerful technique of Artificial Neural Network (ANN) models which can handle fuzzified data. It is already mentioned that identification with crisp data is known and also neural network method has already been used by various researchers for this case. Here, the input and output data may be in fuzzified form. This is because in general we may not get the corresponding input and output values exactly (in crisp form), but we have only the uncertain information of the data. This uncertain data has been assumed to be in terms of fuzzy numbers.

In this paper, the initial design parameters, namely, stiffness and mass and so the frequency of the said problem is known. But after a large span of time, the structure may be subjected to various manmade and natural calamities. Then, the engineers want to know the present health of the structure by system identification methods. It is assumed that only the stiffness is changed and the mass remains the same. As such equipment's are available to get the present values of the frequencies and using these one may get the present parameter values by ANN. But while doing the experiment, one may not get the exact values of the parameters. But we may get those values as uncertain, namely, in fuzzy form. So if sensors are placed to capture the frequency of the floors in fuzzy (uncertain) form, then those may be fed into the proposed new ANN model to get the present stiffness parameters in fuzzified form. In order to train the new ANN model, set of data are generated numerically beforehand. As such, converged ANN model gives the present stiffness parameter values in interval form for each floor. Thus, one may predict the health of the uncertain structure. Corresponding example problems have been solved, and related results are reported to show the reliability and powerfulness of the model.

ANALYSIS AND MODELING

System identification refers to the branch of numerical analysis which uses the experimental input and output data to develop mathematical models of systems which finally identify the parameters. The floor masses for this methodology are assumed to be $[\underline{m_1}, m_1c, \overline{m_1}]$, $[\underline{m_2}, m_2c, \overline{m_2}], \ldots, [\underline{m_n}, m_nc, \overline{m_n}]$, and the stiffness $[\underline{k_1}, k_1c, \overline{k_1}], [\underline{k_2}, k_2c, \overline{k_2}], \ldots, [\underline{k_n}, k_nc, \overline{k_n}]$ are the structural parameters which are to be identified. It may be seen that all the mass and stiffness parameters are taken in fuzzy form. As such here for each mass m_i, we have m_i as the left value,m_ic as the centre value, and m_i as the right value. Similarly for the stiffness parameter for each mass k_i, we have k_i as the left value, k_ic as the center value, and k_i as the right value. The n-storey shear structure is shown in Figure 1. Corresponding dynamic equation of motion for n-storey (supposed as n degrees of freedom) shear structure without damping may be written as

$$\{\tilde{M}\}\{\ddot{\tilde{X}}\} + \{\tilde{K}\}\{\tilde{X}\} = \{\tilde{0}\}, \quad (1)$$

where $\{\ddot{\tilde{x}}\} = \{\underline{\ddot{x}}, \ddot{x}c, \overline{\ddot{x}}\}$, $\{\tilde{x}\} = [\underline{x}, xc, \overline{x}]$.

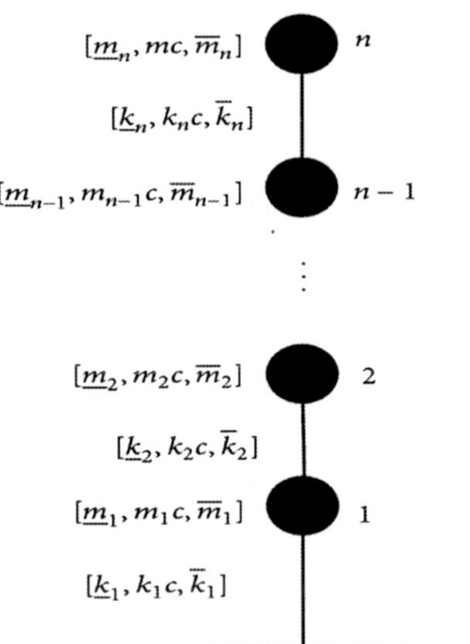

Figure 1: Multistorey shear structure with -levels having fuzzy structural parameters.

$\{\widetilde{M}\} = [\underline{M}, Mc, \overline{M}]$ is $n \times n$ mass matrix of the structure and is given by

$$\{\widetilde{M}\} = \begin{bmatrix} [\underline{m_1}, m_1 c, \overline{m_1}] & 0 & \cdots & \cdots & 0 \\ 0 & [\underline{m_2}, m_2 c, \overline{m_2}] & 0 & \cdots & 0 \\ \cdots & \cdots & \cdots & \cdots & \cdots \\ \cdots & \cdots & 0 & [\underline{m_{n-1}}, m_{n-1} c, \overline{m_{n-1}}] & [\underline{m_n}, m_n c, \overline{m_n}] \\ 0 & \cdots & \cdots & 0 & 0 \end{bmatrix}. \quad (2)$$

$\{\widetilde{K}\} = [\underline{K}, Kc, \overline{K}]$ is $n \times n$ stiffness matrix of the structure and may be written as

$$\{\widetilde{K}\} = \begin{bmatrix} \widetilde{k}_1 + \widetilde{k}_2 & \widetilde{k}_2 & 0 & \cdots & 0 \\ -\widetilde{k}_2 & \widetilde{k}_2 + \widetilde{k}_3 & -\widetilde{k}_3 & \cdots & 0 \\ \cdots & \cdots & & & \cdots \\ 0 & \cdots & -\widetilde{k}_{n-1} & \widetilde{k}_{n-1} + \widetilde{k}_n & \widetilde{k}_n \\ 0 & & \cdots & -\widetilde{k}_n & \widetilde{k}_n \end{bmatrix}, \quad (3)$$

and $\{\widetilde{X}\} = \{\widetilde{x}_1, \widetilde{x}_2, \ldots, \widetilde{x}_n\}^T$ are the vectors of displacement.

We will first solve the above free vibration equation for vibration characteristics, namely, for frequency and mode shapes of the said structural system in order to get the stiffness parameters in fuzzified form. Accordingly putting in free vibration equation (1), we getwhere are eigenvalues or the natural frequency and are mode shapes of the structure, respectively.

BASIC CONCEPT OF FUZZY SET THEORY

Definition 1

Let X be a universal set. Then, the fuzzy subset A of X is defined by its membership function

$$\mu_A : X \longrightarrow [0, 1], \quad (5)$$

which assigns a real number $\mu_A(x)$ in the interval [0, 1], to each element $x \in X$, where the value of $\mu_A(x)$ at x shows the grade of membership of x in A.

Definition 2

Given a fuzzy set A in X and any real number $\alpha \in [0,1]$, then, the α-cut or α-level or cut worthy set of A, denoted by A_α, is the crisp set

$$A_\alpha = \{x \in X \mid \mu_A(x) \geq \alpha\}. \tag{6}$$

The strong α-cut, denoted by $A_{\alpha+}$, is the crisp set

$$A_{\alpha+} = \{x \in X \mid \mu_A(x) \geq \alpha\}. \tag{7}$$

Definition 3

A fuzzy number is a convex normalized fuzzy set of the real line R whose membership function is piecewise continuous.

Definition 4

Triangular fuzzy number A can be defined as a triplet $[a_1, a_2, a_3]$. Its membership function is defined as

$$\mu_A(x) = \begin{cases} 0, & x < a_1 \\ \dfrac{x - a_1}{a_2 - a_1}, & a_1 \leq x \leq a_2 \\ \dfrac{a_3 - x}{a_3 - a_2}, & a_2 \leq x \leq a_3 \\ 0, & x > a_3. \end{cases} \tag{8}$$

Above TFN may be transformed to an interval form A_α by α-cut as

$$A_\alpha = \left[a_1^{(\alpha)}, a_3^{(\alpha)}\right] = [(a_2 - a_1)\alpha + a_1, -(a_3 - a_2)\alpha + a_3]. \tag{9}$$

OPERATION OF FUZZY NUMBER

In this section, we consider arithmetic operation on fuzzy numbers and the result is expressed in membership function:

$$\forall x, y, z \in R. \tag{10}$$

1. Addition: $A(+)B$

$$\mu_{A(+)B}(z) = \bigvee_{z=x+y} (\mu_A(x) \wedge \mu_B(y)). \tag{11}$$

2. Subtraction: $A(-)B$

$$\mu_{A(-)B}(z) = \bigvee_{z=x-y} (\mu_A(x) \wedge \mu_B(y)). \tag{12}$$

3. Multiplication: $A(\cdot)B$

$$\mu_{A(\cdot)B}(z) - \bigvee_{z=x \cdot y} (\mu_A(x) \wedge \mu_B(y)). \tag{13}$$

4. Division: $A(/)B$

$$\mu_{A(/)B}(z) = \bigvee_{z=x/y} (\mu_A(x) \wedge \mu_B(y)). \tag{14}$$

5. Minimum: $A(\wedge)B$

$$\mu_{A(\wedge)B}(z) = \bigvee_{z=x\wedge y} (\mu_A(x) \wedge \mu_B(y)). \tag{15}$$

6. Maximum: $A(\vee)B$

$$\mu_{A(\vee)B}(z) = \bigvee_{z=x\vee y} (\mu_A(x) \wedge \mu_B(y)). \tag{16}$$

ARTIFICIAL NEURAL NETWORK (ANN) AND ERROR-BACK PROPAGATION TRAINING ALGORITHM (EB-PTA) FOR FUZZIFIED DATA

Traditional ANN and EBPTA are well known, but here for the sake of completeness, those are developed for fuzzy case. In ANN, the first layer is considered to be input layer and the last layer is the output layer. Between the input and output layers, there may be more than one hidden layer. Each layer will contain number of neurons or nodes (processing elements) depending upon the problem. These processing elements operate in parallel and are arranged in patterns similar to the patterns found in biological neural nets. The processing elements are connected to each other by adjustable weights. The input/output behavior of the network changes if the weights are changed. So, the weights of the net may be chosen in such a way so as to achieve a desired output. To satisfy this goal, systematic ways of adjusting the weights have to be developed to handle the fuzzified data which are known as training or learning algorithm. Neural network basically depends upon the type of processing elements or nodes, the network topology, and the learning algorithm. Here, error back-propagation training algorithm and feed forward recall have been used but to handle the uncertain system. The typical network is given in Figure 2.

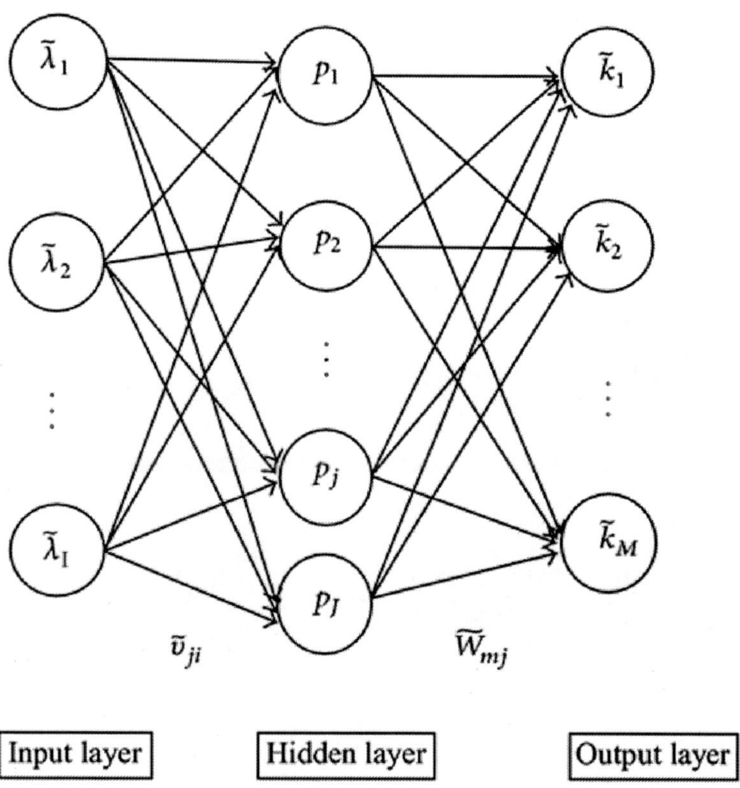

Figure 2: Layered feed-forward fuzzy neural network.

In this Figure, Z_i, P_j, and O_m are input, hidden, and output layers, respectively. The weights between input and hidden layers are denoted by V_{ji}, and the weights between hidden and output layers are denoted by W_{kj} Here, $\tilde{Z}_i = [\underline{\lambda_i}\ \lambda_i c\ \overline{\lambda_i}]$ and $\tilde{O}_k = [\underline{k_m}\ k_m c\ \overline{k_m}]$. and $\tilde{O}_k = [\underline{k_m}\ k_m c\ \overline{k_m}]$.

Given R training pairs $\{\tilde{Z}_1, \tilde{d}_1; \tilde{Z}_2, \tilde{d}_2; \ldots, \tilde{Z}_R, \tilde{d}_R\}$ where $\tilde{Z}_i(I \times 1)$ are input and $\tilde{d}_i(M \times 1)$ are desired values for the given inputs, the error value is computed as

$$\tilde{E} = \frac{1}{2}\left(\tilde{d}_m - \tilde{O}_m\right)^2, \quad m = 1, 2, \ldots M, \tag{17}$$

for the present neural network as

$$\tilde{\delta}_{Om} = 0.5 * \left(\tilde{d}_m - \tilde{O}_m\right)\left(1 - \tilde{O}_m{}^2\right), \quad m = 1, 2, \ldots M,$$

$$\tilde{\delta}_{Pj} = 0.5 * \left(1 - \tilde{P}_j^2\right) \sum_{m=1}^{M} \tilde{\delta}_{Om} \widetilde{W}_{Pj}, \quad j = 1, 2, \ldots J. \tag{18}$$

Consequently, output layer weights (W_{mj}) and hidden layer weights (V_{ji}) are adjusted as

$$\begin{aligned} \widetilde{W}_{mj}^{(New)} &= \widetilde{W}_{mj}^{(Old)} + \eta \tilde{\delta}_{Om} P_j, \quad m = 1, 2, \ldots M, \; j = 1, 2, \ldots J, \\ \tilde{v}_{ji}^{(New)} &= \tilde{v}_{ji}^{(Old)} + \eta \tilde{\delta}_{Pj} Z_i, \quad j = 1, 2, \ldots J, \; i = 1, 2, \ldots I, \end{aligned} \tag{19}$$

RESULTS AND DISCUSSION

To investigate the present method here, examples of one- and two-storey shear structures are considered. So, for example, the floor masses for two-storey shear structure are : $[\underline{m_1}, m_1c, \overline{m_1}]$, $[\underline{m_2}, m_2c, \overline{m_2}]$, and the stiff nesses $[\underline{k_1}, k_1c, \overline{k_1}]$, $[\underline{k_2}, k_2c, \overline{k_2}]$ are the structural parameters. Here, masses are assumed to be constant (as mentioned earlier). So, we will identify the stiffness parameter in fuzzy form using the fuzzy form of the frequency where frequency may be obtained from some experiments. In the following paragraphs, we have used the proposed method to identify the stiffness parameter for one-, two-, five-, and ten-storey frame structures. Here, we have considered the cases with crisp data for five- and ten-storeys and then fuzzified data for one- and two-storeys. The training data are also considered with the influence of noise, namely, in terms of triangular fuzzy number data. Accordingly we have considered the following four cases:

Case(i):Five-storey shear structure with crisp data,

Case(ii):Ten-storey shear structure with crisp data,Case(iii):Single-storey shear structure with fuzzified data,

Case(iv):Double-storey shear structure with fuzzified data.

Computer programs have been written and tested for variety of experiments for the above cases. For the first two cases, namely, Case(i) and Case(ii), the inputs are taken as the crisp frequency values and the outputs are the stiffness parameters which are also in crisp form. On the other hand, for Cases(iii) and (iv), the inputs are taken as the fuzzified frequency values and the outputs are the stiffness parameters again in fuzzified form in the developed Fuzzy Neural Network (FNN) algorithm.

For the first case, an example of a storey shear structure is taken where the masses are $m_1 = m_2 = m_3 = m_4 = m_5 = 36000$ and the stiffness parameters are within the range $k_1 =$ [100000 200000], $k_2 =$ [50000 100000], $k_3 =$ [40000 60000], $k_4 =$ [30000 50000], and $k_5 =$[20000 30000].Acomparison between the desired and ANN values has been presented in Table 1. This table has been plotted in Figure 3.

Table 1: Comparison between the desired and the ANN values of k_1, k_2,k_3,k_4 and k_5 for a five-storey shear structure.

Data number	k_1 (Ann)	k_1 (Des)	k_2 (Ann)	k_2 (Des)	k_3 (Ann)	k_3 (Des)	k_4 (Ann)	k_4 (Des)	k_5 (Ann)	k_5 (Des)
1	181277.7318	181472.3686	57722.68	57880.6541	53111.561	53114.814	44531.8138	44120.9218	24304.5301	24387.4436
2	195883.7223	190579.1937	98497.3362	98529.6391	40890.7789	40714.2336	30510.5884	30636.6569	24013.4116	23815.5846
3	110889.324	112698.6816	97540.2878	97858.3474	56939.1333	56982.5861	35467.0709	35538.4597	27905.0723	27655.1679
4	191334.6369	191337.5856	74367.0906	74268.7824	58151.3678	58679.865	30921.7444	30923.4278	27758.983	27951.999
5	162671.148	163235.9246	90080.9291	90014.0234	53507.0758	53574.7031	31851.263	31942.6356	21775.0509	21868.726
6	109757.8778	109754.0405	57034.3391	57094.3169	55073.904	55154.8026	46360.9403	46469.1566	24899.5619	24897.644
7	127671.411	127849.8219	71003.1282	71088.0641	54999.758	54862.6494	43688.9611	43896.5725	24554.2598	24455.862
8	154429.3614	154688.1519	98500.0073	95786.7763	48031.3148	47844.5404	36250.0047	36341.9896	27719.1389	26463.1301
9	196399.16	195750.6835	89751.9025	89610.3665	53100.0372	53109.5578	48498.0106	49004.441	27950.5364	27093.6483
10	193722.4668	196488.8535	98520.881	97974.6213	43228.929	43423.7338	30822.0268	30688.9216	26813.9637	27546.8668

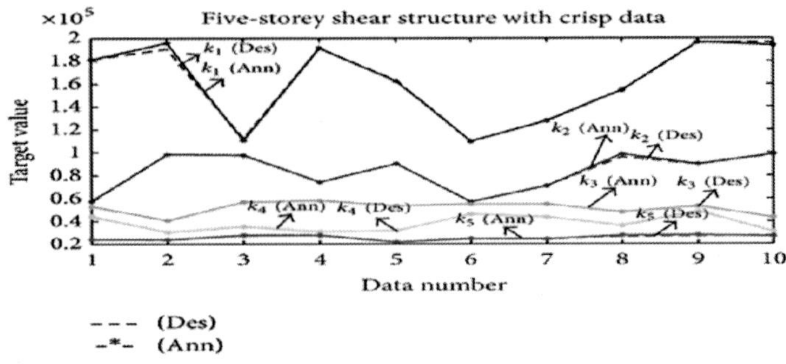

Figure 3 Comparison between the desired and the ANN values of $\bar{k}$ for a single-storey shear structure..

In Case(ii), an example for a ten-storey shear structure has been considered with constant masses similar to Case(i) and the stiffness parameters are in the range k_1=[100000 200000], k_2= k_3= k_4= k_5= k_6= k_7= k_8=k_9= k_{10}= [20000 30000].The desired and ANN values for k_1 to k_5 and k_6 to k_{10} are compared in Tables 2(a) and 2(b), respectively

Table 2: (a) Comparison between the desired and the ANN values of k_1, k_2, k_3, k_4, and k_5 for a ten-storey shear structure.

(b) Comparison between the desired and the ANN values of k_6, k_7, k_8, k_9, and k_{10} for a ten-storey shear structure.

Data number	k_1 (Ann)	k_1 (Des)	k_2 (Ann)	k_2 (Des)	k_3 (Ann)	k_3 (Des)	k_4 (Ann)	k_4 (Des)	k_5 (Ann)	k_5 (Des)
1	116900.6563	114999.7254	23626.293	23947.0748	25255.905	24299.2141	29078.6982	29493.0391	27766.1413	28842.8102
2	137413.4659	135922.821	22400.1311	21970.538	22076.7651	22160.1892	28671.6078	29898.7215	23928.6799	23185.2425
3	174166.5579	171165.6706	26751.8243	27587.6627	28439.4836	28089.9027	28056.19	27636.7332	28909.5075	29349.7909
4	185745.6345	187147.6518	28203.5977	29952.1598	23288.5994	23565.0893	25414.2964	25588.2055	24175.8385	24794.8455
5	131376.8088	132868.9612	22531.4396	21865.7144	20887.9013	20732.4343	22490.5032	21838.4294	21747.4496	22317.9161
6	174687.251	165011.8025	25813.5863	27811.4527	25015.1015	25909.9146	25615.7328	24979.4882	24612.1573	23962.9025
7	185115.3655	197483.6148	24841.291	21957.9798	27352.9705	29101.8783	25184.1779	25178.456	27414.6225	27050.7748
8	107439.5782	107596.7361	28408.1614	29923.5897	22079.0745	21937.6594	29361.5732	29942.4301	25283.6014	25585.5903
9	164872.2954	158701.9167	25498.9862	28022.6157	26269.1879	24323.6779	28505.5766	28548.5168	27421.7863	27566.307
10	134496.3197	136428.6869	23984.6699	23091.3643	26528.5422	27288.6387	20735.4877	20391.8449	26590.0291	26789.4101

(b)

Data number	k_6 (Ann)	k_6 (Des)	k_7 (Ann)	k_7 (Des)	k_8 (Ann)	k_8 (Des)	k_9 (Ann)	k_9 (Des)	k_{10} (Ann)	k_{10} (Des)
1	21170.0974	20899.5068	25777.6655	25605.5953	28204.3487	29899.5021	27503.4171	25859.8704	27163.5463	25814.4649
2	22417.1364	20549.7415	27621.6492	28654.3859	27612.505	28451.7819	28303.9996	29823.0322	22093.3505	22094.0508
3	29672.9685	29638.7013	25998.8211	27124.1481	22438.2305	21982.2179	26315.5549	26153.251	27684.8546	29019.9081
4	19962.2582	19656.5635	21156.2588	20166.7471	22269.5196	21950.7153	23818.7821	23766.1108	27240.5745	27020.6645
5	20161.805	20514.4829	25387.6098	28009.2088	23922.4631	23268.3965	27519.8427	28771.8175	23219.6412	23774.551
6	22307.0935	23043.4895	21527.1166	21425.0932	27311.6444	28803.3786	27670.7454	27848.5243	27234.7985	27349.5593
7	27804.4452	25801.9183	24442.8169	24784.7447	25319.1653	24711.0187	25870.6554	24649.5428	27640.8021	29541.0279
8	25509.2344	25309.6445	22738.1369	22568.3535	23936.8813	24039.6937	28924.1116	28139.7693	25172.6749	25428.1311
9	28341.8519	29012.0809	25380.1928	23690.9169	23071.1828	21792.3148	28034.5751	28984.4414	26519.4395	25401.0583
10	27911.2912	29624.314	26475.8553	24319.8061	21306.3632	21696.0881	25327.5363	24074.5574	24485.2563	23343.2942

For Case(iii), the first example is that of a single-storey shear structure with masses $\bar{M}$= 36000 and the stiffness. Parameters lie within the range K = [100000 200000], K_c =[100010 200010], and$K$ = [100020 200020]. A comparison between desired and the ANN values has been incorporated in Table 3. This table has been plotted in Figure 4. In the second example, a single-storey shear structure is considered with masses $\bar{M}$ = 36000 and the stiffness parameter varying within the range K = [50000 100000], K_c =[50010 100010], and K = [50020 100020]. Comparison between the desired and the ANN values is tabulated in Table 4 and is plotted in Figure 5.

Table 3. Comparison between the desired and the ANN values of $\bar{K}$for a single-storey shear structure.

124932.9319	124189.1286	135932.8213	135095.2381	191905.7285
135763.4956	140411.2146	152464.2896	151324.954	191726.9669
110291.5736	109665.4525	141591.1084	140180.8034	148514.9196
107394.0584	107596.6692	115134.7117	113217.3293	149119.797
124430.5911	123991.6154	134455.7107	133781.941	192947.0787
112574.5401	112331.8935	188853.0283	190015.3846	194542.4439
120988.7913	118390.7788	138166.8698	136934.6781	157619.3944
108960.7756	105997.9543	113526.3083	111130.2755	126504.2017
124700.9011	123497.9913	143556.5197	141726.7069	179985.5092

Table 4 Comparison between the desired and the ANN values of $\bar{K}$ for a single-storey shear structure

Data number	$\underline{k}$ (Ann)	$\underline{k}$ (Des)	kc (Ann)	kc (Des)	$\bar{k}$ (Ann)	$\bar{k}$ (Des)
1	62365.0341	62104.5643	67644.4378	67547.619	95458.8463	95145.8055
2	67613.8959	70215.6073	75826.931	75662.477	95893.1612	97249.3595
3	55005.0087	54842.7263	70556.3936	70090.4017	74368.7997	74553.2046
4	53128.7186	53798.3346	56947.542	56618.6646	74261.1768	74472.6319
5	62246.1626	61995.8077	66881.2194	66895.9705	96278.4523	97122.5295
6	55957.2602	56165.9467	94391.1219	95012.6923	97271.6645	97826.727
7	60056.7259	59195.3894	68223.7328	68472.3391	78385.7211	78780.4298
8	53587.3374	53008.9771	55747.5298	55570.1378	61968.3882	61997.6263
9	62126.6388	61758.9957	71196.546	70863.3535	89991.9346	89022.6034
10	52238.7913	52482.7215	67702.5259	67677.9286	69679.1387	69496.9418

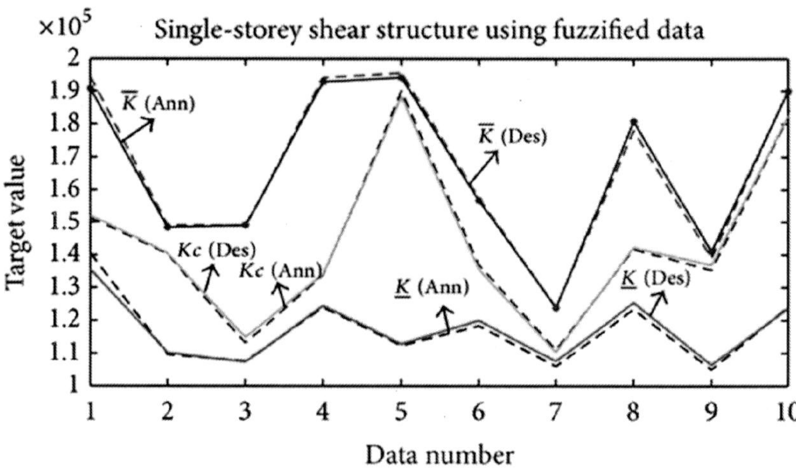

Figure 4. Comparison between the desired and the ANN values of $\bar{k}$ for a single-storey shear structure

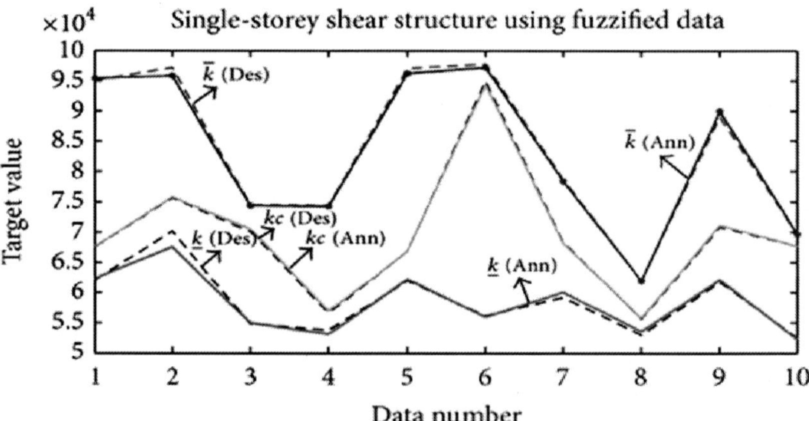

Figure 5. Comparison between the desired and the ANN values of $\bar{k}$ for a single-storey shear.

In Case(iv), the first example of a double-storey shear structure is considered where the masses are $\bar{m}_1 = \bar{m}_2 = 36000$ and the stiffness parameters varying within the range k_1= [100000 200000], k_1c = [100010 200010], k_1= [100020 200020] and k_2= [20000 30000], k_2c =[20010 30010] , and k_2 = [20020 30020]. The desired and ANN values have been compared in Tables 5(a) and 5(b). This table has also been shown in Figures 6(a) and 6(b). In the second example, a double-storey shear structure is implemented with masses $\bar{m}_1 = \bar{m}_2 = 36000$ and the stiffness parameters having the range k_1 = [50000 100000], k_1 c = [50010 100010], k_1 = [50020 100020] and k_2 = [20000 30000], k_2 c = [20010 30010], and k_2 = [20020 30020]. Comparison between the desired and ANN values are again incorporated in Tables 6(a) and 6(b). This table is plotted in Figures 7(a) and 7(b).

Table 5(a). Comparison between the desired and the ANN values of $\bar{k}_1$ for a double-storey shear structure. (b) Comparison between the desired and the ANN values of $\bar{k}_2$ for a double-storey shear structure.

Data number	$\underline{k}_1$ (Ann)	$\underline{k}_1$ (Des)	k_1c (Ann)	k_1c (Des)	$\overline{k_1}$ (Ann)	$\overline{k_1}$ (Des)
1	113258.5422	113317.1008	133858.2555	133969.3413	162741.2326	162807.3359
2	116526.66	117338.8613	128622.4646	129208.408	193447.2534	195183.0465
3	139119.0131	139093.7802	143501.0894	143175.117	191801.5675	192053.204
4	101316.7594	101558.7126	106512.8803	105287.6998	183040.5812	183137.9743
5	173554.7972	173805.8096	180269.037	180336.4392	198199.4731	198416.3724
6	105985.8857	106047.1179	117592.2043	116726.841	127688.8972	126931.9426
7	110472.1362	110631.6345	140132.9188	139925.7771	142461.6007	142303.5615
8	137120.3743	137250.974	152856.9037	152687.5831	155005.6994	154807.0901
9	119783.849	119821.8403	142480.6438	141679.9468	195824.6624	194293.6984
10	141708.5217	141794.4104	148654.6797	148978.7638	165370.4902	165685.9891

(b)

Data number	$\underline{k}_2$ (Ann)	$\underline{k}_2$ (Des)	k_2c (Ann)	k_2c (Des)	$\overline{k_2}$ (Ann)	$\overline{k_2}$ (Des)
1	58488.0205	58566.0533	91472.5908	92796.1403	99954.016	99152.6233
2	51977.6459	51640.041	65679.199	65072.7474	85856.2114	82258.2268
3	69213.7504	68833.6105	77764.8854	78069.9896	85939.2478	85054.9378
4	60124.2902	59566.1848	83319.0924	83316.9426	93794.9834	94103.325
5	71317.3378	71432.6496	76748.5343	76956.3233	83930.3883	83468.7652
6	59384.591	59531.6634	73687.8221	74121.1031	85087.5853	84905.276
7	56031.7629	56050.5807	68215.603	68455.8273	83728.3652	83326.3957
8	58849.1438	58906.6227	72741.8224	73046.2969	79796.3231	79495.3742
9	57077.8681	56400.72	61035.9761	61329.384	95110.8992	99091.8975
10	57858.7023	57830.2476	69404.8867	69250.9562	99433.354	99954.0197

Table 6(a). Comparison between the desired and the ANN values of $\bar{k}_1$ for a double-storey shear structure. (b) Comparison between the desired and the ANN values of $\bar{k}2$ for a double-storey shear structure.

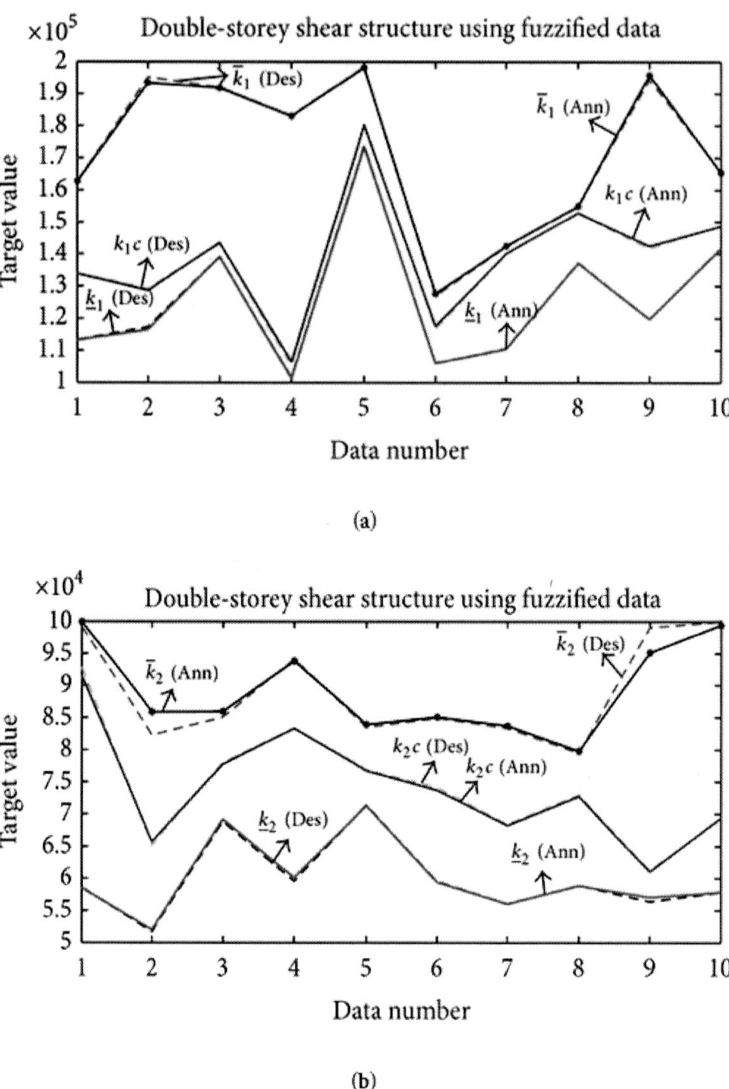

Figure 6(a). Comparison between the desired and the ANN values of $\bar{k}_1$ for a double-storey shear structure. (b) Comparison between the desired and the ANN values of $\bar{k}_2$ for a double-storey shear structure.

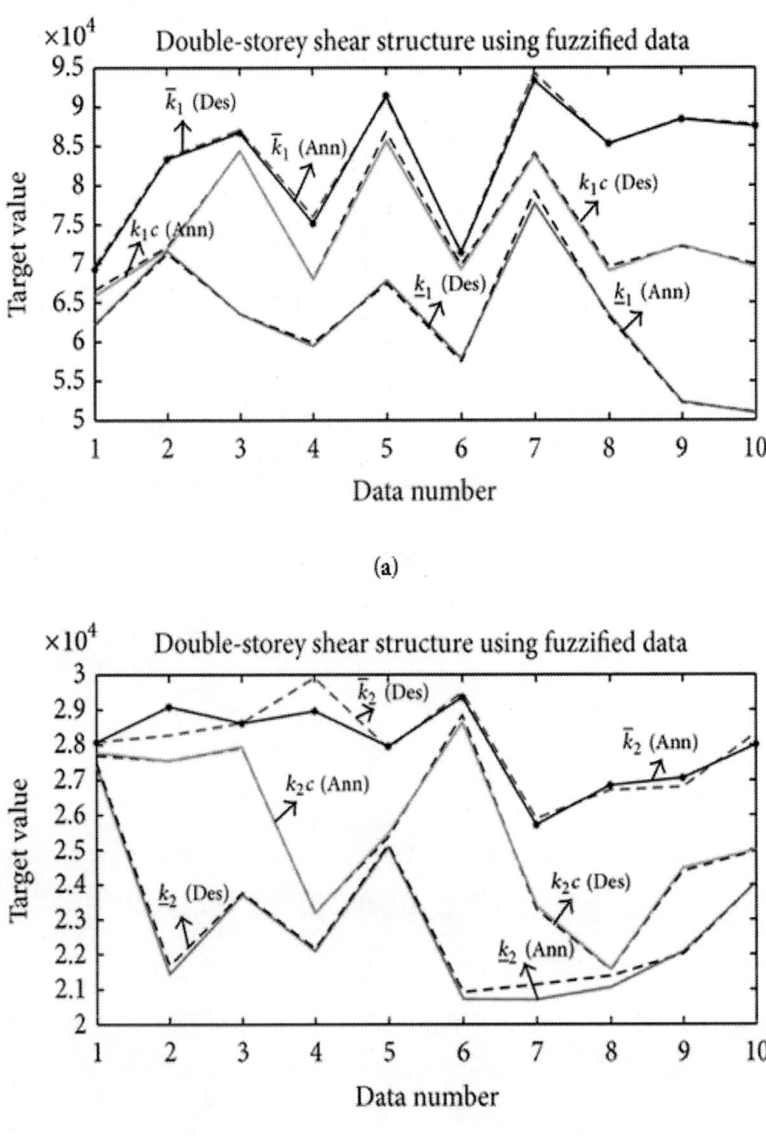

Figure 7(a). Comparison between the desired and the ANN values of $\bar{k}_1$ for a double-storey shear structure. (b) Comparison between the desired and the ANN values of $\bar{k}_2$ for a double-storey shear structure.

The training data with the influence of noise for two-storey shear structure in TFN form for five sets of data have been presented here. Accordingly, Figures 8(a) and 8(b) refer the fuzzy plot of frequency. Moreover, the Triangular Fuzzy Number (TFN) plots of identified stiffness are cited in Figures 9(a) and 9(b). Also for different alpha values such as , and , the comparison between the desired and ANN values with another five sets of data has been given in Tables 7(a), and 7(b), and 7(c).

Table 7 (a). Comparison between the desired and the ANN values of k_1, $\overline{k}_1$ and k_2, $\overline{k}_2$ for a double-storey shear structure for $\alpha = 0.3$. (b)Comparison between the desired and the ANN values of k_1, $\overline{k}_1$ and k_2, $\overline{k}_2$ for a double-storey shear structure for $\alpha = 0.5$. (c) Comparison between the desired and the ANN values of k_1, k_1 and k_2, k_2 for a double-storey shear structure for $\alpha = 0.8$..

(a)

Data number	$\underline{k}_1$ (Ann)	$\underline{k}_1$ (Des)	$\overline{k}_1$ (Ann)	$\overline{k}_1$ (Des)	$\underline{k}_2$ (Ann)	$\underline{k}_1$ (Des)	$\overline{k}_2$ (Ann)	$\overline{k}_2$ (Des)
1	109470	109250	124660	123870	63676	63908	81668	81670
2	119370	119420	141760	141590	59687	59772	79075	78865
3	141840	141880	154360	154170	63017	63149	77680	77561
4	126590	126380	179820	178510	58265	57879	84888	87763
5	143790	143950	160360	160670	61323	61256	90425	90743

(b)

Data number	$\underline{k}_1$ (Ann)	$\underline{k}_1$ (Des)	$\overline{k}_1$ (Ann)	$\overline{k}_1$ (Des)	$\underline{k}_2$ (Ann)	$\underline{k}_1$ (Des)	$\overline{k}_2$ (Ann)	$\overline{k}_2$ (Des)
1	111790	111390	122640	121830	66536	66826	79388	79513
2	125300	125280	141300	141110	62124	62253	75972	75891
3	144990	144970	153930	153750	65795	65976	76269	76271
4	131130	130750	169150	167990	59057	58865	78073	80211
5	145180	145390	157010	157330	63632	63541	84419	84602

(c)

Data number	$\underline{k}_1$ (Ann)	$\underline{k}_1$ (Des)	$\overline{k}_1$ (Ann)	$\overline{k}_1$ (Des)	$\underline{k}_2$ (Ann)	$\underline{k}_1$ (Des)	$\overline{k}_2$ (Ann)	$\overline{k}_2$ (Des)
1	115270	114590	119610	118770	70827	71203	75968	76278
2	134200	134070	140600	140400	65779	65975	71318	71430
3	149710	149600	153290	153110	69963	70218	74153	74336
4	137940	137310	153150	152200	60244	60344	67851	68882
5	147270	147540	152000	152320	67096	66967	75411	75392

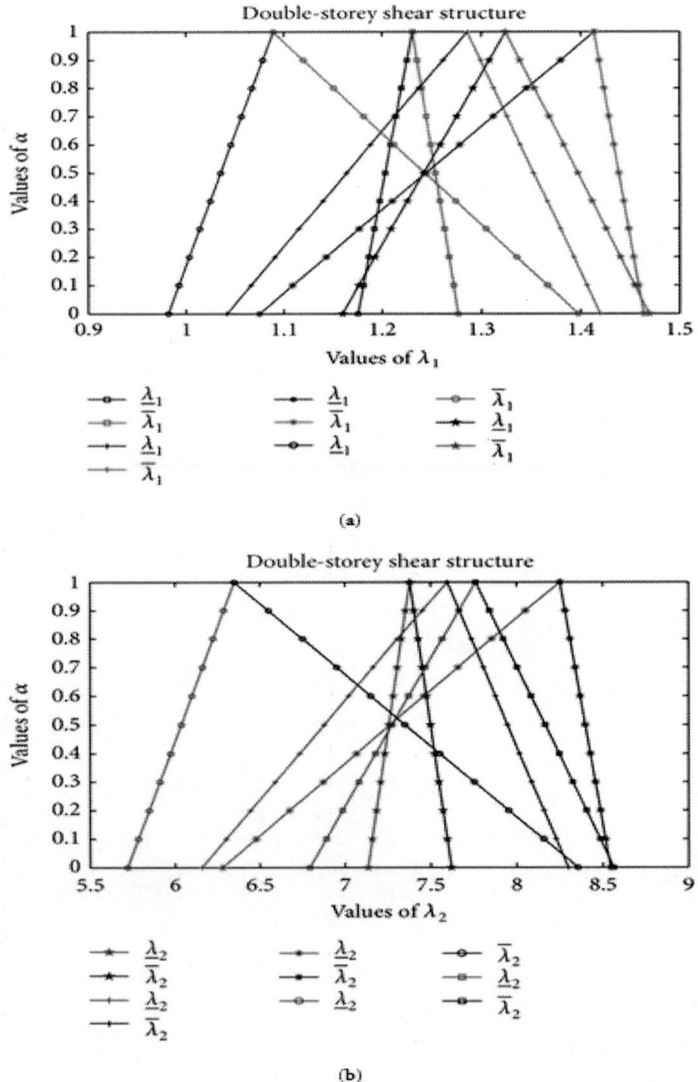

Figure 8 (a). Comparison of λ_1 and $\bar{\lambda}_1$ with respect to α. (b) Comparison of λ_2 and $\bar{\lambda}_2$ with respect to α.

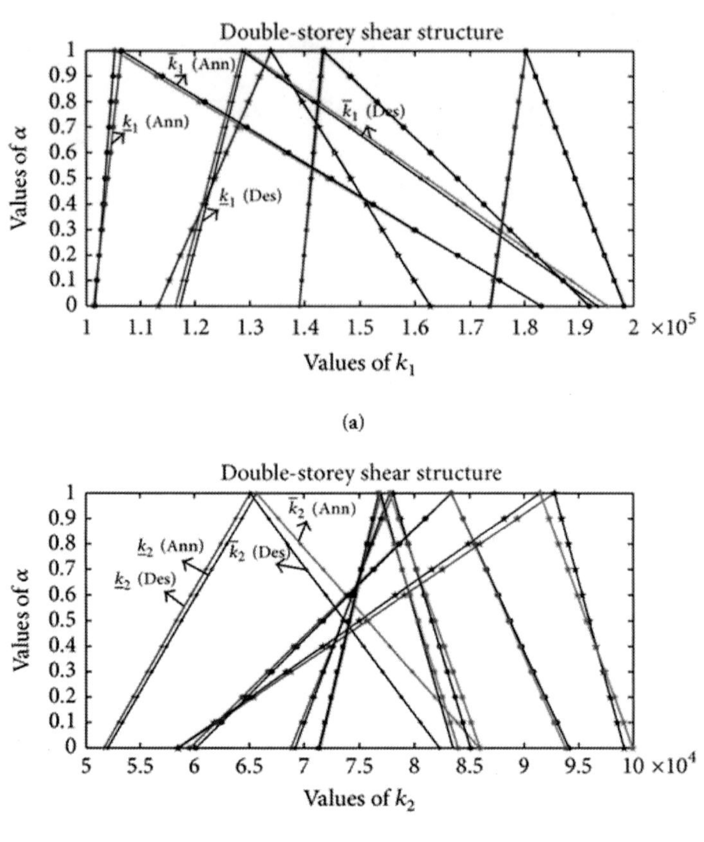

Figure 9 (a). Comparison of k_1 and $\overline{k}_1$ with respect to α. (b) Comparison of k_1 and $\overline{k}_2$ with respect to α.

CONCLUSION

Here, the procedure is demonstrated to identify stiffness parameters for multistorey shear structure using fuzzified data in ANN. The present study considers example problems of one-, two-, five-, and ten-storey shear structures. Identification study for five- and ten-storey shear structures has been done with crisp data. Then, fuzzified data has been considered for one- and two-storey shear structures for the present identification procedure. Initial design parameters, namely, stiffness and mass and so the frequency of the said problem is known in term of fuzzy numbers. The engineers want to know the present health of the structure by system identification methods. It is assumed that only the stiffness is changed and the mass remains the same. The present values of the frequencies may be obtained by available equipments, and using these, one may get the present parameter values by ANN. So, if sensors are placed to capture the frequency of the floors in fuzzy (uncertain) form, then, those may be fed into the proposed new ANN model to get the present stiffness parameters. The methods of one- and two-storey shear structures with fuzzified data may very well be extended for higher storey structures following the present procedure. As regards the influence of noise, it may be seen that the input and output data for two-storey shear structure are actually in terms of Triangular Fuzzy Number (TFN) which themselves dictate the noise in both monotonic increasing and decreasing senses. In order to train the new ANN model, set of data are generated numerically beforehand. As such, converged ANN model gives the present stiffness parameter values in fuzzified form for each floor. Thus, one may predict the health of the structure. Corresponding example problems (as mentioned) have been solved, and related results are reported to show the reliability and powerfulness of the model.

ACKNOWLEDGMENTS

The authors would like to acknowledge funding from the Ministry of Earth Sciences, New Delhi, India. They are also thankful to the anonymous reviewers for their valuable suggestion to improve the paper.

REFERENCES

1. E. Khanmirza, N. Khaji, and V. J. Majd, "Model updating of multistory shear buildings for simultaneous identification of mass, stiffness and damping matrices using two different soft-computing methods," Expert Systems with Applications, vol. 38, no. 5, pp. 5320–5329, 2011.
2. M. I. Friswell, D. J. Inman, and D. F. Pilkey, "The direct updating of damping and stiffness matrices," AIAA Journal, vol. 36, no. 3, pp. 491–493, 1998.

3. M. Tanaka and H. D. Bui, Inverse Problems in Engineering Mechanics, Balkema, Rotterdam, The Netherlands, 1994.
4. K. F. Alvin, A. N. Robertson, G. W. Reich, and K. C. Park, "Structural system identification: from reality to models," Computers and Structures, vol. 81, no. 12, pp. 1149–1176, 2003.
5. S. D. Fassois and J. S. Sakellariou, "Time-series methods for fault detection and identification in vibrating structures," Philosophical Transactions of the Royal Society A, vol. 365, no. 1851, pp. 411–448, 2007.
6. S. F. Marsi, G. A. Bekey, H. Sassi, and T. K. Caughey, "Non-parametric identification of a class of non-linear multi degree dynamic systems," Earthquake Engineering & Structural Dynamics, vol. 10, no. 1, pp. 1–30, 1982.
7. P. Ibanez, "Review of analytical and experimental techniques for improving structural dynamic models," Welding Research Council Bulletin, no. 249, 1979.
8. A. K. Datta, M. Shrikhande, and D. K. Paul, "System identification of buildings: a review," in Proceedings of 11th Symposium on Earthquake Engineering, University of Roorkee, Roorkee, India.
9. C.-H Loh and I.-C Tou, "A system identification approach to the detection of changes in both linear and non-linear structural parameters," Earthquake Engineering & Structural Dynamics, vol. 24, no. 1, pp. 85–97, 1995.
10. P. Yuan, Z. Wu, and X. Ma, "Estimated mass and stiffness matrices of shear building from modal test data," Earthquake Engineering and Structural Dynamics, vol. 27, no. 5, pp. 415–421, 1998.
11. C. H. Chen, "Structural identification from field measurement data using a neural network," Smart Materials and Structures, vol. 14, no. 3, pp. S104–S115, 2005.
12. C. S. Huang, S. L. Hung, C. M. Wen, and T. T. Tu, "A neural network approach for structural identification and diagnosis of a building from seismic response data," Earthquake Engineering and Structural Dynamics, vol. 32, no. 2, pp. 187–206, 2003.
13. C. Y. Kao and S. L. Hung, "Detection of structural damage via free vibration responses generated by approximating artificial neural networks," Computers and Structures, vol. 81, no. 28-29, pp. 2631–2644, 2003.
14. Z. Wu, B. Xu, and K. Yokoyama, "Decentralized parametric damage detection based on neural networks," Computer-Aided Civil and Infrastructure Engineering, vol. 17, no. 3, pp. 175–184, 2002.
15. B. Xu, Z. Wu, G. Chen, and K. Yokoyama, "A localized identification method with neural networks and its application to structural health monitoring," Journal of Structural Engineering A, vol. 48, pp. 419–427, 2002.
16. B. Xu, Z. Wu, G. Chen, and K. Yokoyama, "Direct identification of structural parameters from dynamic responses with neural networks," Engineering Applications of Artificial Intelligence, vol. 17, no. 8, pp. 931–943, 2004.
17. S. Chakraverty, "Identification of structural parameters of multistorey

shear buildings from modal data," Earthquake Engineering and Structural Dynamics, vol. 34, no. 6, pp. 543–554, 2005.

18. M. J. Perry, C. G. Koh, and Y. S. Choo, "Modified genetic algorithm strategy for structural identification," Computers and Structures, vol. 84, no. 8-9, pp. 529–540, 2006.
19. G. S. Wang, "Application of hybrid genetic algorithm to system identification," Structural Control and Health Monitoring, vol. 16, no. 2, pp. 125–153, 2009.
20. S. Yoshitomi and I. Takewaki, "Noise-bias compensation in physical-parameter system identification under microtremor input," Engineering Structures, vol. 31, no. 2, pp. 580–590, 2009.
21. Y. Lu and Z. Tu, "A two-level neural network approach for dynamic FE model updating including damping," Journal of Sound and Vibration, vol. 275, no. 3–5, pp. 931–952, 2004.
22. C. G. Koh, Y. F. Chen, and C. Y. Liaw, "A hybrid computational strategy for identification of structural parameters," Computers and Structures, vol. 81, no. 2, pp. 107–117, 2003.
23. H. Tang, S. Xue, and C. Fan, "Differential evolution strategy for structural system identification, "Computers and Structures, vol. 86, no. 21-22, pp. 2004–2012, 2008.

Chapter 5

COMPARISON OF ARTIFICIAL NEURAL NETWORK ARCHITECTURE IN SOLVING ORDINARY DIFFERENTIAL EQUATIONS

Susmita Mall and S. Chakraverty

Department of Mathematics, National Institute of Technology, Rourkela, Odisha-769008, India

ABSTRACT

This paper investigates the solution of Ordinary Differential Equations (ODEs) with initial conditions using Regression Based Algorithm (RBA) and compares the results with arbitrary- and regression-based initial weights for different numbers of nodes in hidden layer. Here, we have used feed forward neural network and error back propagation method for minimizing the error function and for the modification of the parameters (weights and biases). Initial weights are taken as combination of random as well as by the proposed regression based model. We present the method for solving a variety of problems and the results are compared. Here, the number of nodes in hidden layer has been fixed according to the degree of polynomial in the regression fitting. For this, the input and output data are fitted first with various degree polynomials using regression analysis and the coefficients involved are taken as initial weights to start with the neural training. Fixing of the hidden nodes depends upon the degree of the polynomial. For the example problems, the analytical results have been compared with neural results with arbitrary and regression based weights with four, five, and six nodes in hidden layer and are found to be in good agreement.

INTRODUCTION

Differential equations play vital role in various fields of engineering and science. The exact solution of differential equations may not be always possible [1]. So various types of well known numerical methods such as Euler, Runge-kutta, Predictor-Corrector, finite element, and finite difference methods, are used for solving these equations. Although these numerical methods provide good approximations to the solution, but these may be challenging for higher dimension problems. In recent years, many researchers tried to find new methods for solving differential equations. As such here Artificial Neural Network (ANN) based models are used to solve ordinary differential equations with initial conditions.

Lee and Kang [2] first introduced a method to solve first order differential equation using Hopfield neural network models. Then, another approach by Meade and Fernandez [3, 4] has been proposed for both linear and nonlinear differential equations using -splines and feed forward neural network. Artificial neural networks based on Broyden-Fletcher-Goldfarb-Shanno (BFGS) optimization technique for solving ordinary and partial differential equations have been excellently presented by Lagaris et al. [5]. Also Lagaris et al. [6] investigated neural network methods for boundary value problems with irregular boundaries. Parisi et al. [7] presented unsupervised feed forward neural network for the solution of differential equations. The potential of the hybrid and optimization technique to deal with differential equation of lower order as well as higher order has been presented by Malek and Shekari Beidokhti [8]. Choi and Lee [9] discussed comparison of generalizing ability on solving differential equation using back propagation and reformulated radial basis function network. Yazdi et al. [10] used unsupervised kernel least mean square algorithm for solving ordinary differential equations. A new algorithm for solving matrix Riccati differential equations has been developed by Selvaraju and Abdul Samant [11]. He et al. [12] investigated a class of partial differential equations using multilayer neural network. Kumar and Yadav [13] surveyed multilayer perceptrons and radial basis function neural network methods for the solution of differential equations. Tsoulos et al. [14] solved differential equations with neural networks using a scheme based on grammatical evolution. Numerical solution of elliptic partial differential equation using radial basis function neural networks has been presented by Jianyu et al. [15]. Shirvany et al. [16] proposed multilayer perceptron and radial basis function (RBF) neural networks with a new unsupervised training method for numerical solution of partial differential equations. Mai-Duy and Tran-Cong [17] discussed numerical solution of differential equations using multiquadric radial basis function networks. Fuzzy linguistic model in neural network to solve differential equations is presented by Leephakpreeda [18]. Franke and Schaback [19] solved partial differential equations by collocation using radial basis functions. Smaoui and Al-Enezi [20] presented the dynamics of two nonlinear partial differential equations using artificial neural networks. Differential equations with genetic programming have been analyzed by Tsoulos and Lagaris [21]. McFall and Mahan [22] used artificial neural network for solution of boundary value problems with exact satisfaction of arbitrary boundary conditions. Hoda and Nagla [23] solved mixed boundary value problems using multilayer perceptron neural network method.

As per the review of the literatures, it reveals that authors have taken the parameters (weights/biases) as arbitrary (random) and the numbers of nodes in hidden layer are considered by trial and error method. In this paper, we propose a method for solving ordinary differential equations using feed forward neural network as a basic approximation element and error back propagation algorithm [24, 25] by fixing hidden nodes as per the required accuracy. The trial solution of the model is generated by training the algorithm. The approximate solution by ANN has many benefits compared with traditional numerical methods. The ANN trial solution is written as sum of two terms, first one satisfies initial/boundary conditions and the second part involves regression based neural network with adjustable parameters. The computational complexity does not increase considerably with the number of sampling points. The method is general so it can be applied to solve linear and nonlinear ordinary and partial differential equations. The modification of parameters has been done without direct use of optimization technique. For which computation of the gradient of error with respect to the network parameters is required. A regression based artificial neural network with combinations of initial weights (arbitrary and regression based) in the connections is first proposed by Chakraverty et al. [26] and then by Singh et al. [27]. Here, number of nodes in hidden layer may be fixed according to the degree of polynomial required for the accuracy. We have considered a first order and an application problem such as damped free vibration problem to show the comparison of different ANN models. Mall and Chakraverty [28] proposed regression-based neural network model for solving ordinary differential equations.

Rest of the paper is organized as follows. In Section 2, we describe the general formulation of the proposed approach and computation of gradient of the error function. Section 3 gives details of problem formulation and construction of the appropriate form of trial solution. The proposed regression based artificial neural network method has been presented in Section 4. Numerical examples and its results are presented in Section 5. In this section, we compare arbitrary and regression based weight results and those are shown graphically. Section 6 incorporates the discussion and analysis part. Lastly conclusion is outlined in Section 7.

GENERAL FORMULATION FOR DIFFERENTIAL EQUATIONS

Let us consider the following general differential equations which represent both ordinary and partial differential equations [4]:

$$G\left(x, \psi(x), \nabla\psi(x), \nabla^2\psi(x) \cdots\right) = 0, \quad x \in D, \tag{1}$$

Subject to some initial or boundary conditions, where ,

$x = (x_1, x_2, \ldots, x_n) \in R^n$, $D \subset R^n$ denotes the domain, and $\psi(x)$ is the solution to be computed. Here, G is the function which defines the structure of the differential equation and ∇ is a differential operator. For the solution of the differential equation, a discretized domain $\overline{D}$ over finite set of points in D is considered. Thus, the problem transformed into the system of equations as follows:

$$G\left(x_i, \psi(x_i), \nabla\psi(x_i), \nabla^2\psi(x_i) \cdots\right) = 0, \quad x \in \overline{D}. \tag{2}$$

Let $\psi_t(x, p)$ denote the trail solution with adjustable parameters (weights, biases) , and then the problem may be formulated as

$$G\left(x_i, \psi_t(x_i, p), \nabla\psi_t(x_i, p), \ldots, \nabla^m\psi_t(x_i, p) \cdots\right) = 0. \tag{3}$$

Corresponding error function with respect to every input data is written as

$$\min_p \sum_{x_i \in \overline{D}} \left(G\left(x_i, \psi_t(x_i, p), \nabla\psi_t(x_i, p), \ldots, \nabla^m\psi_t(x_i, p)\right)\right)^2. \tag{4}$$

Now, $\psi_t(x, p)$ may be written as the sum of two terms

$$\psi_t(x, p) = A(x) + F(x, N(x, p)), \tag{5}$$

where $A(x)$ satisfies initial or boundary condition and contains no adjustable parameters, whereas $N(x, p)$ is the output of feed forward neural network with the parameters p and input data x The second term $F(x, N(x, p))$ makes no contribution to initial or boundary but this is used to a neural network model whose weights and biases are adjusted to minimize the error function.

Computation of the Gradient

The error computation not only involves the outputs but also the derivatives of the network output with respect to its inputs. So, it requires finding out the gradient of the network derivatives with respect to its inputs. Let us now consider a multilayered perceptron with one input node, a hidden layer with nodes (fixed number of nods as proposed), and one output unit. For the given inputs $x = (x_1, x_2, \dots x_n)$, the output is given by

$$N(x, p) = \sum_{j=1}^{m} v_j \sigma(z_j), \tag{6}$$

where $z_j = \sum_{i=1}^{n} w_{ji} x_i + u_j$, w_{ji} denotes the weight from input unit *i* to the hidden unit j, v_j denotes weight from the hidden unit *j* to the output unit, u_j denotes the biases, and $\sigma(z_j)$ is the sigmoid activation function.

The derivatives of *N*(*x*, *p*)with respect to input x_i is

$$\frac{\partial^k N}{\partial x_i^k} = \sum_{j=1}^{m} v_j w_{ji}^k \sigma_j^{(k)}, \tag{7}$$

where $\sigma = \sigma(z_j)$ and $\sigma^{(k)}$ denotes the *k*th order derivative of sigmoid function.

Let N_ϑ denote the derivative of the network with respect to its inputs and then we have the following relation [4]:

$$N_{\vartheta} = D^{n}N = \sum_{i=1}^{n} v_i P_i \sigma_i^{(n)}, \tag{8}$$

Where

$$P_j = \prod_{k=1}^{n} w_{jk}^{\lambda_k}, \quad \kappa = \sum_{i=1}^{n} \lambda_i. \tag{9}$$

The derivative of N_{ϑ} with respect to other parameters may be obtained as

$$\frac{\partial N_{\vartheta}}{\partial v_j} = P_j \sigma_j^{(\kappa)}, \tag{10}$$

$$\frac{\partial N_{\vartheta}}{\partial u_j} = v_j P_j \sigma_j^{(\kappa+1)}, \tag{11}$$

$$\frac{\partial N_{\vartheta}}{\partial w_{ji}} = x_i v_j P_j \sigma_j^{(\kappa+1)} + v_j \lambda_i w_{ji}^{\lambda_i - 1} \left(\prod_{k=1, k \neq i} w_{ji}^{\lambda_k} \right) \sigma_j^{(\kappa)}. \tag{12}$$

FORMULATION OF FIRST ORDER ORDINARY DIFFERENTIAL EQUATION

Let us consider first order ordinary differential equation as below

$$\frac{d\psi}{dx} = f(x, \psi), \quad x \in [a, b], \tag{13}$$

with initial condition $\psi(a) = A.$

In this case, the ANN trail solution may be written as

$$\psi_t(x,p) = A + (x-a)N(x,p), \tag{14}$$

where $N(x, p)$ is the neural output of the feed forward network with one input data x with parameters p. The trial solution $\psi_t(x, p)$ satisfies the initial condition. We differentiate the trial solution $\psi_t(x, p)$ to get

$$\frac{d\psi_t(x,p)}{dx} = N(x,p) + (x-a)\frac{dN(x,p)}{dx}. \tag{15}$$

For evaluating the derivative term in the right hand side of (15), we use (5)–(11).

The error function for this case may be formulated as

$$E(p) = \sum_{i=1}^{n}\left(\frac{d\psi_t(x_i,p)}{dx} - f(x_i,\psi_t(x_i,p))\right)^2. \tag{16}$$

The weights from input to hidden are modified according to the following rule

$$w_{ji}^{r+1} = w_{ji}^{r} - \eta\left(\frac{\partial E}{\partial w_{ji}^{r}}\right), \tag{17}$$

Where

$$\frac{\partial E}{\partial w_{ji}^{r}} = \frac{\partial}{\partial w_{ji}^{r}}\left(\sum_{i=1}^{n}\left(\frac{d\psi_t(x_i,p)}{dx} - f(x_i,\psi_t(x_i,p))\right)^2\right). \tag{18}$$

Here, η is the learning rate and r is the iteration step. The weights from hidden to output layer may be updated in a similar formulation as done for input to hidden.

Formulation of Second Order Ordinary Differential Equation

In this case, the second order ordinary differential equation may be written in general as

$$\frac{d^2\psi}{dx^2} = f\left(x, \psi, \frac{d\psi}{dx}\right), \quad x \in [a,b], \tag{19}$$

with initial conditions $\psi(a) = A, \psi'(a) = A'$.

The ANN trail solution may be discussed as

$$\psi_t(x,p) = A + A'(x-a) + (x-a)^2 N(x,p), \tag{20}$$

where $N(x, p)$ is the neural output of the feed forward network with one input data x with parameters p and the trial solution $\psi_t(x, p)$ satisfies the initial conditions.

The error function to be minimized for second order ordinary differential equation will be

$$E(p) = \sum_{i=1}^{n} \left(\frac{d^2\psi_t(x_i, p)}{dx^2} - f\left(x_i, \psi_t(x_i, p), \frac{d\psi}{dx}\right)\right)^2. \tag{21}$$

Next, the following weight updating rule is applied for weights from input to hidden connections:

$$w_{ji}^{r+1} = w_{ji}^{r} - \eta\left(\frac{\partial E}{\partial w_{ji}^{r}}\right), \tag{22}$$

Where

$$\frac{\partial E}{\partial w^r_{ji}} = \frac{\partial}{\partial w^r_{ji}}\left(\sum_{i=1}^{n}\left(\frac{d^2\psi_t(x_i,p)}{dx^2} - f\left[x_i,\psi_t(x_i,p),\frac{d\psi}{dx}\right]\right)^2\right). \tag{23}$$

Again, we update the weights from hidden to output layer, as discussed for input to hidden.

PROPOSED REGRESSION-BASED ALGORITHM

Three layer architecture of ANN for the present problem is considered. Usually numbers of nodes in the hidden layer are taken by trial and error method. Here, we fix the number of nodes in hidden layer by using regression-based weight generation [24, 25]. Figure 1 shows the proposed model, in which the input layer consist of single input unit and the output layer consist of one output unit. Numbers of nodes in the hidden layer are fixed according to degree of polynomial to be considered. If nth degree polynomial is considered, then the number of nodes in hidden layer will be $n + 1$ and coefficients (constants) of the polynomial may be considered as initial weights from input to hidden as well as hidden to output layers or any combination of random and regression based weight. Network architecture with five degree polynomial has been shown in Figure 1, the six coefficients (constants) are taken as initial weights in two stages from input to hidden and hidden to output layer. The constants of the polynomial, that is, a_i are taken as initial weights and six nodes for the six constants in the hidden layer are considered.

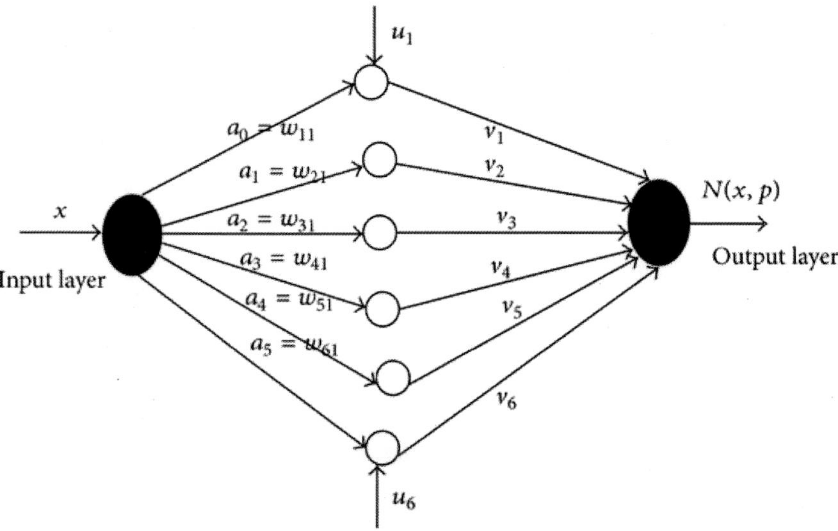

Figure 1. Three-layered neural network architecture with single input and single output node.

NUMERICAL EXAMPLES

In this section, we present solution of two example problems as mentioned earlier. In all cases, we have used error back propagation algorithm and one hidden layer. The weights are taken as arbitrary and regression based for comparison of the training method. Sigmoid function is considered as an activation function for hidden unit.

Example 1. Let us consider the first order ordinary differential equation as follows:

$$\frac{d\psi}{dx} + \left(x + \frac{1+3x^2}{1+x+x^3}\right)\psi = x^3 + 2x + x^2\left(\frac{1+3x^2}{1+x+x^3}\right), \qquad (24)$$

$$x \in [0,1],$$

with initial condition $\psi(0) = 1$.

The trial solution is written as

$$\psi_t(x,p) = 1 + xN(x,p). \qquad (25)$$

We have trained the network for 20 equidistant points in [0, 1] and compared results between analytical and neural with arbitrary and regression based weights with four, five, and six nodes fixed in hidden layer. Comparison between analytical and neural results with arbitrary and regression based weights is given in Table 1. Analytic results are incorporated in second column. Neural results for arbitrary weights (from input to hidden layer) and $v(A)$ (from hidden to output layer) with four, five, and six nodes are cited in third, fifth, and seventh column, respectively. Similarly neural results with regression weights $v(R)$ (from input to hidden layer) and (from hidden to output layer) with four, five, and six nodes are given in fourth, sixth, and ninth column, respectively.

Table 1. Analytical and neural solutions with arbitrary and regression based weights (Example 1)

Input data	Analytical	Neural results							
		$w(A), v(A)$ (four nodes)	$w(R), v(R)$ (four nodes)	$w(A), v(A)$ (five nodes)	$w(R), v(R)$ (five nodes)	$w(A), v(A)$ (six nodes)	Deviation%	$w(R), v(R)$ (six nodes)	Deviation%
0	1.0000	1.0000	1.0000	1.0000	1.0000	1.0000	0.00	1.0000	0.00
0.05	0.9536	1.0015	0.9998	1.0002	0.9768	0.9886	3.67	0.9677	1.47
0.10	0.9137	0.9867	0.9593	0.9498	0.9203	0.9084	0.58	0.9159	0.24
0.15	0.8798	0.9248	0.8986	0.8906	0.8802	0.8906	1.22	0.8815	0.19
0.20	0.8514	0.9088	0.8869	0.8564	0.8666	0.8587	0.85	0.8531	0.19
0.25	0.8283	0.8749	0.8630	0.8509	0.8494	0.8309	0.31	0.8264	0.22
0.30	0.8104	0.8516	0.8481	0.8213	0.9289	0.8013	1.12	0.8114	0.12
0.35	0.7978	0.8264	0.8030	0.8186	0.8051	0.7999	0.26	0.7953	0.31
0.40	0.7905	0.8137	0.7910	0.8108	0.8083	0.7918	0.16	0.7894	0.13
0.45	0.7889	0.7951	0.7908	0.8028	0.7948	0.7828	0.77	0.7845	0.55
0.50	0.7931	0.8074	0.8063	0.8007	0.7960	0.8047	1.46	0.7957	0.32
0.55	0.8033	0.8177	0.8137	0.8276	0.8102	0.8076	0.53	0.8041	0.09
0.60	0.8200	0. 8211	0.8190	0.8362	0.8246	0.8152	0.58	0.8204	0.04
0.65	0.8431	0.8617	0.8578	0.8519	0.8501	0.8319	1.32	0.8399	0.37
0.70	0.8731	0.8896	0.8755	0.8685	0.8794	0.8592	1.59	0.8711	0.22
0.75	0.9101	0.9281	0.9231	0.9229	0.9139	0.9129	0.31	0.9151	0.54
0.80	0.9541	0.9777	0.9613	0.9897	0.9603	0.9755	2.24	0.9555	0.14
0.85	1.0053	1.0819	0.9930	0.9956	1. 0058	1.0056	0.03	0.9948	1.04
0.90	1.0637	1.0849	1.1020	1.0714	1.0663	1.0714	0.72	1.0662	0.23
0.95	1.1293	1.2011	1.1300	1.1588	1.1307	1.1281	0.11	1.1306	0.11
1.00	1.2022	1.2690	1.2195	1.2806	1.2139	1.2108	0.71	1.2058	0.29

Analytical and neural results with arbitrary and regression based weights for six nodes in hidden layer are compared in Figures 2 and 3. The error plot is shown in Figure 4. Absolute deviations in % values have been calculated in Table 1 and the maximum deviation for arbitrary weights neural results (six hidden nodes) is 3.67 (eighth column) and for regression based weights it is 1.47 (tenth column). From Figures 2 and 3, one may see that results from the regression-based weights agree exactly at all points with analytical results but for results with arbitrary weights they are not so. Thus, one may see that the neural results with regression based weights are more accurate.

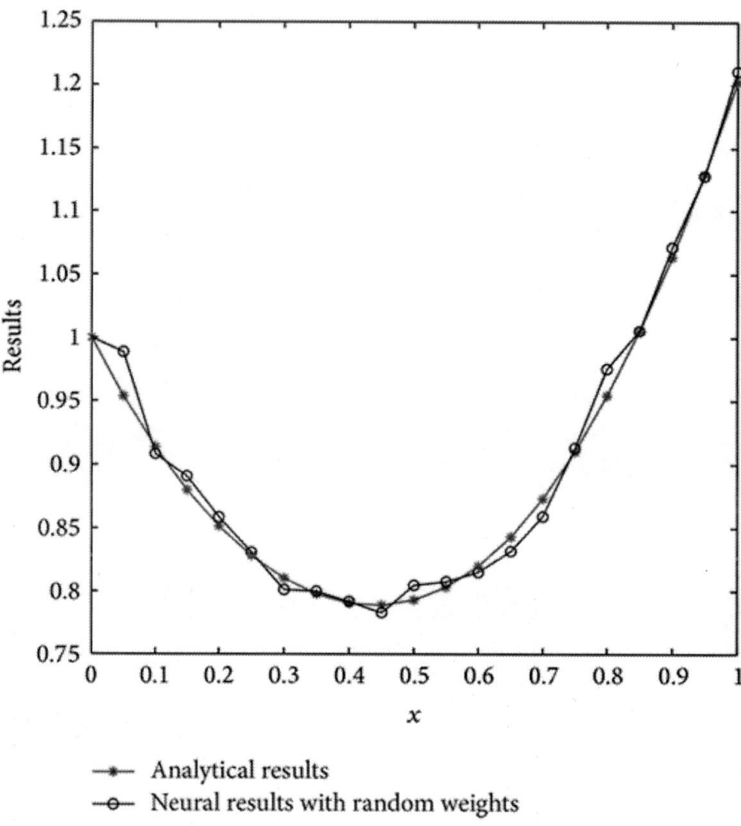

Figure 2. Plot of comparison between (analytical results) and (neural results) with arbitrary weights (Example 1).

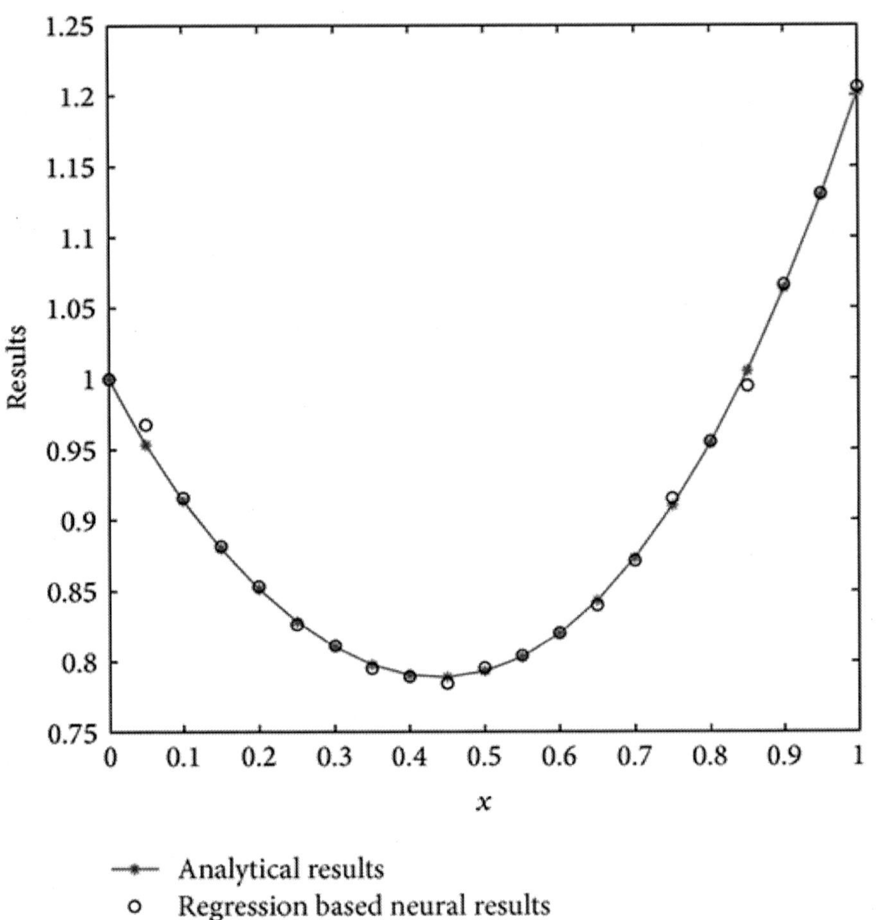

Figure 3. Plot of comparison between (analytical results) and (neural results) with regression-based weights for six nodes (Example 1).

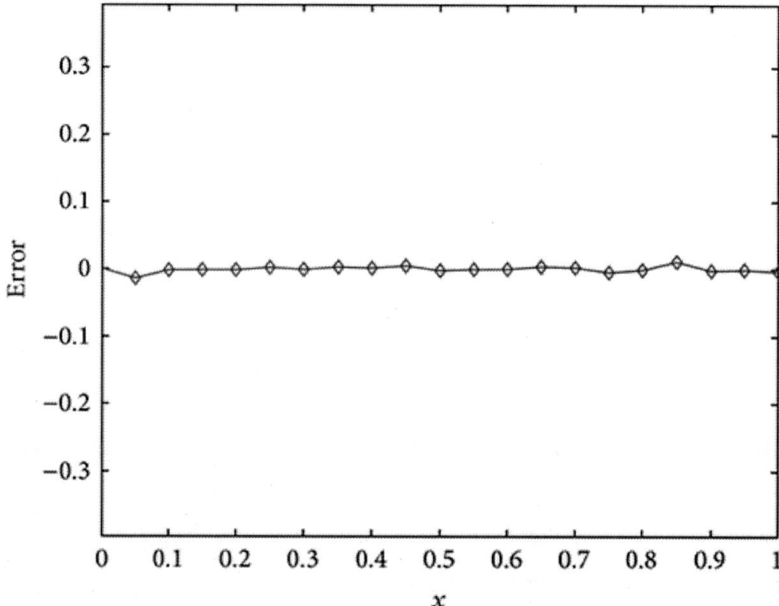

Figure 4. Error plot between analytical- and regression-based weights approximation solution (Example 1).

It may be seen that by increasing the number of nodes in hidden layer from four to six, the results are found to be better. Although the authors increased the number of nodes in hidden layer beyond six, but the results were not improving.

The first problem has also been solved by a well-known numerical method, namely, using Euler and Runge-kutta method. Table 2 shows comparison between the neural results (with six hidden nodes) and other numerical results (Euler and Runge-Kutta results).

Table 2. Comparison of the results (Example 1)

Input data	Analytical	Euler	Runge-Kutta	$w(R), v(R)$ (Six nodes)
0	1.0000	1.0000	1.0000	1.0000
0.0500	0.9536	0.9500	0.9536	0.9677
0.1000	0.9137	0.9072	0.9138	0.9159
0.1500	0.8798	0.8707	0.8799	0.8815
0.2000	0.8514	0.8401	0.8515	0.8531
0.2500	0.8283	0.8150	0.8283	0.8264
0.3000	0.8104	0.7953	0.8105	0.8114
0.3500	0.7978	0.7810	0.7979	0.7953
0.4000	0.7905	0.7721	0.7907	0.7894
0.4500	0.7889	0.7689	0.7890	0.7845
0.5000	0.7931	0.7717	0.7932	0.7957
0.5500	0.8033	0.7805	0.8035	0.8041
0.6000	0.8200	0.7958	0.8201	0.8204
0.6500	0.8431	0.8178	0.8433	0.8399
0.7000	0.8731	0.8467	0.8733	0.8711
0.7500	0.9101	0.8826	0.9102	0.9151
0.8000	0.9541	0.9258	0.9542	0.9555
0.8500	1.0053	0.9763	1.0054	0.9948
0.9000	1.0637	1.0342	1.0638	1.0662
0.9500	1.1293	1.0995	1.1294	1.1306
1.000	1.2022	1.1721	1.2022	1.2058

Example 2. Let us consider the following second order damped free vibration equation:

$$\frac{d^2\psi}{dx^2} + 4\frac{d\psi}{dx} + 4\psi = 0, \quad x \in [0,4]. \tag{26}$$

With initial conditions $\psi(0) = 1, \psi'(0) = 1.$.

As discussed above, we can write the trail solution as

$$\psi_t(x,p) = 1 + x + x^2 N(x,p). \tag{27}$$

Then, the network is trained for 40 equidistant points in [0, 4] and with four, five, and six hidden nodes according to arbitrary and regression-based algorithm. In Table 3, we compare the analytical solutions with neural solutions taking arbitrary- and regression-based weights for four, five, and six nodes in hidden layer. Here, analytic results are cited in second column of Table 3. Neural results for arbitrary weights $w(A)$ (from input to hidden layer) and $v(A)$ (from hidden to output layer) with four, five, and six nodes are shown in third, fifth, and seventh column, respectively. Neural results with regression-based weights $v(R)$ (from input to hidden layer) and $w(R)$ (from hidden to output layer) with four, five and six nodes are cited in fourth, sixth, and eighth column, respectively.

Analytical and neural results which are obtained for random initial weights are depicted in Figure 5. Figure 6 shows comparison between analytical and neural results for regression-based initial weights for six hidden nodes. Finally, the error plot between analytical and RBNN results are shown in Figure 7.

Table 3. Analytical and neural solutions with arbitrary- and regression-based weights (Example 2)

Input data	Analytical	Neural results					
		$w(A), v(A)$ (four nodes)	$w(R), v(R)$ (four nodes)	$w(A), v(A)$ (five nodes)	$w(R), v(R)$ (five nodes)	$w(A), v(A)$ (six nodes)	$w(R), v(R)$ (six nodes)
0	1.0000	1.0000	1.0000	1.0000	1.0000	1.0000	1.0000
0.1	1.0643	1.0900	1.0802	1.0910	1.0878	1.0923	1.0687
0.2	1.0725	1.1000	1.0918	1.0858	1.0715	1.0922	1.0812
0.3	1.0427	1.0993	1.0691	1.0997	1.0518	1.0542	1.0420
0.4	0.9885	0.9953	0.9732	0.9780	0.9741	0.8879	0.9851
0.5	0.9197	0.9208	0.9072	0.9650	0.9114	0.9790	0.9122
0.6	0.8433	0.8506	0.8207	0.8591	0.8497	0.8340	0.8082
0.7	0.7645	0.7840	0.7790	0.7819	0.7782	0.7723	0.7626
0.8	0.6864	0.7286	0.6991	0.7262	0.6545	0.6940	0.6844
0.9	0.6116	0.6552	0.5987	0.6412	0.6215	0.6527	0.6119
1.0	0.5413	0.5599	0.5467	0.5604	0.5341	0.5547	0.5445
1.1	0.4765	0.4724	0.4847	0.4900	0.4755	0.4555	0.4634
1.2	0.4173	0.4081	0.4035	0.4298	0.4202	0.4282	0.4172
1.3	0.3639	0.3849	0.3467	0.3907	0.3761	0.3619	0.3622
1.4	0.3162	0.3501	0.3315	0.3318	0.3274	0.3252	0.3100
1.5	0.2738	0.2980	0.2413	0.2942	0.2663	0.2773	0.2759
1.6	0.2364	0.2636	0.2507	0.2620	0.2439	0.2375	0.2320
1.7	0.2036	0.2183	0.2140	0.2161	0.2107	0.2177	0.1921
1.8	0.1749	0.2018	0.2007	0.1993	0.1916	0.1622	0.1705
1.9	0.1499	0.1740	0.1695	0.1665	0.1625	0.1512	0.1501
2.0	0.1282	0.1209	0.1204	0.1371	0.1299	0.1368	0.1245
2.1	0.1095	0.1236	0.1203	0.1368	0.1162	0.1029	0.1094
2.2	0.0933	0.0961	0.0942	0.0972	0.0949	0.0855	0.09207
2.3	0.0794	0.0818	0.0696	0.0860	0.0763	0.0721	0.0761
2.4	0.0675	0.0742	0.0715	0.0849	0.0706	0.0526	0.0640
2.5	0.0573	0.0584	0.0419	0.0609	0.0543	0.0582	0.0492
2.6	0.0485	0.0702	0.0335	0.0533	0.0458	0.0569	0.0477
2.7	0.0411	0.0674	0.0602	0.0581	0.0468	0.0462	0.0409
2.8	0.0348	0.0367	0.0337	0.0387	0.0328	0.0357	0.03460
2.9	0.0294	0.0380	0.0360	0.0346	0.0318	0.0316	0.0270
3.0	0.0248	0.0261	0.0207	0.0252	0.0250	0.0302	0.0247
3.1	0.0209	0.0429	0.0333	0.0324	0.0249	0.0241	0.0214
3.2	0.0176	0.0162	0.0179	0.0154	0.0169	0.0166	0.0174
3.3	0.0148	0.0159	0.0137	0.0158	0.0140	0.0153	0.0148
3.4	0.0125	0.0138	0.0135	0.0133	0.0130	0.0133	0.0129
3.5	0.0105	0.0179	0.0167	0.0121	0.0132	0.0100	0.0101
3.6	0.0088	0.0097	0.0096	0.0085	0.0923	0.0095	0.0090
3.7	0.0074	0.0094	0.0092	0.0091	0.0093	0.0064	0.0071
3.8	0.0062	0.0081	0.0078	0.0083	0.0070	0.0061	0.0060
3.9	0.0052	0.0063	0.0060	0.0068	0.0058	0.0058	0.0055
4.0	0.0044	0.0054	0.0052	0.0049	0.0049	0.0075	0.0046

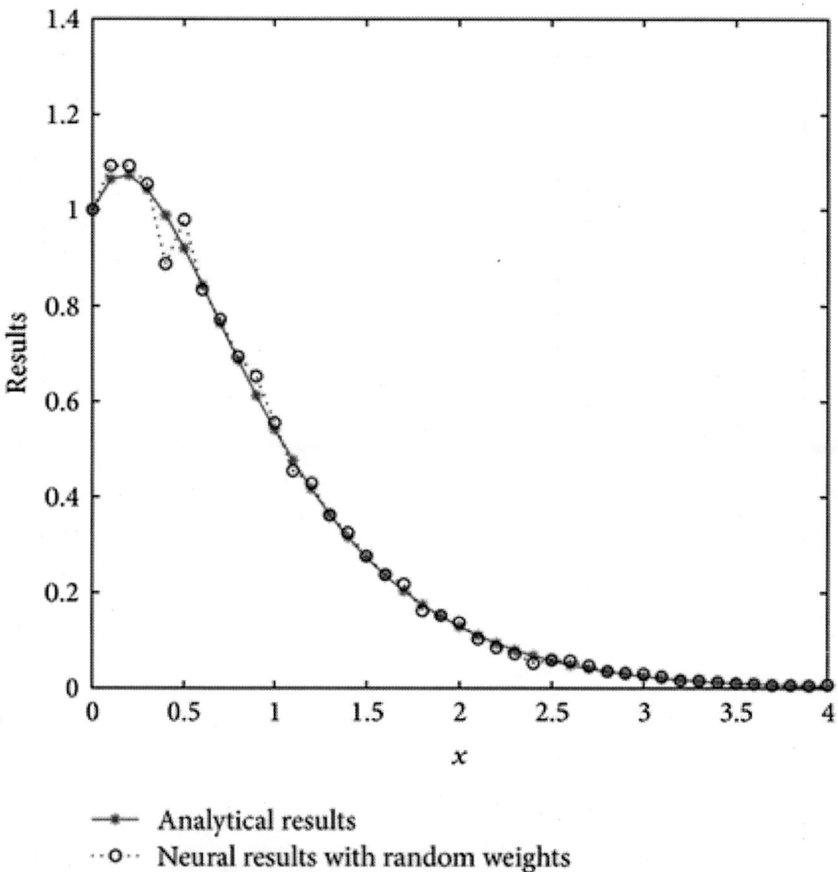

Figure 5. Plot of comparison between (analytical results) and (neural results) with arbitrary weights (for six nodes) (Example 2).

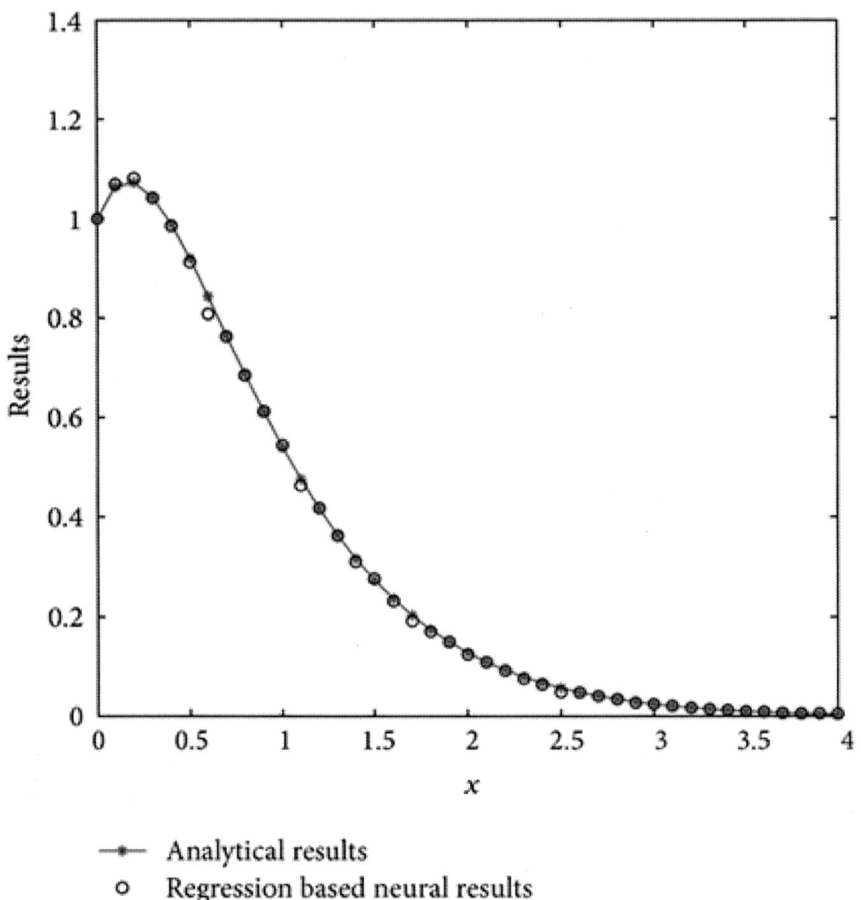

Figure 6. Plot of comparison between (analytical solutions) and (neural solutions) with regression based weights (for six nodes) (Example 2).

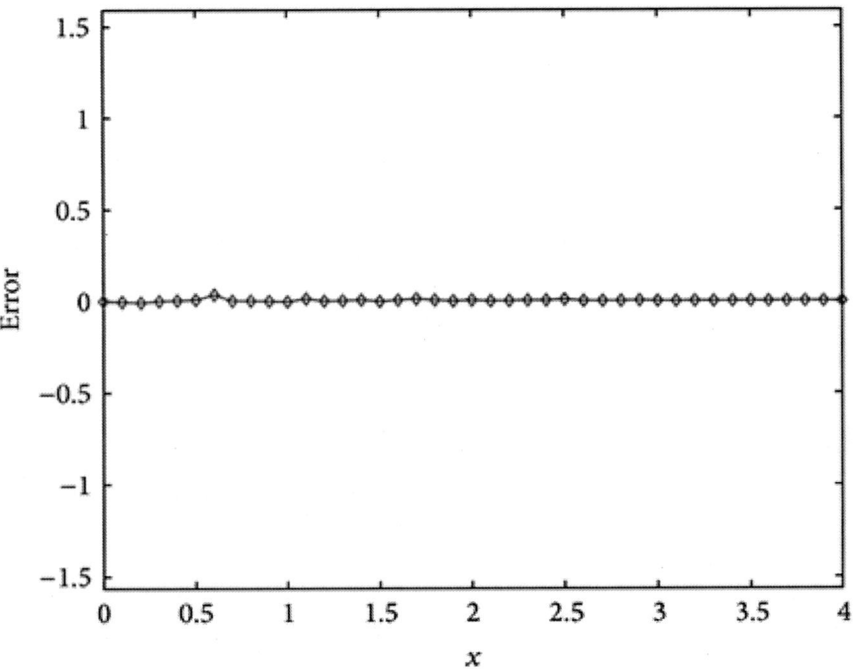

Figure 7. Error plot between analytical, and regression-based weights solution (Example 2).

Example 3. Now we consider an initial value problem as follows:

$$\frac{dy}{dx} + 5y = e^{-3x}, \tag{28}$$

subject to . $\psi(0) = 0$

The ANN trial solution is written as

$$\psi_t(x, p) = xN(x, p). \tag{29}$$

Ten equidistant points in the given domain which are taken with four, five, and six hidden nodes according to arbitrary and regression-based algorithms have been considered. Comparison of analytical and neural results with arbitrary- and regression-based weights have been shown in Table 4. Also, other numerical results, namely, Euler and Runge-Kutta results are compared with neural results in this table.

Analytical and traditional neural results obtained using random initial weights with six nodes are depicted in Figure 8. Similarly, Figure 9 shows comparison between analytical and neural results with regression-based initial weights for six hidden nodes. Finally, the error plot between analytical and RBNN results are cited in Figure 10.

Table 4. Analytical and neural solutions with arbitrary- and regression-based weights (Example 3)

Input data	Analytical	Euler	Runge-Kutta	Neural results					
				$w(A), v(A)$ (four nodes)	$w(R), v(R)$ (four nodes)	$w(A), v(A)$ (five nodes)	$w(R), v(R)$ (five nodes)	$w(A), v(A)$ (six nodes)	$w(R), v(R)$ (six nodes)
0	0	0	0	0	0	0	0	0	0
0.1	0.0671	0.1000	0.0671	0.0440	0.0539	0.0701	0.0602	0.0565	0.0670
0.2	0.0905	0.1241	0.0904	0.0867	0.0938	0.0877	0.0927	0.0921	0.0907
0.3	0.0917	0.1169	0.0917	0.0849	0.0926	0.0889	0.0932	0.0931	0.0918
0.4	0.0829	0.0991	0.0829	0.0830	0.0876	0.0806	0.0811	0.0846	0.0824
0.5	0.0705	0.0797	0.0705	0.0760	0.0748	0.0728	0.0714	0.0717	0.0706
0.6	0.0578	0.0622	0.0577	0.0492	0.0599	0.0529	0.0593	0.0536	0.0597
0.7	0.0461	0.0476	0.0461	0.0433	0.0479	0.0410	0.0453	0.0450	0.0468
0.8	0.0362	0.0360	0.0362	0.0337	0.0319	0.0372	0.0370	0.0343	0.0355
0.9	0.0280	0.0271	0.0280	0.0324	0.0308	0.0309	0.0264	0.0249	0.0284
1.0	0.0215	0.0203	0.0215	0.0304	0.0282	0.0255	0.0247	0.0232	0.0217

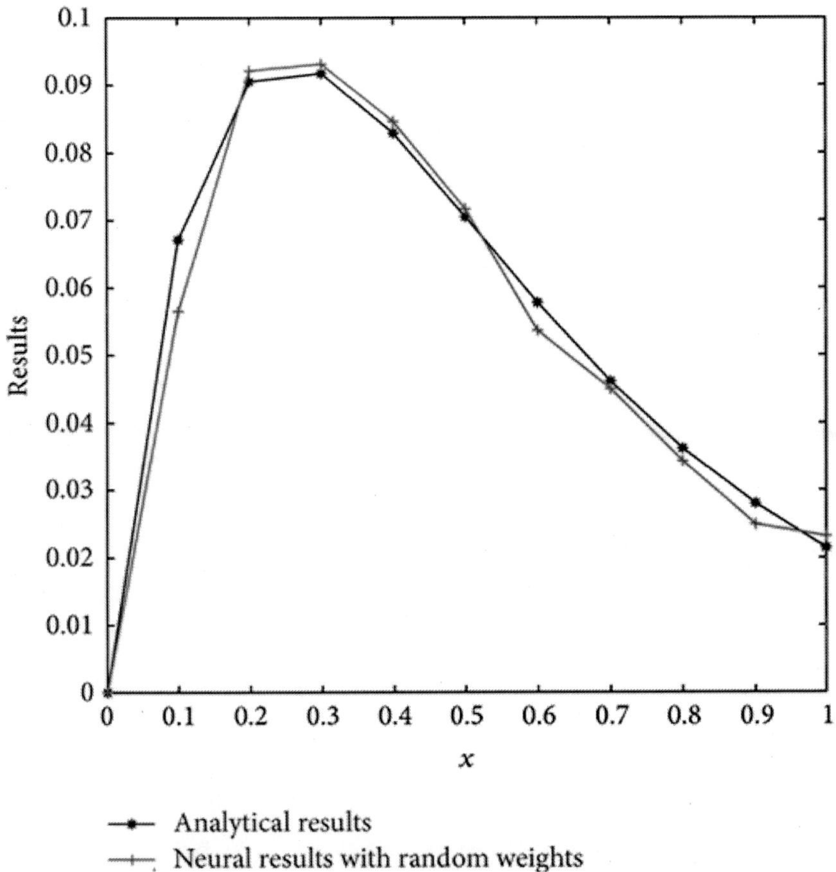

Figure 8. Plot of comparison between (analytical results) and (neural results) with arbitrary weights (for six nodes) (Example 3).

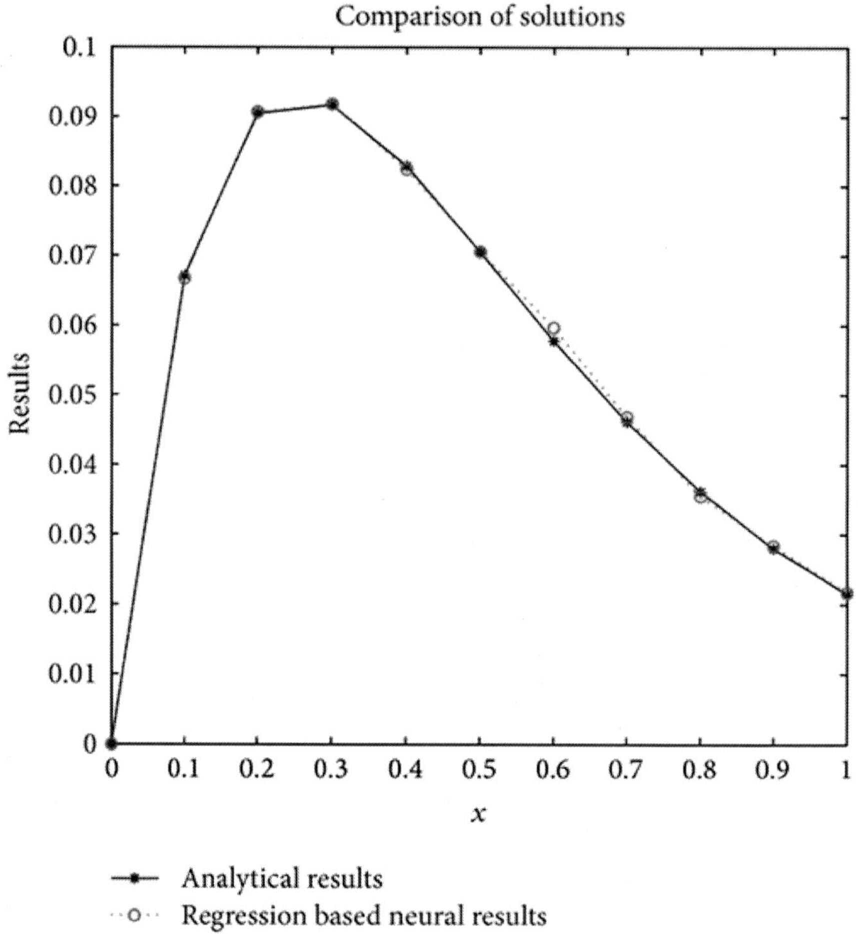

Figure 9. Plot of comparison between (analytical solutions) and (neural solutions) with regression based weights (for six nodes) (Example 3).

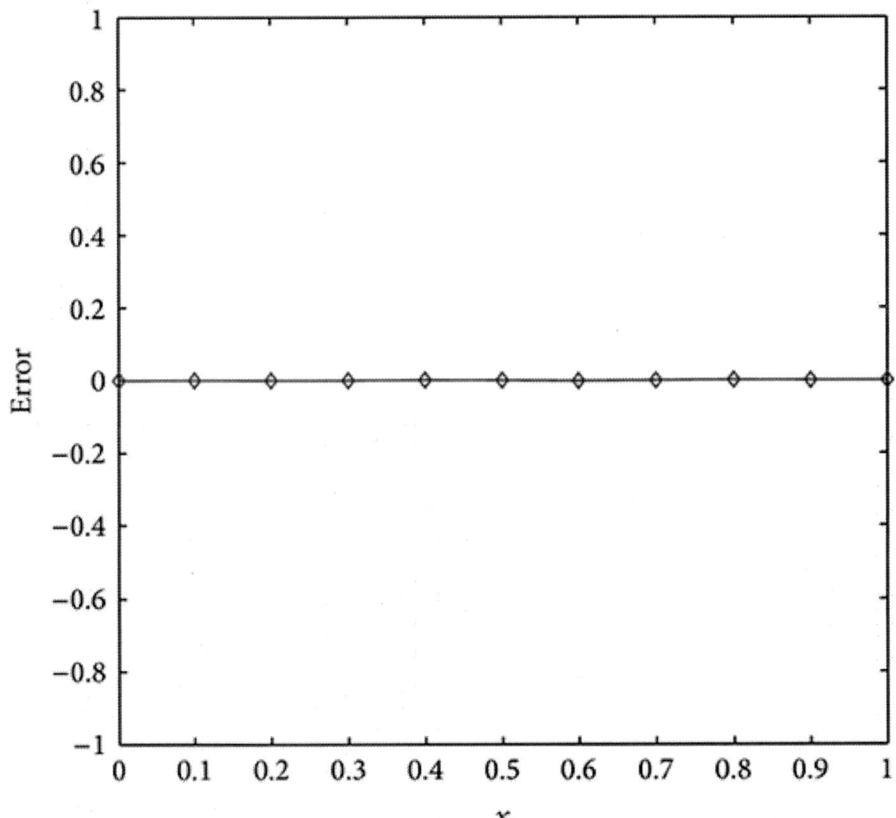

Figure 10. Error plot between analytical, and regression-based weights solution (Example 3).

Example 4. Here, we consider a standard differential equation which represents exponential growth as follows:

$$\frac{dy}{dx} = \alpha y, \tag{30}$$

with initial condition $y(0) = 1$.

Here $1/\alpha$ represents time constant or characteristic time.

Analytic result may be found as

$$y = e^{\alpha x}. \tag{31}$$

Considering $\alpha = 1$, we have the analytical solution as y = e^x.

The ANN trial solution in this case is

$$\psi_t(x, p) = 1 + xN(x, p). \tag{32}$$

Now, the network is trained for ten equidistant points in the domain [0, 1] with four, five, and six hidden nodes according to arbitrary- and regression-based algorithm. Comparison of analytical and neural results with arbitrary- $(w(A), v(A))$ and regression-based weights $(w(R), v(R))$ has been given in Table 5. Analytical and traditional neural results obtained using random initial weights with six nodes are shown in Figure 11. Figure 12 depicts comparison between analytical and neural results with regression-based initial weights for six hidden nodes. Error plot between analytical and RBNN results is cited in Figure 13.

Table 5. Analytical and neural solutions with arbitrary- and regression-based weights (Example 4)

Input data	Analytical	Neural results					
		$w(A), v(A)$ (four nodes)	$w(R), v(R)$ (four nodes)	$w(A), v(A)$ (five nodes)	$w(R), v(R)$ (five nodes)	$w(A), v(A)$ (six nodes)	$w(R), v(R)$ (six nodes)
0	1.0000	1.0000	1.0000	1.0000	1.0000	1.0000	1.0000
0.1000	1.1052	1.1069	1.1061	1.1093	1.1060	1.1075	1.1051
0.2000	1.2214	1.2337	1.2300	1.2250	1.2235	1.2219	1.2217
0.3000	1.3499	1.3543	1.3512	1.3600	1.3502	1.3527	1.3498
0.4000	1.4918	1.4866	1.4921	1.4930	1.4928	1.4906	1.4915
0.5000	1.6487	1.6227	1.6310	1.6412	1.6456	1.6438	1.6493
0.6000	1.8221	1.8303	1.8257	1.8205	1.8245	1.8234	1.8220
0.7000	2.0138	2.0183	2.0155	2.0171	2.0153	2.0154	2.0140
0.8000	2.2255	2.2320	2.2302	2.2218	2.2288	2.2240	2.2266
0.9000	2.4596	2.4641	2.4625	2.4664	2.4621	2.4568	2.4597
1.0000	2.7183	2.7373	2.7293	2.7232	2.7177	2.7111	2.7186

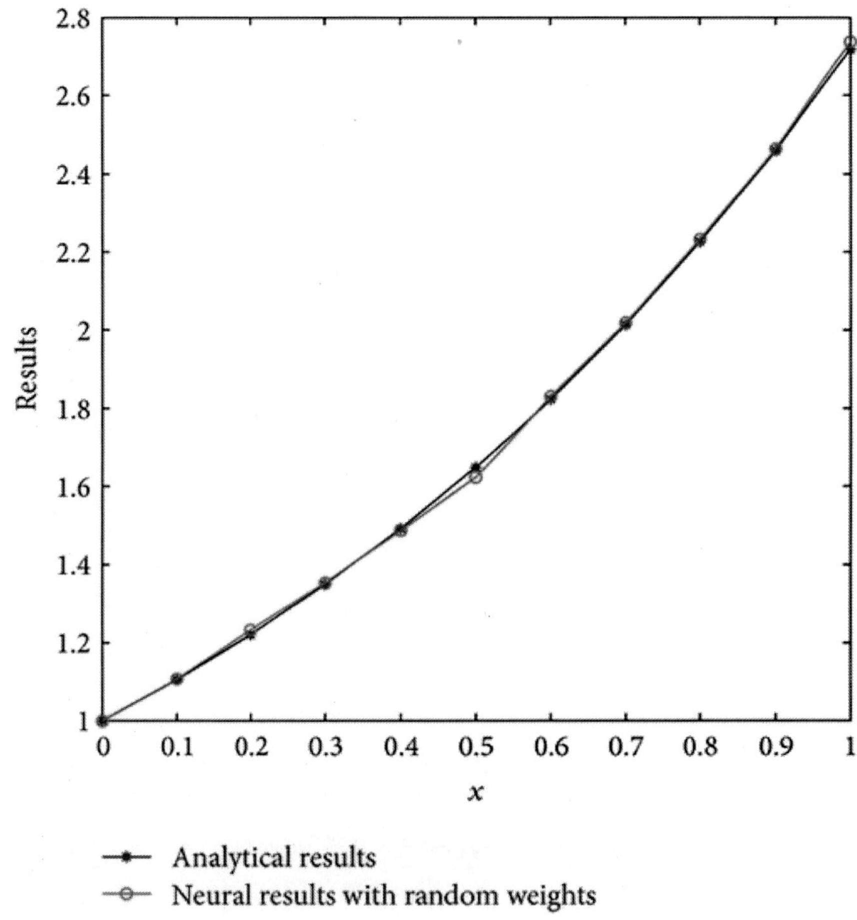

Figure 11. Plot of comparison between (analytical results) and (neural results) with arbitrary weights (for six nodes) (Example 4).

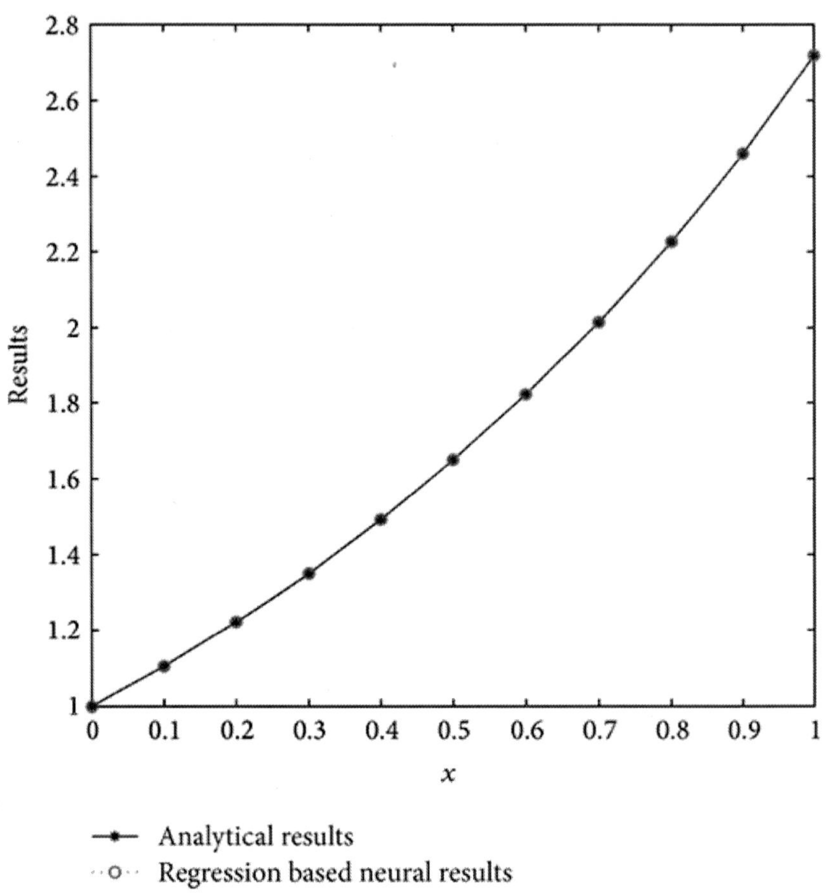

Figure 12. Plot of comparison between (analytical solutions) and (neural solutions) with regression based weights (for six nodes) (Example 4).

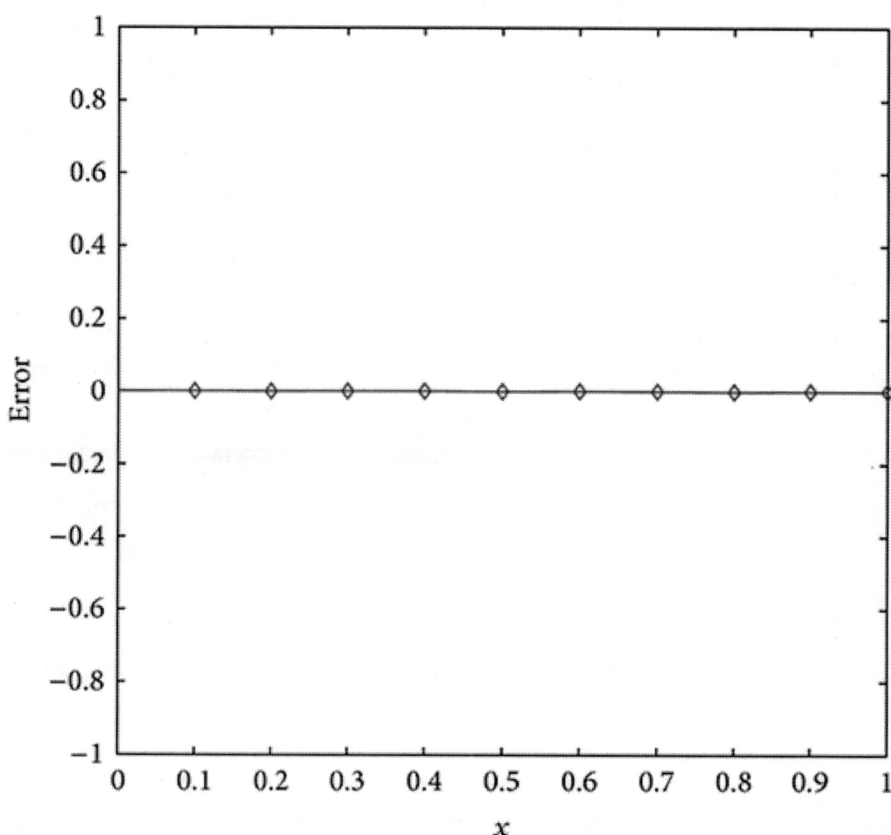

Figure 13. Error plot between analytical and regression based weights solution (Example 4).

DISCUSSION AND ANALYSIS

In traditional artificial neural network, the parameters (weights/ biases) are usually taken as arbitrary (random) and the number of nodes in hidden layer is considered by trial and error method. Also, few authors have used optimization technique to minimize the error. In this investigation, a regression-based artificial neural network with combinations of initial weights (arbitrary and regression based) in the connections is considered. We have fixed the number of nodes in hidden layer according to the degree of polynomial of regression fitting. The initial weights from input to hidden and hidden to output layer are taken by using regression-based weight generation. Back propagation algorithm has been employed for modification of the parameters without use of any optimization technique. Also, time of computation is less than traditional artificial neural architecture. Table 6 shows the computation of training time in hours with four, five, and six hidden nodes.

Table 6. Time of computation

Problems	Time of computation in hours					
	Traditional ANN			Proposed ANN (four nodes)	Proposed ANN (five nodes)	Proposed ANN (six nodes)
	Four nodes	Five nodes	Six nodes			
Example 1	1.57 hrs	1.51	1.49	1.31	1.27	1.09
Example 2	3.06	3.00	2.44	2.23	1.55	1.38

It is well known that the other numerical methods are usually iterative in nature, where we fix the step size before the start of the computation. After the solution is obtained, if we want to know the solution in between steps, then again the procedure is to be repeated from initial stage. ANN may be one of the reliefs where we may overcome this repetition of iterations. The authors are not claiming that the method presented is most accurate. As it may be seen by the comparison in Tables 2 and 4 that Runge-Kutta method although it gives better result but the above repetitive nature is required for each step size. Here, after getting the converged ANN, we may use it as a black box to get numerical results of any arbitrary point in the domain.

Here, we have considered three, four, and five degree polynomial for regression fitting. One may consider higher degree polynomial in the simulation but it has been seen that by increasing the degree of the polynomials, the accuracy does not usually increase. In the future, it needs to develop a methodology about what degree polynomial one should use to get a result with acceptable accuracy. This is however not of the scope of this paper and the authors are working in this direction and hope to communicate the findings in the future.

CONCLUSION

This paper presents a new approach to solve ordinary differential equations by using regression based artificial neural network model. Accuracy of the proposed method has been examined by solving a first order and a second order damped free vibration problem. The main value of the paper is that the numbers of nodes in hidden layer are fixed according to the degree of polynomial in the regression. Accordingly, here, comparisons of different neural architectures corresponding to different regression models are investigated. Moreover, the algorithm is unsupervised and error back propagation algorithm is used to minimize the error function. Corresponding initial weights from input to hidden and hidden to output are all obtained by the proposed procedure. The trail solution is closed and differentiable. One may see from the tables and graphs that the initial weights generated by regression model make the results more accurate. Lastly, it may be mentioned that the implemented Regression Based Neural Network (RBNN) algorithm is simple, computationally efficient, and straight forward.

Conflict of Interests

The authors declare that there is no conflict of interests regarding the publication of this paper.

ACKNOWLEDGMENT

The first author is thankful to the Department of Science and Technology (DST), Government of India for the financial support under Women Scientist Scheme-A.

REFERENCES

1. H. J. Ricardo, A Modern Introduction to Differential Equations, Elsevier, 2nd edition, 2009.
2. H. Lee and I. S. Kang, "Neural algorithm for solving differential equations," Journal of Computational Physics, vol. 91, no. 1, pp. 110–131, 1990. View at Publisher · View at Google Scholar · View at Scopus
3. A. J. Meade Jr. and A. A. Fernandez, "The numerical solution of linear ordinary differential equations by feedforward neural networks," Mathematical and Computer Modelling, vol. 19, no. 12, pp. 1–25, 1994. View at Scopus
4. A. J. Meade Jr. and A. A. Fernandez, "Solution of nonlinear ordinary differential equations by feedforward neural networks," Mathematical and Computer Modelling, vol. 20, no. 9, pp. 19–44, 1994. View at Scopus
5. I. E. Lagaris, A. Likas, and D. I. Fotiadis, "Artificial neural networks for solving ordinary and partial differential equations," IEEE Transactions on Neural Networks, vol. 9, no. 5, pp. 987–1000, 1998. View at Publisher · View at Google Scholar · View at Scopus
6. I. E. Lagaris, A. C. Likas, and D. G. Papageorgiou, "Neural-network methods for boundary value problems with irregular boundaries," IEEE Transactions on Neural Networks, vol. 11, no. 5, pp. 1041–1049, 2000. View at Publisher · View at Google Scholar · View at Scopus
7. D. R. Parisi, M. C. Mariani, and M. A. Laborde, "Solving differential equations with unsupervised neural networks," Chemical Engineering and Processing, vol. 42, no. 8-9, pp. 715–721, 2003. View at Publisher · View at Google Scholar · View at Scopus
8. A. Malek and R. Shekari Beidokhti, "Numerical solution for high order differential equations using a hybrid neural network-Optimization method," Applied Mathematics and Computation, vol. 183, no. 1, pp. 260–271, 2006. View at Publisher · View at Google Scholar · View at Scopus
9. B. Choi and J.-H. Lee, "Comparison of generalization ability on solving differential equations using backpropagation and reformulated radial basis function networks," Neurocomputing, vol. 73, no. 1–3, pp. 115–118, 2009. View at Publisher · View at Google Scholar · View at Scopus
10. H. S. Yazdi, M. Pakdaman, and H. Modaghegh, "Unsupervised kernel least mean square algorithm for solving ordinary differential equations," Neurocomputing, vol. 74, no. 12-13, pp. 2062–2071, 2011. View at Publisher · View at Google Scholar · View at Scopus
11. N. Selvaraju and J. Abdul Samant, "Solution of matrix Riccati differential equation for nonlinear singular system using neural networks," International Journal of Computer Applications, vol. 29, pp. 48–54, 2010.
12. S. He, K. Reif, and R. Unbehauen, "Multilayer neural networks for solving a class of partial differential equations," Neural Networks, vol. 13, no. 3, pp. 385–396, 2000. View at Publisher · View at Google Scholar · View at Scopus

13. M. Kumar and N. Yadav, "Multilayer perceptrons and radial basis function neural network methods for the solution of differential equations: a survey," Computers and Mathematics with Applications, vol. 62, no. 10, pp. 3796-3811, 2011. View at Publisher · View at Google Scholar · View at Scopus
14. I. G. Tsoulos, D. Gavrilis, and E. Glavas, "Solving differential equations with constructed neural networks," Neurocomputing, vol. 72, no. 10–12, pp. 2385–2391, 2009. View at Publisher · View at Google Scholar · View at Scopus
15. L. Jianyu, L. Siwei, Q. Yingjian, and H. Yaping, "Numerical solution of elliptic partial differential equation using radial basis function neural networks," Neural Networks, vol. 16, no. 5-6, pp. 729–734, 2003. View at Publisher · View at Google Scholar · View at Scopus
16. Y. Shirvany, M. Hayati, and R. Moradian, "Multilayer perceptron neural networks with novel unsupervised training method for numerical solution of the partial differential equations," Applied Soft Computing Journal, vol. 9, no. 1, pp. 20–29, 2009. View at Publisher · View at Google Scholar · View at Scopus
17. N. Mai-Duy and T. Tran-Cong, "Numerical solution of differential equations using multiquadric radial basis function networks," Neural Networks, vol. 14, no. 2, pp. 185–199, 2001. View at Publisher · View at Google Scholar · View at Scopus
18. T. Leephakpreeda, "Novel determination of differential-equation solutions: universal approximation method," Journal of Computational and Applied Mathematics, vol. 146, no. 2, pp. 443–457, 2002. View at Publisher · View at Google Scholar · View at Scopus
19. C. Franke and R. Schaback, "Solving partial differential equations by collocation using radial basis functions," Applied Mathematics and Computation, vol. 93, no. 1, pp. 73–82, 1998. View at Scopus
20. N. Smaoui and S. Al-Enezi, "Modelling the dynamics of nonlinear partial differential equations using neural networks," Journal of Computational and Applied Mathematics, vol. 170, no. 1, pp. 27–58, 2004. View at Publisher · View at Google Scholar · View at Scopus
21. I. G. Tsoulos and I. E. Lagaris, "Solving differential equations with genetic programming," Genetic Programming and Evolvable Machines, vol. 7, no. 1, pp. 33–54, 2006. View at Publisher · View at Google Scholar · View at Scopus
22. K. S. McFall and J. R. Mahan, "Artificial neural network method for solution of boundary value problems with exact satisfaction of arbitrary boundary conditions," IEEE Transactions on Neural Networks, vol. 20, no. 8, pp. 1221-1233, 2009. View at Publisher · View at Google Scholar · View at Scopus
23. S. A. Hoda and H. A. Nagla, "Neural network methods for mixed boundary value problems," International Journal of Nonlinear Science, vol. 11, pp. 312–316, 2011.
24. J. M. Zurada, Introduction to Artificial Neural Network, West Publishing, 1994.

25. S. Haykin, Neural Networks a Comprehensive Foundation, Prentice Hall, New York, NY, USA, 1999.

26. S. Chakraverty, V. P. Singh, and R. K. Sharma, "Regression based weight generation algorithm in neural network for estimation of frequencies of vibrating plates," Computer Methods in Applied Mechanics and Engineering, vol. 195, no. 33–36, pp. 4194–4202, 2006. View at Publisher · View at Google Scholar · View at Scopus

27. V. P. Singh, S. Chakraverty, R. K. Sharma, and G. K. Sharma, "Modeling vibration frequencies of annular plates by regression based neural network," Applied Soft Computing Journal, vol. 9, no. 1, pp. 439–447, 2009. View at Publisher · View at Google Scholar · View at Scopus

28. S. Mall and S. Chakraverty, "Regression Based Neural network training for the solution of ordinary differential equations," International Journal of Mathematical Modelling and Numerical Optimisation, vol. 4, pp. 136–149, 2013. View at Publisher · View at Google Scholar

Chapter 6

ARTIFICIAL NEURAL NETWORK MODELING FOR BIOLOGICAL REMOVAL OF ORGANIC CARBON AND NITROGEN FROM SLAUGHTERHOUSE WASTEWATER IN A SEQUENCING BATCH REACTOR

Pradyut Kundu, Anupam Debsarkar, and Somnath Mukherjee

Environmental Engineering Division, Civil Engineering Department, Jadavpur University, Kolkata 700032, India

ABSTRACT

The present paper deals with treatment of slaughterhouse wastewater by conducting a laboratory scale sequencing batch reactor (SBR) with different input characterized samples, and the experimental results are explored for the formulation of feedforward backpropagation artificial neural network (ANN) to predict combined removal efficiency of chemical oxygen demand (COD) and ammonia nitrogen (-N). The reactor was operated under three different combinations of aerobic-anoxic sequence, namely, (4 + 4), (5 + 3), and (5 + 4) hour of total react period with influent COD and -N level of 2000 ± 100 mg/L and 120 ± 10 mg/L, respectively. ANN modeling was carried out using neural network tools, with Levenberg-Marquardt training algorithm. Various trials were examined for training of three types of ANN models (Models "A," "B," and "C") using number of neurons in the hidden layer varying from 2 to 30. All together 29, data sets were used for each three types of model for which 15 data sets were used for training, 7 data sets for validation, and 7 data sets for testing. The experimental results were used for testing and validation of three types of ANN models. Three ANN models (Models "A," "B," and "C") were trained and tested reasonably well to predict COD and -N removal efficiently with 3.33% experimental error.

INTRODUCTION

The sequencing batch reactor (SBR) is the most promising and viable of the proposed activated sludge modifications for the removal of organic carbon and nutrients [1]. Due to its simplicity and flexibility of operation, it has become increasingly popular for the biological treatment of domestic and industrial wastewater [2]. The most common (aerated) SBR is a fill-and-draw activated sludge system for wastewater treatment. Equalization, aeration, and clarification can all be performed in a single batch reactor. In general, SBR systems have a relatively small footprint; they are useful for areas where the available land is limited. In addition, system cycles can be easily modified, making SBRs extremely flexible to adapt to more restrictive effluent quality standards by public authorities. The determination of the influent characteristics and effluent requirements, site specific parameters such as temperature, and key design parameters such as nutrient-to-biomass ratio, treatment cycle duration, suspended solids, and hydraulic retention time is imperative to establish the operation sequence of the SBR. It allows calculating the number of cycles per day, number of basins (batches), decanting volume, reactor size, and detention times. For most industrial wastewater applications, treatability studies have typically been required to determine the optimum operating sequence. Slaughterhouse wastewater is mainly composed of diluted blood, protein, fat, and suspended solids. Organic carbon and nitrogen are major contaminants of concern in the wastewater. The aim of this study consists in the identification of suitable operation conditions for a cycle according to characteristics of influent wastewater, treatment requirements, and effluent quality using a SBR technology for simultaneous removal of organic carbon and nitrogen from slaughterhouse wastewater and discusses some aspects on process optimization based on artificial neural network (ANN) model.

Artificial neural networks (ANNs) are now used in many areas of science and engineering and considered as promising tool because of their simplicity towards simulation, prediction, and modeling [3, 4]. The advantages of ANN are that the mathematical description of the phenomena involved in the process is not required; less time is required for model development than the traditional mathematical models and prediction ability with limited numbers of experiments [5–7]. Application of ANN to solve environmental engineering problems has been reported in many articles. ANNs were applied in biological wastewater treatment and physicochemical wastewater treatment [8–10].

ANNs are mathematical systems comprised of a number of "processing units" that are linked via weighted interconnections. The tool helps in mapping a set of input data into a corresponding set of output data after learning a series of past process data from a given system. Moreover, the neural network model possesses a distinctive ability of learning nonlinear functional relationship without requiring a structural knowledge of the process to be modeled. Several examples of successful development of software sensor mechanism based on the neural network approach are described in the literature [11–14]. The application of ANN modeling in environmental engineering field is, however, still being undergone. A sizeable number of ANN modeling in wastewater treatment are used to explore its application potential for predicting experimental data aiming for enhancing efficiency and optimizing the WWTP [15–18].

The objective of the present study was application of feedforward backpropagation artificial neural network (ANN) modeling to predict the performance of a laboratory scale sequencing batch reactor operated under three different combinations of aerobic-anoxic sequential hours of cycles, namely, (4 hour aerobic + 4 hour anoxic), (5 hour aerobic + 3 hour anoxic), and (5 hour aerobic + 4 hour anoxic) of total react period in terms of COD removal and -N reduction from real life slaughterhouse wastewater as output parameters in correspondence with various input parameters of influent COD and -N concentration, microbial concentration, contact time, pH, dissolved oxygen (DO), and so forth. The data used for ANN formulation were obtained from experimental investigation as carried out in the laboratory by the authors.

MATERIAL AND METHODS

Seed Acclimatization for Combined Carbon Oxidation and Nitrification

Heterotrophic microbes were actively acclimatized in the laboratory environment by inoculating sludge collected from an aeration pond of a small-scale slaughterhouse located nearby to the institute. The mixture of sludge was continuously aerated with intermittent feeding with dextrose solution having concentrations of 1000 mg/L and ammonium chloride (NH_4Cl) having concentration of 200 mg/L as a carbon and nitrogen source, respectively. The acclimatization process was continued for an overall period of 90 days. The biomass growth was monitored by the magnitude of sludge volume index (SVI) and mixed liquor suspended solid (MLVSS) concentration in the reactor. pH in the reactor was maintained in the range 6.8–7.5 by adding required amount of sodium carbonate (Na_2CO_3) and phosphate buffer. The seed acclimatization phase was considered to be over when a steady state condition was observed in terms of equilibrium COD and -N reduction with respect to a steady level of MLVSS concentration and SVI in the reactor.

Denitrifying seed was cultured separately in 2.0 L capacity aspirator bottle under anoxic condition. 500 gm of digested sludge obtained from a local sewage treatment plant (STP) was added to 1.0 L of distilled water. The solution was filtered and added to 500 mL of untreated slaughterhouse wastewater. The resulting solution was acclimatized for denitrification purpose using dextrose as carbon source and potassium nitrate (KNO_3) as the source of nitrate nitrogen (-N). Magnetic stirrer was provided for proper mixing of the solution. Denitrifying seed was acclimatized against a nitrate-nitrogen concentration varying from 10 to 90 mg/L as N, over a period of three months.

Experimental Setup

The experiment that was performed in a laboratory scale sequencing batch reactor of 20.0 L effective volume was fabricated by Plexiglass sheet of 6 mm thickness which is shown schematically in Figure 1. The feed solution was kept in a 25.0 L capacity carboy placed up on an elevated wooden platform. A feed tube as inlet was connected from the bottom of carboy to the inlet spout of the reactor. The air is supplied through a belt-driven air compressor. The air from compressor supplied to a diffuser system which is made up of glass tube with 2 mm opening size in a single assembly and provided 50 mm above the bottom of the SBR. The compressed air was supplied to the reactor through the above openings. Treated water was withdrawn from an outlet placed at 100 mm above the bottom of the reactor. A stirrer of 0.3 hp capacity is installed centrally for agitating and mixing the content of the reactor. The air supply was stopped during anoxic mode of the react period. During this phase only, the stirrer was allowed to operate. A timer was connected to compressor for controlling the aeration period. A sludge withdrawal port was also provided near the bottom of the reactor.

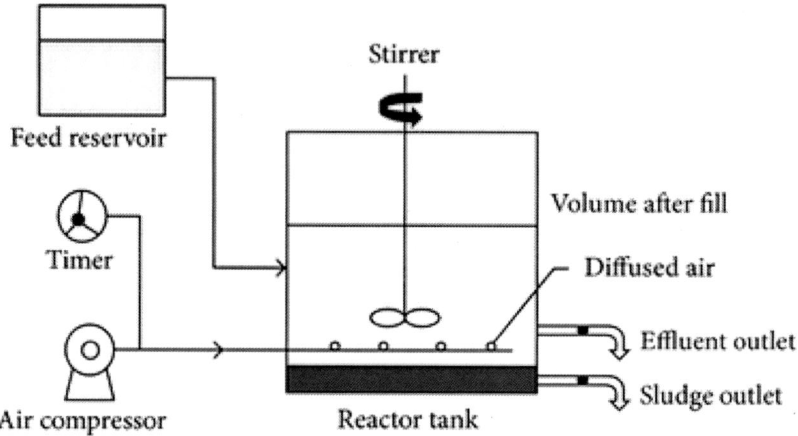

Figure 1. Experimental setup of SBR.

Experimental Procedure

The treatability study of slaughterhouse wastewater in SBR was investigated for the wastewater sample collected from outlet of the slaughterhouse, as mentioned above. The raw and primary-treated wastewater was first characterized and subsequently treatability experiment was carried out in the laboratory scale SBR unit. The following analytical parameters, namely, pH, TSS, VSS, DO, BOD5 at 20°C, COD, TKN, and -N were estimated for the wastewater characterization of the slaughterhouse effluent. The analytical parameters were determined following the protocols as described in "Standard Methods" [19]. For each parameter testing three sets of replicates were considered. A mixed liquor of 2.5 L, containing mixed sludge as acclimatized previously, was taken into SBR containing 20.0 L volume of pretreated slaughterhouse wastewater. The performance study was carried out with pretreated slaughterhouse wastewater having an average initial chemical oxygen demand (COD) of mg/L and ammonia nitrogen (-N) concentration of mg/L. The volatile suspended solid (VSS) to suspended (SS) ratio of the sludge was 0.783. After seeding, MLVSS concentration in the SBR reactor was found to be mg/L. The duration of a complete cycle was

10.0 to 11.0 hour, giving two complete cycles per day. The total cycle period consisted of a fill period of 0.5 hour, overall react period of 8.0 to 9.0 hour, settle period of 1.0 hour, and decant period of 0.5 hour with two cycles per day. In the carbon oxidation and nitrogen removal study, the overall react period was divided into aerobic and anoxic react periods with following three combinations:

Combination-1: 4-hour aerobic react period and 4-hour anoxic react period;

Combination-2: 5-hour aerobic react period and 3-hour anoxic react period;

Combination-3: 5-hour aerobic react period and 4-hour anoxic react period.

In the ammoniacal nitrogen removal phase, the reactor was continuously aerated by a compressor of capacity 0.25 hp. during the fill period and for the entire aerobic react phase. The mechanical mixer was operated continuously with a speed of 400 rpm from the beginning of the fill phase to the end of the total react phase for proper mixing of liquid in the reactor. During the draw phase, the supernatant wastewater that was decanted until the liquid volume in the reactor decreased to 4.0 L. SRT (solid retention time) was manually controlled by withdrawal of volume of the mixed liquor from the reactor every day at the onset of the commencement of settle phase. The reactor was continuously run for 120 days. The treated volume of slaughterhouse wastewater was taken as 16 L. The initial pH values in the reactor were kept in between 7.0 and 8.0, whereas the sludge volume index (SVI) has been kept within the range of 75–85 mL/gm, for obtaining good settling property of the biomass. The SRT of 20–25 days is maintained for carbon oxidation and nitrification in the present SBR system for treatment of wastewater as suggested by Tremblay et al. [20].

During the time course of the study, 100 mL of sample was collected from the outlet of the reactor at every 1.0 hour interval, after completion of the fill period. The samples were analyzed for the following parameters, namely, pH, DO, MLSS, MLVSS, COD, -N, -N, and -N as per "Standard Methods" [19]. The pH of the solution was measured by a digital pH meter. -N, -N, and -N were estimated by respective ion selective electrodes meter. COD was analyzed by closed reflux method in digester. Dissolved oxygen (DO) was measured electrometrically by digital DO meter. Mixed liquor suspended solids (MLSS) and mixed liquor volatile suspended solids (MLVSS) were measured by gravimetric method at the temperature of 103–105°C in oven and °C in muffle furnace, respectively.

Artificial Neural Network Modeling

The architecture of ANN consists of input layer, one or more hidden layer, and output layer. Each layer of the network consists of a number of interconnected processing elements called as neurons. These neurons interact with each other with the help of the weight. Each neuron is connected to all the neurons in the next layer. The data is presented to the neural network in the input layer. The output of the neural network is presented by output layer for the given input data. The hidden layers enable these networks to compute complicated relations between input and output. The structure of feedforward neural network is exhibited in Figure 2.

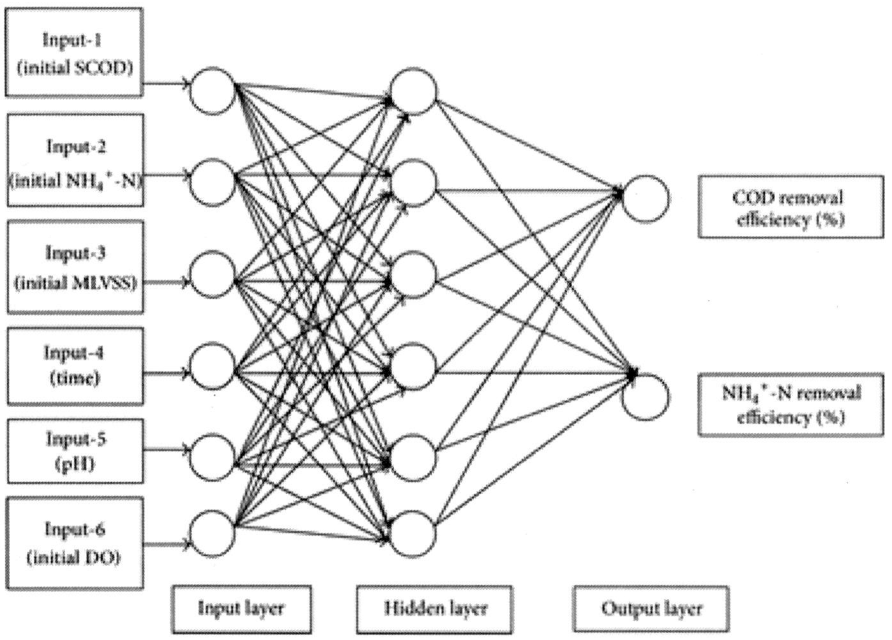

Figure 2. Architecture of ANN Model.

The number of hidden layers is to be selected in respect of the complexity of the problem. Generally one hidden layer is sufficient for investigation of most of the problem. The number of neurons in the hidden layer is selected by trial and error method starting from minimum value and then to be increased depending on the nature of problem. The training of neural network is carried out by presenting a series of input data and target output values. The parameters affecting the output should be selected as input parameters. The backpropagation training algorithm has been widely used to model various problems in environmental engineering. In the backpropagation training algorithm, the neurons in the hidden layer and output layer process its input by multiplying each input by its weight, summing the product, and then processing the sum using a nonlinear transfer function, also called activation function, to produce results. The most common transfer function used is the sigmoid function. The learning in the neural network takes place by modifying weights of the neurons according to the error between the actual output value and the target output values. The changes in weight are proportional to negative of the derivative of the error.

The backpropagation is essentially a gradient descending method to minimize the network error function equation:

$$E = \sum_{j=1}^{k}\sum_{i=1}^{n}(e_i(j) - t_i(j)), \quad (1)$$

where $e_i(j)$ and $t_i(j)$ are estimated and targeted values, respectively. "n" is the number of output nodes, and "k" is the number of training samples.

Before starting training of an ANN, weights are initially randomized. Based on the error propagation, weights are adjusted based on

$$\Delta W_{ij}(n) = \alpha\frac{dE}{dW_{ij}} + \eta\Delta W_{ij}(n-1), \quad (2)$$

where $W_{ij}(n)$ and $W_{ij}(n-1)$ are the weights increment between nodes i and j during the adjacent iteration α and η are learning rate and momentum factor. Careful selection and appropriate adjustment of the learning rate are very much necessary for successful training of backpropagation neural network. Some earlier contributory works were cited in various literatures in reference to ANN modeling on nutrient removal in biological reactor [21, 22].

The training of ANN model was carried out by presenting the complete input data set to the network and continued till the average MSE is minimized. After the training is over, the trained neural network deemed to be reproduced by the target output values for provided training data. Weights of the trained neurons are then stored in the neural network memory. Testing of the trained network is carried out by presenting the set of test data and then comparing the output of the network with the actual values of the output. The performance of formulated ANN model can be measured by several statistical parameters, such as coefficient of determination (R), MSE, and RMSE. A well-trained model should have R value close to 1 and error should be least.

The numbers of input and output neurons are fixed according to the nature of the problem. In the present study, only one hidden layer was selected. The number of neurons in the hidden layer was selected from 2 to 30. The inputs to the neural network include the amount of MLVSS (mg/L), initial concentration of COD (mg/L), initial concentration of NH_4^+-N (mg/L), pH, and contact time (hour). The percentage removal of COD and NH_4^+-N was selected as targets.

Data Preprocessing

The input and output variables in the present study consist of different characteristics and importance level, resulting into varying response to the neural network. The ANN model training would be more efficient if preprocessing steps are to be performed on the input and target data, by making the preprocessing exercise useable in real applications. The input parameters were scaled up in the range 0.2 to 0.8. The preprocessing of the data could be performed by the algorithm as given in

$$X_i\,(\text{net}) = 0.2 + 0.6\frac{(X_{im} - \min\,(X_i))}{\max\,(X_i) - \min\,(X_i)}, \tag{3}$$

where $X_i(\text{net})$ is normalized value of *i*th variable; X_{im} is observed value of *i*th variable; $\min(X_i)$ is minimum value of *i*th observed variable in the training data-set; $\max(X_i)$ is maximum value of *i*th observed variable in the training data-set.

After preprocessing of the training data set, the new input sets are fed into the trained networks with minimum and maximum vectors for the training set. In order to compare the neural network results with the observed results, the rescaled outputs need to be converted back within the same range for the original targets. The algorithm as given in (4) was used for this purpose:

$$Y_{i(p)} = \min Y_i + \frac{(\max Y_i - \min Y_i)}{0.6} \times (X_i(\text{net}) - 0.2), \tag{4}$$

where $Y_{i(p)}$ is predicted value of th output variable; $X_i(\text{net})$ is normalized value of *i*th output variable; $\min Y_i$ is minimum value of *i*th observed variable in the training data-set; $\max Y_i$ is maximum value of *i*th observed variable in the training data-set.

ANN Software

A three-layered feedforward neural network with backpropagation training algorithm was used to validate the ANN model. The tangent-sigmoid transfer functions (tansig) in between input and hidden layer and a linear transfer function (purelin) in between hidden layer and output layer were used. The Levenberg-Marquardt algorithm was used for ANN model training. During training process, small weights were assigned to the connection between neurons in a random way. Weights were modified until the error between the predicted and experimental values of adsorption efficiency are minimized. It is desired that the difference between predicted and observed values should be as small as possible. During testing process, the network was tested for its generalization ability with the observed output after the training process was completed. When the neural networks are tested successfully, they can be used for prediction.

The feedforward backpropagation (BP) algorithm with Levenberg-Marquardt training was applied for neural network model development. The BP is an approximate steepest descent algorithm where an MSE is used as performance function. In the neural network development, different number of hidden layers, the number of neurons in each layer, and the type of transfer function for each neuron were analyzed all with a learning rate of 1.0 [23] and training goal of 10−5. Then, the trained networks were tested using the testing data sets and the MSE method by modifying the network weights.

Performance of Developed ANN Model

In order to measure the pollutant removal efficiency and the performance of three neural network models developed for biological system, different types of statistical parameters were used to estimate the error. In the present work, ME, MSE, and RMSE were selected to measure the network performance of Models "A," "B," and "C" under three different combinations of aerobic-anoxic sequence, namely,(4 + 4), (5 + 3), and (5 + 4) hour of total react period, respectively, for treatment of slaughterhouse wastewater in SBR. Furthermore, a linear regression analysis between the predicted values and actual experimental values was carried out to investigate the network response for establishing the removal efficiencies of organic matter as COD and nitrogen matter as NH_4^+-N in SBR system.

Optimization of ANN Model

The optimal architecture of the ANN model and its parameter variation were determined based on the minimum value of the MSE of the training and prediction set as suggested by Ekici and Aksoy [24]. To start the training, initially 2 neurons were taken in the hidden layer and it was then increased up to 30 neurons:

$$\mathrm{MSE} = \frac{1}{N}\sum_{i=1}^{N}(T_i - A_i), \tag{5}$$

where N is number of data points; T_i is network predicted value at the ith data; A_i is experimental value at the ith data; i is an index of the data.

RESULTS AND DISCUSSIONS

Characterization of Slaughterhouse Wastewater

The slaughterhouse wastewater samples were collected from two different locations: (i) the raw (untreated) wastewater from the main collection pit and (ii) the primary treated effluent from the inlet box of aeration basin. The wastewater samples were collected 6 (six) times over the entire course of the study in 25.0 L plastic containers and stored in a refrigerator at approximately 4.0°C. The above wastewater samples (raw and primary treated) were characterized in the laboratory with respect to the parameters as exhibited in Table 1. The performance of the present study was carried out with wastewater having an average initial chemical oxygen demand (COD) of 2000 ± 100 mg/L and ammonia nitrogen (NH_4^+-N) concentration of 120 ± 10 mg/L as N.

Table 1. Characteristics and composition of slaughterhouse wastewater

Parameters (all units are in mg/L except pH)	Raw wastewater range	Pre treated wastewater range
pH	8.0–8.5	7.5–8.5
Total suspended solids	10120–14225	4255–5340
Total dissolved solids	6345–7840	2800–3830
COD	4185–5240	1930–2096
BOD_5 at 20°C	3000–3500	1010–1465
Total Kjeldahl nitrogen (TKN)	450–560	315–412
NH_4^+-N (as N)	215–310	110–130

Treatment of Slaughterhouse Wastewater for Carbon Oxidation and Nitrogen Removal in SBR

The performance of the SBR system in the slaughterhouse wastewater treatment for combined carbon and nitrogen removal has been plotted in Figures 3, 4, and 5. The aerobic period was operated long enough (4.0 to 5.0 hours) to achieve nitrification to improve effluent quality. The presence of low DO (2.4 mg/L) level at the beginning of the aerobic react phase and subsequently increased progressively and reached to its maximum value at the end of the aeration period. The organic loading was decreased substantially at the beginning of anoxic period followed by a reduction in DO level. Generally, DO concentration, in the range of 2.4–4.5 mg/L prevailed in the reactor during the aerobic react period, which was beneficial for ammonium oxidation. The effluent NH_4^+-N was below 18.15 mg/L, giving an average NH_4^+-N removal of 85.52% under (4 + 4) hour react period combination. The effluent NH_4^+-N remained less than 13.28 mg/L, yielding an average NH_4^+-N removal of 88.78% under (5 + 3) hour react period combination. Under (5 + 4) hour react period combination, improved performance, in terms of NH_4^+-N oxidation, was observed that produced a final treated effluent having NH_4^+-N concentration less than 12.55 mg/L as N indicating an average 90.28% NH_4^+-N removal.

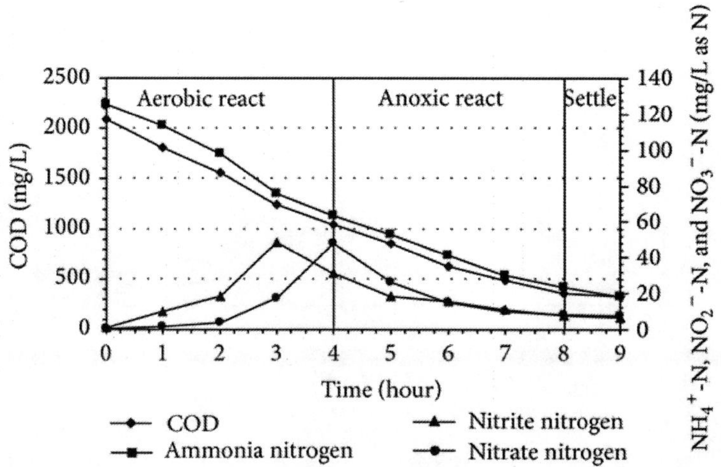

Figure 3. Carbon oxidation, nitrification, and denitrification profiles for slaughterhouse wastewater treatment in (4 + 4) hour react cycle.

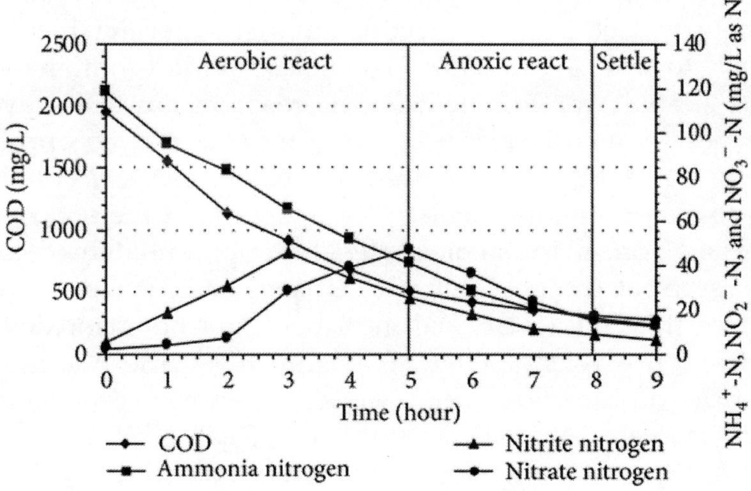

Figure 4. Carbon oxidation, nitrification, and denitrification profiles for slaughterhouse wastewater treatment in (5 + 3) hour react cycle.

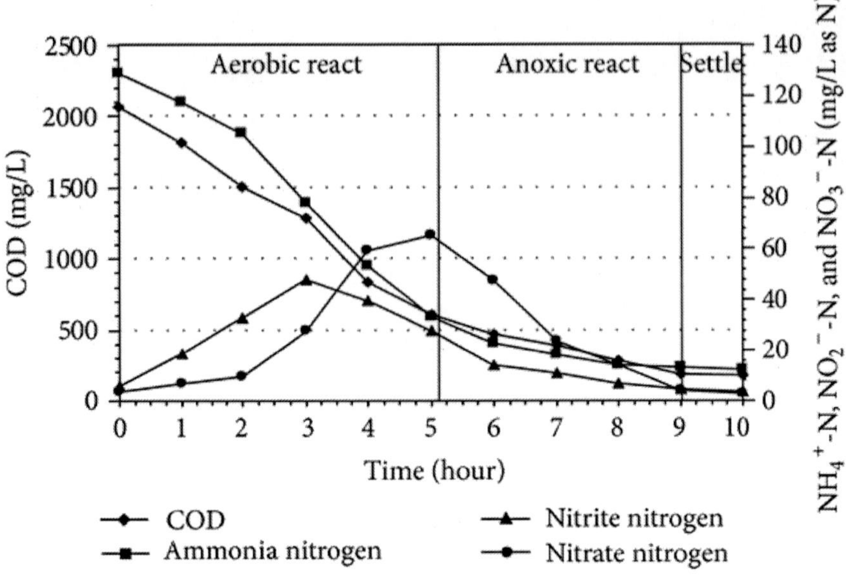

Figure 5. Carbon oxidation, nitrification, and denitrification profiles for slaughterhouse wastewater treatment in (5 + 4) hour react cycle.

At the end of anoxic react period, under (4 + 4) hour react period combination, 82.58% of nitrate reduction was achieved which descent noticeably to 67.65% under (5 + 3) hour react period combination due to nonavailability of sufficient anoxic reaction time. However, the nitrate reduction efficiency was found to be improved appreciably under (5 + 4) hour react period in the extent of 93.62% yielding a nitrate concentration less than 4.18 mg/L as N at the end of anoxic react period from an initial nitrate level of approximately 65.43 mg/L as N, present at the beginning of anoxic phase. It was interesting to observe that, by a marginal increment of 1-hour anoxic period, denitrification efficiency changes positively. In the present study, most of the nitrates were removed in the anoxic react phase. The amount of nitrate removal was as much as 82.58, 67.65 and 93.62% in (4 + 4), (5 + 3), and (5 + 4) hour combination, respectively.

Development ANN Models for Combined Carbon Oxidation and Nitrification of Slaughterhouse Wastewater in SBR

Three models were developed for combined carbon oxidation and nitrification of slaughterhouse wastewater in the following combinations:

Model "A" (Combination-1): 4-hour aerobic and 4-hour anoxic react period in SBR system;

Model "B" (Combination-2): 5-hour aerobic and 3-hour anoxic react period in SBR system;

Model "C" (Combination-3): 5-hour aerobic and 4-hour anoxic react period in SBR system.

The ANN model was developed for biological removal of combined organic carbon and nitrogen of a slaughterhouse wastewater in a sequencing batch reactor using experimental data. Table 2 represents the input parameters for developing the ANN studies. Total 29 experimental data sets were available for each aerobic/anoxic react period combination in SBR system. These data were divided into 50% for training set (15 data sets), 25% for validation set (7 data sets), and 25% for testing data set (7 data sets). The training set was used to develop the neural network. The validation data set was used to determine when the network's general performance was maximized through early stopping, and the testing data set was used to evaluate the generalization ability of the trained network. The 29 data sets used for development of ANN model in SBR system for each combination of aerobic/anoxic react period are presented in Tables 3, 4, and 5.

Table 2. Range of variables in ANN study

Serial number	Variables	Ranges
1	Initial MLVSS concentration (mg/L)	1810–2600
2	Initial concentration of COD (mg/L)	1910–2096
3	Initial concentration of NH_4^+-N (mg/L)	112–130
4	pH	7.0-8.0
5	Initial DO level (mg/L)	2.4–4.5
6	Total react time (hour)	8-9
7	COD/NH_4^+-N removal efficiency (%)	0–100

Table 3. Data set for ANN Model "A" under (4 + 4) hour aerobic-anoxic react period

Serial number	Initial COD (mg/L)	Initial NH_4^+-N (mg/L)	Initial MLVSS (mg/L)	Time (hour)	pH	Initial DO (mg/L)	% COD removal efficiency	% NH_4^+-N removal efficiency
1	2004.25	112.41	2155.41	8	7.1	3.8	86.45	86.92
2	2077.11	118.55	1844.22	8	7.4	2.4	88.11	88.52
3	1922.64	117.34	1863.57	8	7.1	3.5	89.62	88.81
4	1913.21	121.46	2482.36	8	7.0	2.7	85.37	84.44
5	2030.25	117.52	2272.21	8	7.2	3.6	89.33	85.83
6	1938.48	120.25	2212.54	8	7.0	3.7	83.21	85.11
7	1925.41	124.36	2475.45	8	8.0	3.8	80.19	84.9
8	2024.17	122.24	1940.26	8	7.0	4.4	86.08	85.25
9	2094.40	113.84	2131.22	8	7.5	4.0	88.25	86.54
10	2040.33	116.55	2075.35	8	7.0	2.8	88.65	82.97
11	1998.34	125.52	2322.14	8	7.0	3.0	85.22	88.54
12	1917.24	127.84	2391.22	8	7.2	3.0	85.39	89.31
13	1989.17	128.66	1917.27	8	7.5	3.6	84.11	82.58
14	1997.57	129.88	1968.26	8	8.0	3.5	86.05	90.31
15	2085.27	124.24	2012.55	8	7.0	3.0	90.42	84.22
16	2054.22	122.26	2048.22	8	7.4	3.0	91.94	86.27
17	2014.11	122.31	2144.24	8	7.2	3.7	84.18	88.55
18	1984.27	116.27	1950.25	8	7.1	3.8	84.62	89.33
19	1932.92	127.57	1995.27	8	7.5	4.3	85.21	86.28
20	2015.28	123.94	2212.51	8	7.5	4.4	85.22	82.85
21	2008.15	122.27	2352.81	8	7.0	4.2	83.64	81.22
22	2017.47	126.67	2432.55	8	7.6	4.0	88.52	81.6
23	2037.81	120.76	2245.28	8	7.6	4.2	91.39	82.27
24	1938.58	119.41	2185.35	8	7.4	3.6	85.35	85.22
25	2096.55	125.22	2265.21	8	7.5	3.5	84.29	85.52
26	2036.28	115.48	2258.36	8	7.1	3.4	86.55	87.22
27	1965.25	114.88	2424.37	8	7.4	4.0	87.56	84.25
28	1975.27	126.48	2575.36	8	7.0	2.9	86.34	87.54
29	2072.55	128.85	1850.29	8	7.5	3.0	90.22	88.25

Table 4. Data set for ANN Model "B" under (5 + 3) hour aerobic-anoxic react period

Serial number	Initial COD (mg/L)	Initial NH_4^+-N (mg/L)	Initial MLVSS (mg/L)	Time (hour)	pH	Initial DO (mg/L)	% COD removal efficiency	% NH_4^+-N removal efficiency
1	2044.23	113.01	2055.46	8	7.2	2.8	84.42	88.90
2	2057.15	119.56	1944.22	8	7.5	3.4	84.16	86.55
3	1972.65	118.32	1963.51	8	7.0	3.2	86.62	89.88
4	1943.22	120.44	2382.33	8	7.5	2.9	82.35	86.45
5	2050.22	116.50	2172.24	8	7.4	3.1	88.34	89.85
6	1918.08	130.24	2412.52	8	7.5	3.5	84.26	87.15
7	1955.47	121.35	2575.44	8	8.0	3.8	82.39	86.96
8	2044.12	123.28	1940.22	8	7.5	4.0	85.58	88.24
9	2084.00	117.81	2431.25	8	7.5	4.1	87.27	89.50
10	2060.31	115.56	2275.32	8	7.0	2.6	86.66	88.95
11	1948.35	124.50	2522.13	8	7.0	3.0	87.28	89.55
12	1927.26	128.86	2491.21	8	7.3	3.8	82.30	89.30
13	1979.14	127.64	2417.22	8	7.5	3.4	86.18	88.55
14	1947.51	128.80	2568.21	8	8.0	3.5	86.85	91.35
15	2075.26	120.25	2212.54	8	8.0	3.2	89.46	90.25
16	2034.28	125.28	2148.25	8	7.6	3.0	90.93	91.22
17	2024.15	125.36	2044.21	8	7.6	3.7	84.68	87.57
18	1974.26	115.23	1850.24	8	7.2	3.6	84.62	88.37
19	1922.92	126.50	1895.21	8	7.5	4.2	87.26	89.25
20	2045.28	122.93	2412.52	8	7.0	4.5	87.25	86.80
21	2088.15	112.20	2352.01	8	7.0	4.4	85.64	88.25
22	2077.48	129.64	2132.55	8	7.8	4.0	89.53	91.60
23	2057.84	122.36	2045.28	8	7.6	4.1	90.38	82.25
24	1948.58	118.91	2085.33	8	7.0	3.4	84.37	86.26
25	1962.45	118.55	2165.21	8	7.0	4.5	85.51	88.78
26	2066.21	119.58	2158.32	8	7.6	3.8	87.50	89.28
27	1925.24	124.68	2024.32	8	7.4	4.0	86.57	88.24
28	1915.24	127.58	2175.33	8	7.0	2.8	85.33	88.50
29	2042.54	129.85	1950.23	8	7.8	3.0	89.28	90.26

Table 5. Data set for ANN Model "C" under (5 + 4) hour aerobic-anoxic react period

Serial number	Initial COD (mg/L)	Initial NH_4^+-N (mg/L)	Initial MLVSS (mg/L)	Time (hour)	pH	Initial DO (mg/L)	% COD removal efficiency	% NH_4^+-N removal efficiency
1	1914.23	115.65	2155.46	9	7.8	3.8	94.45	88.52
2	2057.15	118.54	1844.22	9	8.0	4.4	90.11	89.82
3	1982.65	124.36	1863.51	9	8.0	4.2	93.60	90.41
4	1963.22	123.43	2282.33	9	7.0	3.9	95.37	90.64
5	2050.22	121.55	2072.24	9	7.0	4.1	90.33	87.73
6	1978.08	122.21	2212.52	9	7.2	4.5	93.21	91.21
7	1965.47	120.33	2475.44	9	7.6	3.8	90.19	88.93
8	2044.12	124.26	1840.22	9	7.2	3.0	92.08	88.35
9	2084.00	127.88	2331.25	9	7.7	3.1	89.25	87.44
10	2070.31	117.54	2175.32	9	7.1	3.6	89.65	86.45
11	1978.35	120.56	2422.13	9	7.4	4.0	95.22	92.54
12	1967.26	124.87	2591.21	9	7.5	2.8	95.39	91.33
13	1949.14	124.67	2517.22	9	7.8	4.4	94.11	92.48
14	1977.51	125.82	2068.21	9	8.0	4.5	93.05	90.61
15	2075.26	119.26	2112.54	9	8.0	4.2	92.42	89.62
16	2034.28	124.29	2248.25	9	7.6	4.0	94.94	89.77
17	2044.15	123.34	2244.21	9	7.7	2.7	94.18	87.65
18	2084.26	125.26	1950.24	9	7.6	3.6	94.62	90.43
19	2032.92	128.52	1895.21	9	7.6	3.2	95.21	91.88
20	2045.28	129.92	2112.52	9	7.2	3.5	95.22	92.95
21	2078.15	116.26	2052.01	9	7.2	3.4	93.64	88.22
22	2057.48	126.66	2332.55	9	7.9	3.0	89.52	86.65
23	2027.84	123.34	2545.28	9	7.5	3.1	92.39	89.24
24	1948.58	119.94	1985.33	9	7.5	4.4	95.35	91.54
25	2065.25	128.92	2365.21	9	7.0	4.0	91.36	90.28
26	2066.21	118.53	1958.32	9	7.3	4.2	90.55	85.32
27	1945.24	124.61	1824.32	9	7.0	3.0	92.56	89.45
28	1955.24	126.56	2275.33	9	8.0	3.8	88.34	85.64
29	2022.54	122.80	2550.23	9	8.0	4.0	91.22	89.65

During the training process, small weights were assigned to the connection between neurons in a random way. The weights were modified until the error between the predicted and experimental values of COD and ammonia nitrogen removal efficiency in SBR is minimized. The feedforward backpropagation (BP) algorithm with Levenberg-Marquardt (LM) training was applied for development of all three ANN models.

The BP is an approximate steepest descent algorithm with MSE used as performance function. In the neural network development, different number of hidden layers, number of neurons in each layer, and type of transfer function for each neuron were analyzed with a learning rate of 1.0 and training goal of 10−5. Then, the trained networks were tested using the testing data sets and MSE method by modifying the network weights. It was found that network with one hidden layer of neurons was successful.

The tansig transfer function was used in the hidden layer and linear transfer function in the output layer. The training of the network was carried out with different number of neurons in the hidden layer with training goal of 10−5. It is observed from Figure 6 that MSE value of 0.15584 is much higher for 2 neurons in one hidden layer. With the increase of neuron numbers in the hidden layer, there was a gradual decrease in MSE values attaining a minimum value of 0.00575 with 18 neurons in one hidden layer. With the further increase of hidden neurons, there was a sharp increase in MSE values. Hence, 18 hidden neurons were considered for optimization in the present study.

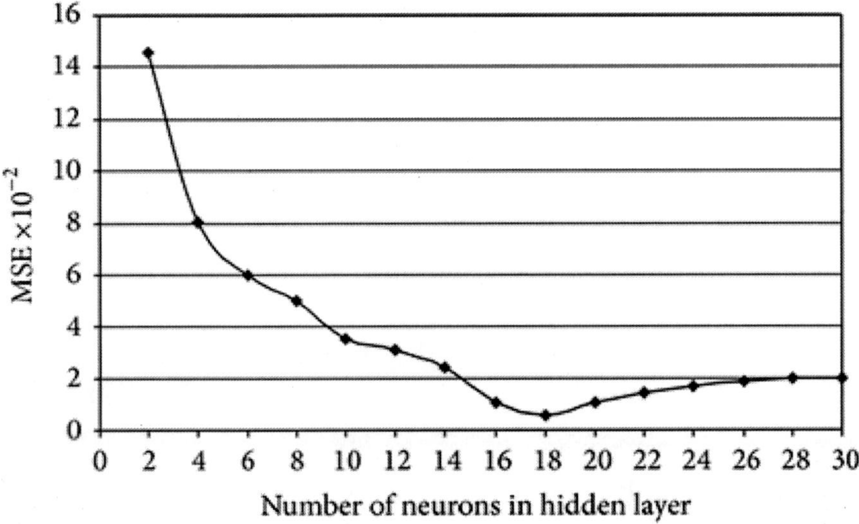

Figure 6. Relation between MSE and number of neurons in hidden layer.

A regression analysis of the network response between the output and the corresponding target was also performed with 18 hidden neurons layer. Figures 7, 8, and 9 exhibit the training, validation, and test squared error for the Levenberg-Marquardt algorithm for Model "A," "B," and "C," respectively, under three different combinations of aerobic-anoxic sequence, namely, (4 + 4), (5 + 3), and (5 + 4) hour of total react period. It was observed that Models "A," "B," and "C" took 7, 6, and 5 epochs, respectively, for training, validation, and testing of 29 data sets in each model. Finally, an optimal three-layered ANN with tangent sigmoid transfer function (tansig) at hidden layer with 18 neurons and linear transfer function (purelin) at output layer with Levenberg-Marquardt (LM) training algorithm was chosen to predict the COD and ammonia nitrogen removal efficiency in Models "A," "B," and "C," respectively.

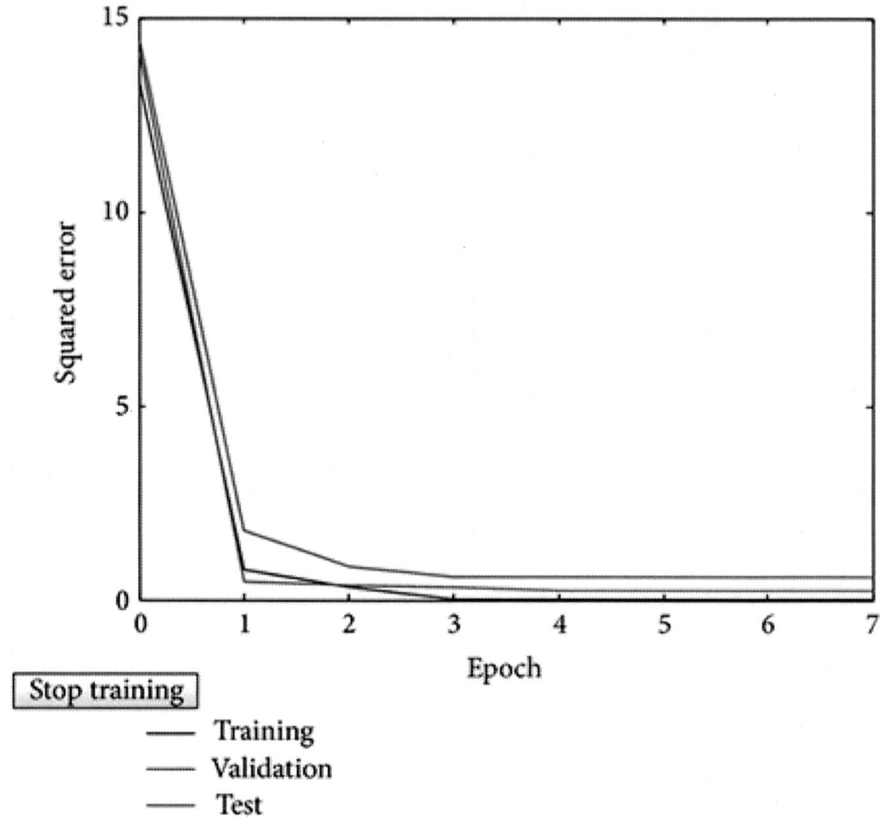

Figure 7. ANN Model "A" training, validation, and test squared error for the Levenberg-Marquardt algorithm for prediction of COD and NH_4^+-N removal efficiency during (4 + 4) aerobic-anoxic react period combination in SBR system.

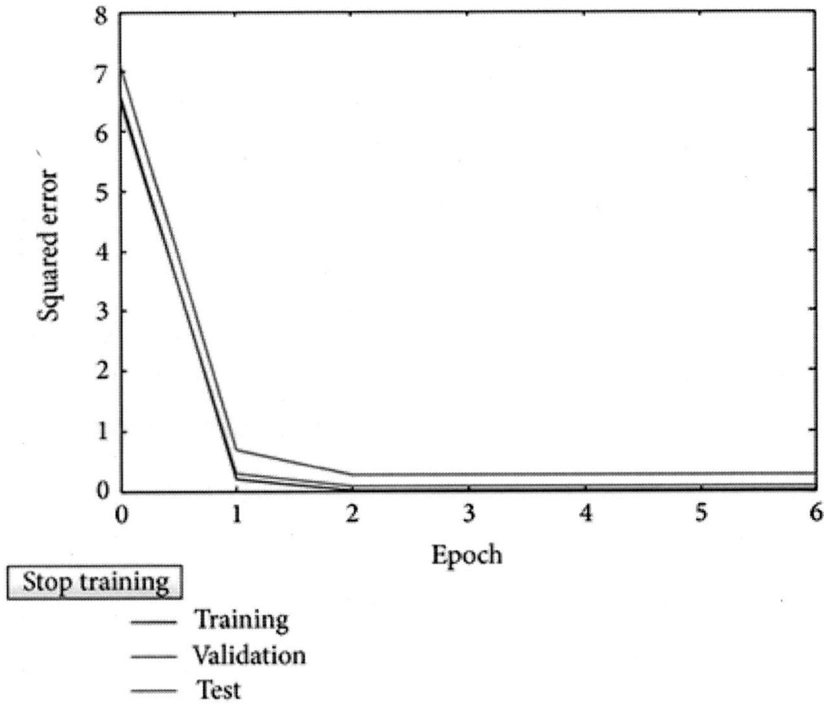

Figure 8. ANN Model "B" training, validation, and test squared error for the Levenberg-Marquardt algorithm for prediction of COD and NH_4^+-N removal efficiency during (5 + 3) aerobic-anoxic react period combination in SBR system.

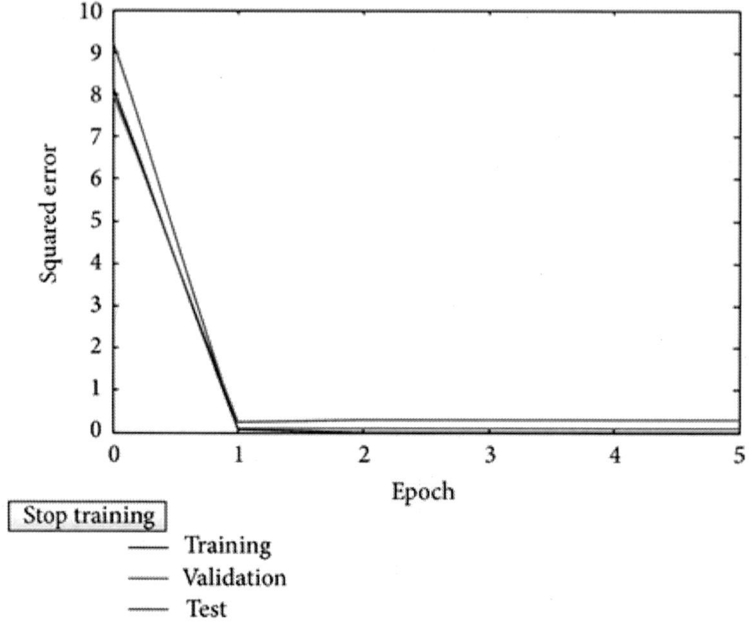

Figure 9. ANN Model "C" training, validation, and test squared error for the Levenberg-Marquardt algorithm for prediction of COD and NH_4^+-N removal efficiency during (5 + 4) aerobic-anoxic react period combination in SBR system.

The scattered diagrams of linear regression analysis for three model were plotted in Figures 10 and 11 for Model "A," Figures 12 and 13 for Model "B," and Figures 14 and 15 for Model "C" in correspondence with comparison between experimental and ANN predicted values of COD and NH_4^+-N removal efficiencies of each models, respectively. The two lines were used to show the success of the prediction. The one is the perfect fit line (predicted data equal to experimental data), on which all the data of an ideal model are lying. Another line corresponds to best fits to scatter plot for chaotic data with equation that is obtained with regression analysis based on the minimization of the squared errors. The plotting of the results as obtained through ANN exercise using the experimental data satisfactorily predicted the success of the experimental data and validated the model. The values of coefficient of determination (R) above 0.90 with slope approaching 1 and Y intercept value closer to zero were achieved through results of statistical analysis for removal of COD and NH_4^+-N in SBR.

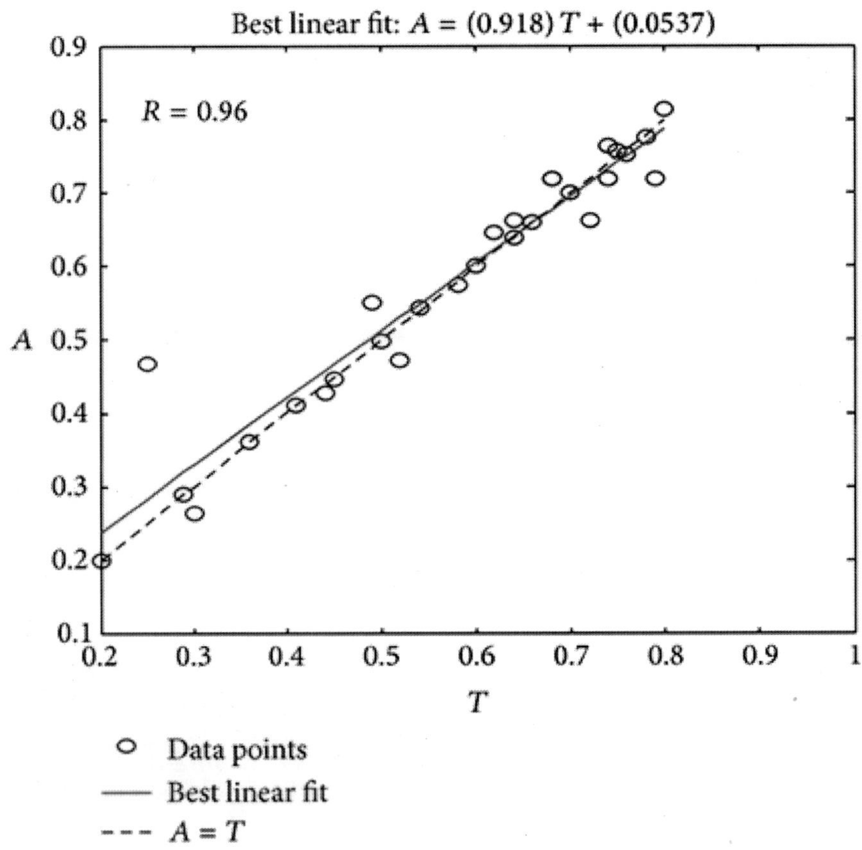

Figure 10. Linear regression analysis of ANN Model "A" for COD removal efficiency during (4 + 4) aerobic-anoxic react period combination in SBR system (*A*: simulated values, *T*: experimental values).

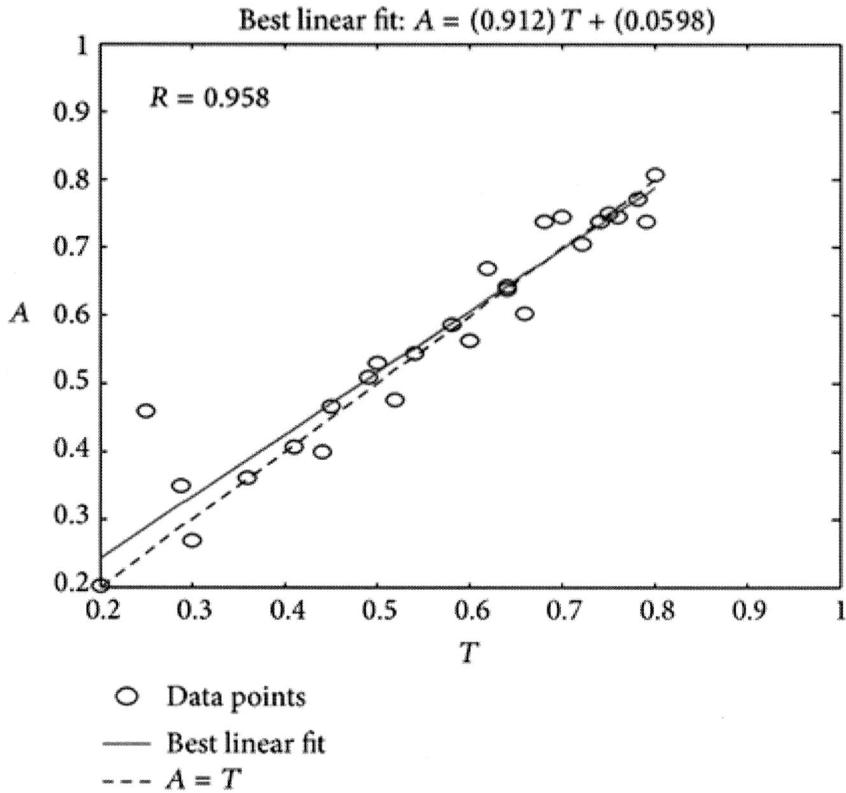

Figure 11. Linear regression analysis of ANN Model "A" for NH_4^+-N removal efficiency during (4 + 4) aerobic-anoxic react period combination in SBR system (*A*: simulated values, *T*: experimental values).

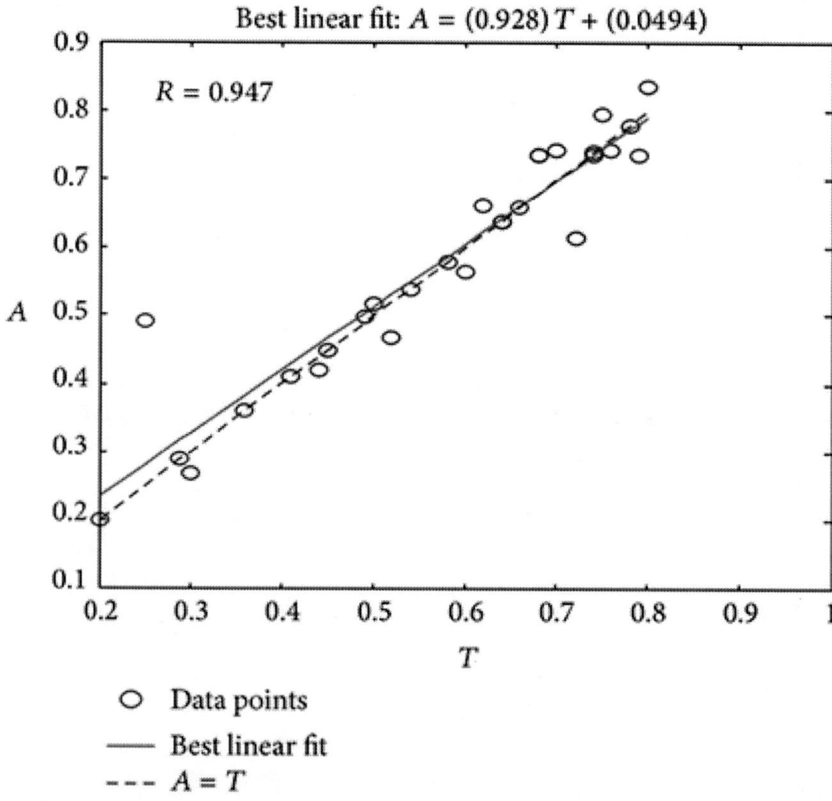

Figure 12. Linear regression analysis of ANN Model "B" for COD removal efficiency during (5 + 3) aerobic-anoxic react period combination in SBR system (*A*: simulated values, *T*: experimental values).

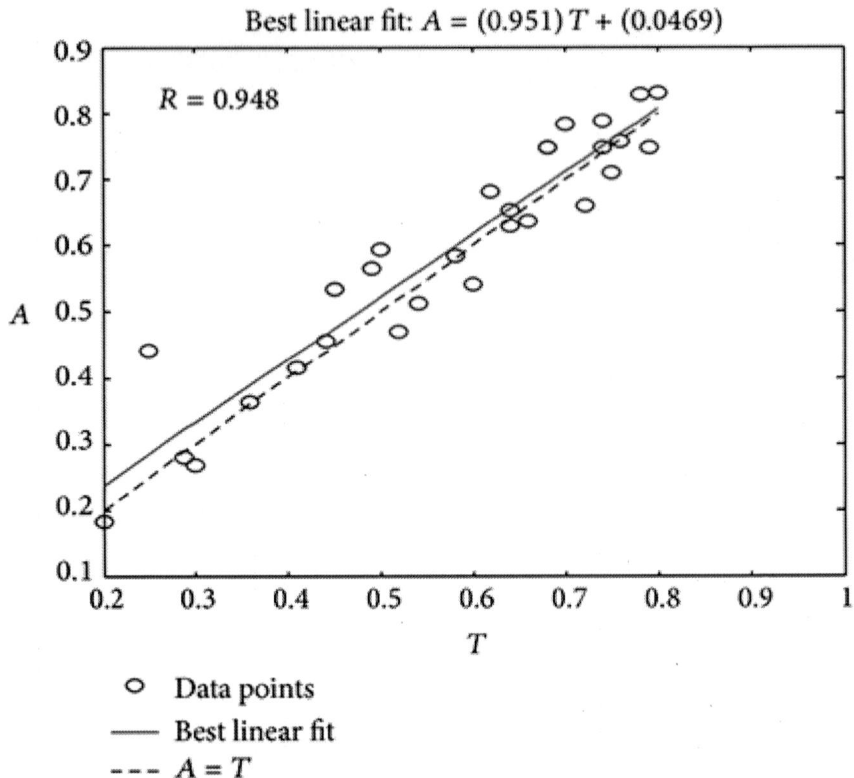

Figure 13. Linear regression analysis of ANN Model "B" for NH_4^+-N removal efficiency during (5 + 4) aerobic-anoxic react period combination in SBR system (*A*: simulated values, *T*: experimental values).

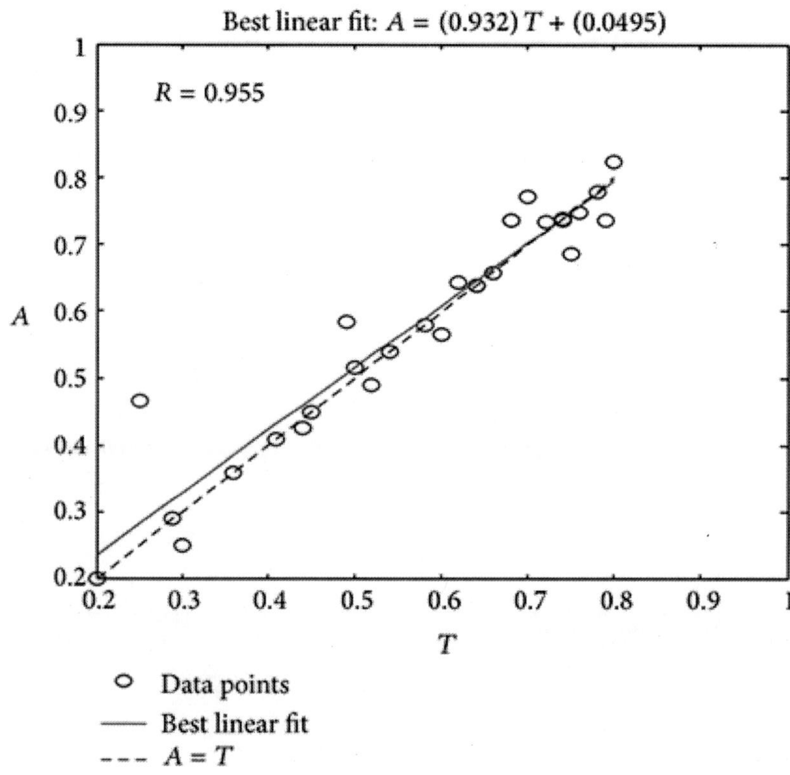

Figure 14. Linear regression analysis of ANN Model "C" for COD removal efficiency during (5 + 4) aerobic-anoxic react period combination in SBR system (*A*: simulated values, *T*: experimental values).

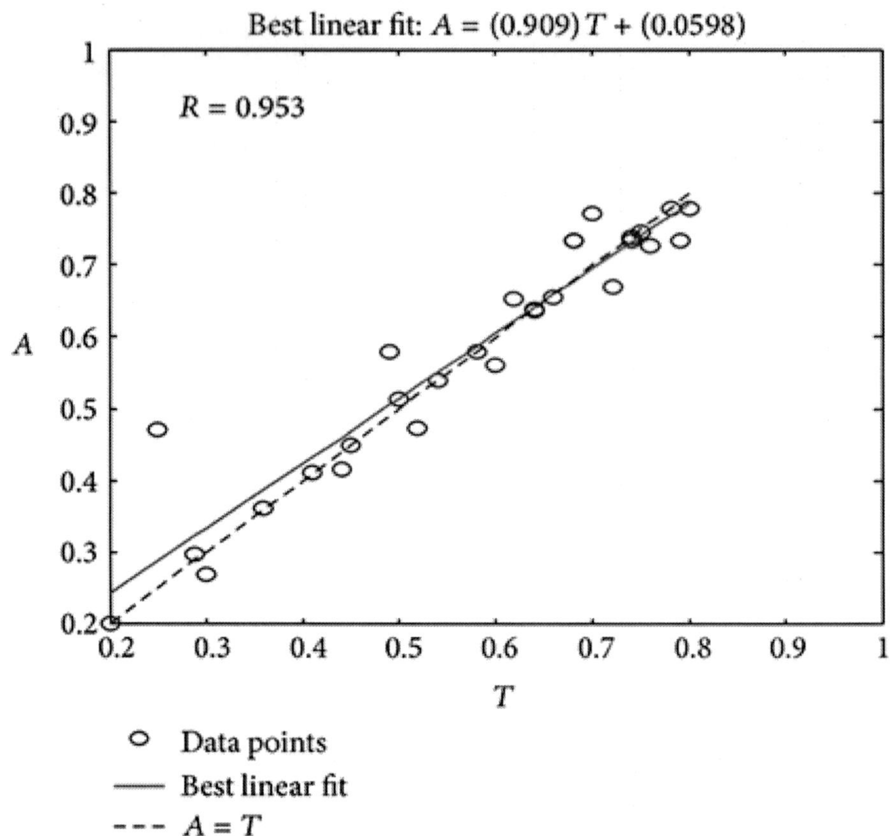

Figure 15. Linear regression analysis of ANN Model "C" for NH_4^+-N removal efficiency during (5 + 4) aerobic-anoxic react period combination in SBR system (*A*: simulated values, *T*: experimental values).

The coefficient of determination is also presented as *R*. The values of coefficient of determination (*R*) for COD and NH_4^+-N removal are found to be 0.947 and 0.960, respectively, which indicate a reasonable fitting to experimental data. Smith [25] suggested the following values of coefficient of determination (*R*) between 0.0 and 1.0 for different sets of variable:

$R \geq 0.8$ strong correlation exists between two sets of variables;

$0.2 \leq R \leq 0.8$ correlations exist between the two sets of variables;

$R \leq 0.2$ weak correlation exists between the two sets of variables.

The linear regression between the network outputs and the corresponding targets showed that the neural network outputs (forecasted data) were obviously agreed with the experimental values. The correlation between ANN testing outputs and the experimental values of COD and NH_4^+-N removal efficiency for all test data (7 data sets) of Models "A," "B," and "C" are shown in Figures 16, 17, and 18, respectively. This results are reasonable, since the experimental and ANN model predicted data set error has similar characteristics, and it does not show that any significant change over fitting has occurred. Comparison of the ANN model's results and experimental results of COD and NH_4^+-N removal efficiencies for all test data of Models "A," "B," and "C" are presented in Tables 6, 7, and 8, respectively. The performance error of experimental and ANN model predicted values for COD and NH_4^+-N removal efficiency in SBR is visualized within limit of 4%. The statistical analysis of the results of the network performance is presented in Table 9. The values of ME, MSE, and RMSE of all three models for COD and NH_4^+-N removal efficiency are on lower side range. It was found that the predicted values of COD and NH_4^+-N removal efficiency by ANN model are very close to the experimental values for all data sets in test series of Models "A," "B," and "C."

Table 6. Comparison of ANN Model "A" output and experimental values for test data set

Serial number	COD removal efficiency (%)		NH_4^+-N removal efficiency (%)		Error (%)	
	Experimental values	ANN predicted values	Experimental values	ANN predicted values	COD	NH_4^+-N
1	86.45	87.32	86.92	85.54	−0.87	1.38
2	89.33	90.52	85.83	87.22	−1.19	−1.39
3	88.65	86.15	82.97	84.19	2.50	−1.22
4	90.42	88.95	84.22	85.12	1.47	−0.90
5	85.22	84.55	82.85	82.12	0.67	0.73
6	84.29	87.15	85.52	84.28	−2.86	1.24
7	90.22	89.51	88.25	86.45	0.71	1.80

Table 7. Comparison of ANN Model "B" output and experimental values for test data set

Serial number	COD removal efficiency (%)		NH_4^+-N removal efficiency (%)		Error (%)	
	Experimental values	ANN predicted values	Experimental values	ANN predicted values	COD	NH_4^+-N
1	82.35	83.18	86.45	85.15	-0.83	1.30
2	85.58	84.72	88.24	87.27	0.86	0.97
3	82.30	84.15	89.30	90.56	-1.85	-1.26
4	90.93	91.25	91.22	88.95	-0.32	2.27
5	87.25	86.12	86.80	88.16	1.13	-1.36
6	84.37	82.78	86.26	85.75	1.59	0.51
7	85.33	84.62	88.50	90.78	0.71	-2.28

Table 8. Comparison of ANN Model "C" output and experimental values for test data set

Serial number	COD removal efficiency (%)		NH_4^+-N removal efficiency (%)		Error (%)	
	Experimental values	ANN predicted values	Experimental values	ANN predicted values	COD	NH_4^+-N
1	93.60	95.24	90.41	88.35	-1.64	2.06
2	90.19	92.85	88.93	90.18	-2.66	-1.25
3	95.22	93.28	92.54	90.76	1.94	1.78
4	94.18	95.15	87.65	88.25	-0.97	-0.60
5	95.21	91.88	91.88	92.85	3.33	-0.97
6	92.39	90.74	89.24	90.12	1.65	-0.88
7	92.56	91.25	89.45	87.48	1.31	1.97

Table 9. Comparison of performance statistics of three ANN models

Model number	Pollutant removal efficiency	ME	MSE	RMSE	Coefficient of determination	Slope	Y-axis intercept
Model "A"	COD removal	0.06	2.81	1.67	0.960	0.918	0.0537
	NH_4^+-N removal	0.23	1.63	1.27	0.958	0.912	0.0598
Model "B"	COD removal	0.18	1.32	1.14	0.947	0.928	0.0494
	NH_4^+-N removal	0.02	2.38	1.54	0.948	0.951	0.0469
Model "C"	COD removal	0.42	4.28	2.06	0.955	0.932	0.0495
	NH_4^+-N removal	0.30	2.13	1.45	0.953	0.909	0.0598

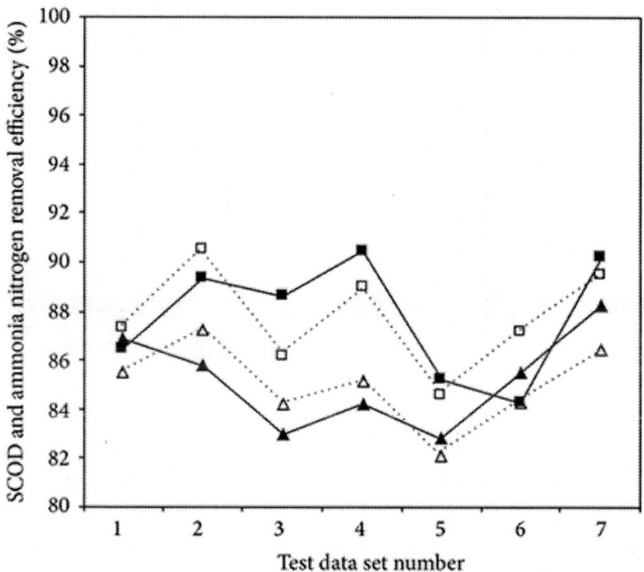

Figure 16. Stimulation results of Model "A" for test data sets.

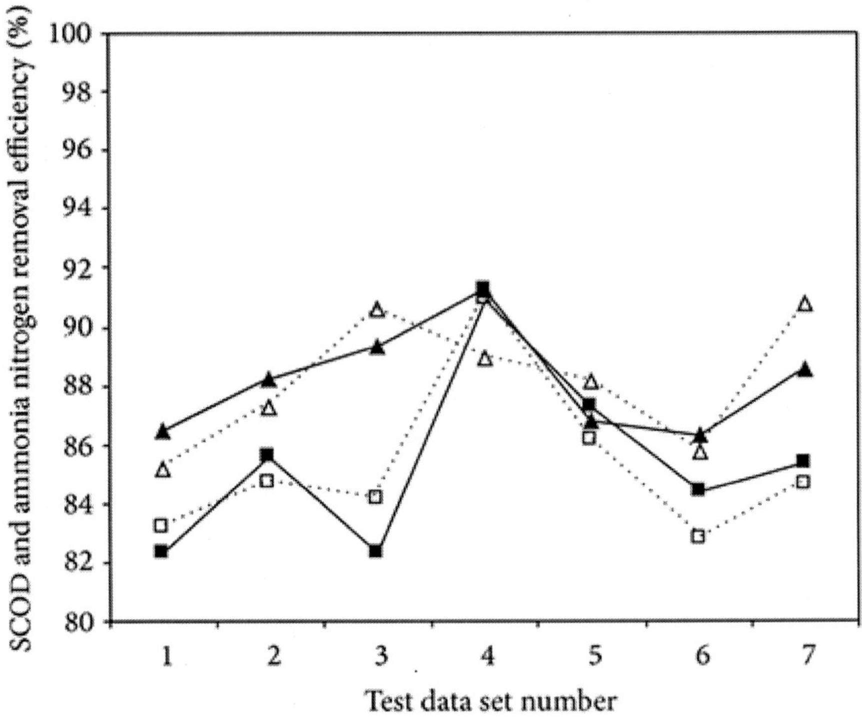

Figure 17. Stimulation results of Model "B" for test data sets.

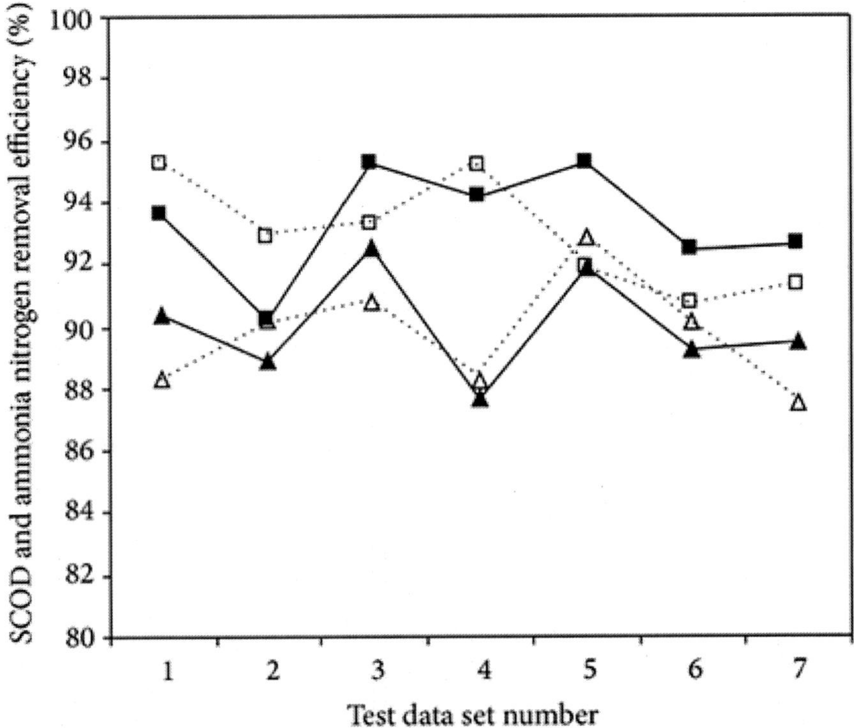

Figure 18. Stimulation results of Model "C" for test data sets.

CONCLUSION

Based on performing all relevant experiment and analysis of results, it is concluded that SBR is a reasonable alternative option for simultaneous removal of high COD and -N containing wastewater that finds slaughterhouse effluent with others. The experimental values indicated that both COD and NH_4^+-N could effectively be treated by heterotrophic facultative bacteria. It was found that under aerobic condition, maximum removal efficiency of about 95.57% of COD and 92.95% NH_4^+-N could be achieved over a react period of 9 hours for pretreated slaughterhouse wastewater in SBR. The combination of 5.0-hour aerobic react period and 4.0-hour anoxic react period is found to be reasonable from the view point of both organic carbon oxidation and nitrogen removal aspects. A steady increase in MLVSS level has been occurred during experiment. The overall increase in MLVSS in both the phases demonstrated the favourable microbial activity for organic carbon oxidation, nitrification, and denitrification.

The three neural network Models "A," "B," and "C" under three different combinations of aerobic-anoxic sequence, namely,(4 + 4), (5 + 3), and (5 + 4) hour of total react period, were successfully trained and tested which could forecast pollutant removal efficiency for combined carbon oxidation and nitrification of slaughterhouse wastewater in SBR. Based on the results obtained from the ANNs trained and limited to the architecture of the ANNs that had been trained, it is found that the ANN-based models can provide an efficient and a robust tool in predicting SBR performance. It was also found that after training, three ANN-based models were able to generalize very well when tested against any unknown data set. This observation yielded that the ANN-based models can be identified without detailed information of the kinetics of the system. In other words, as compared to statistical methods, ANNs can provide a more general framework for determining relationships between data and do not require specification of any functional form. Based on experimental results, the error of ANN model output was well within 3.33% and also the coefficient of determination above 0.94 and slope approaching 1 with intercept value closer to zero. The study also indicated that the ANN model technique has a great potential in prediction of organic carbon and nutrients removal efficiency in biological system.

CONFLICT OF INTERESTS

The authors disclosed the fact that this paper has been prepared for academic purpose for research persuasion and exchange of knowledge. There is no bearing on any financial relation with any commercial identities and also avoiding any conflict of interests.

ACKNOWLEDGMENT

This study was supported by the research funds of Jadavpur University, Jadavpur, Kolkata-32.

REFERENCES

1. Metcalf and Eddy, Wastewater Engineering-Treatment, Disposal and Reuse, Tata McGraw-Hill, New York, NY, USA, 4th edition, 1995.
2. J. Grady, G. Daigger, and H. Lim, Biological Wastewater Treatment, Marcel Dekker, New York, NY, USA, 1999.
3. N. Bhat and T. J. McAvoy, "Use of neural nets for dynamic modeling and control of chemical process systems," Computers and Chemical Engineering, vol. 14, no. 4-5, pp. 573–582, 1990. View at Scopus
4. M.-J. Syu and G. T. Tsao, "Neural network modeling of batch cell growth pattern," Biotechnology and Bioengineering, vol. 42, no. 3, pp. 376–380, 1993. View at Scopus
5. M. J. Willis, C. Di Massimo, G. A. Montague, M. T. Tham, and A. J. Morris, "Artificial neural networks in process engineering," IEE Proceedings D, vol. 138, no. 3, pp. 256–266, 1991. View at Scopus
6. G. A. Montague, A. J. Morris, and M. T. Tham, "Enhancing bioprocess operability with generic software sensors," Journal of Biotechnology, vol. 25, no. 1-2, pp. 183–201, 1992. View at Scopus
7. S. Linko, J. Luopa, and Y.-H. Zhu, "Neural networks as "software sensors" in enzyme production," Journal of Biotechnology, vol. 52, no. 3, pp. 257–266, 1997. View at Publisher · View at Google Scholar · View at Scopus
8. M. M. Hamed, M. G. Khalafallah, and E. A. Hassanien, "Prediction of wastewater treatment plant performance using artificial neural networks," Environmental Modelling and Software, vol. 19, no. 10, pp. 919–928, 2004. View at Publisher · View at Google Scholar · View at Scopus
9. D. Aguado, A. Ferrer, A. Seco, and J. Ferrer, "Comparison of different predictive models for nutrient estimation in a sequencing batch reactor for wastewater treatment," Chemometrics and Intelligent Laboratory Systems, vol. 84, no. 1-2, pp. 75–81, 2006. View at Publisher · View at Google Scholar · View at Scopus
10. M. Häck and M. Köhne, "Estimation of wastewater process parameters using neural networks," Water Science and Technology, vol. 33, no. 1, pp. 101–115, 1996. View at Publisher · View at Google Scholar · View at Scopus

11. M. Bongards, "Improving the efficiency of a wastewater treatment plant by fuzzy control and neural networks," Water Science and Technology, vol. 43, no. 11, pp. 189–196, 2001. View at Scopus

12. Y.-S. T. Hong, M. R. Rosen, and R. Bhamidimarri, "Analysis of a municipal wastewater treatment plant using a neural network-based pattern analysis," Water Research, vol. 37, no. 7, pp. 1608–1618, 2003. View at Publisher · View at Google Scholar · View at Scopus

13. W. C. Chen, N.-B. Chang, and J.-C. Chen, "Rough set-based hybrid fuzzy-neural controller design for industrial wastewater treatment," Water Research, vol. 37, no. 1, pp. 95–107, 2003. View at Publisher · View at Google Scholar · View at Scopus

14. S. Eslamian and N. Lavaei, "Modelling nitrate pollution of groundwater using artificial neural network and genetic algorithm in an arid zone," International Journal of Water, vol. 5, no. 2, pp. 194–203, 2009. View at Publisher · View at Google Scholar · View at Scopus

15. H. Zhao, O. J. Hao, T. J. McAvoy, and C.-H. Chang, "Modeling nutrient dynamics in sequencing batch reactor," Journal of Environmental Engineering, vol. 123, no. 4, pp. 311–318, 1997. View at Scopus

16. N. Al-Mutairi, N. Kartam, P. Koushki, and M. Al-Mutairi, "Modeling and predicting biological performance of contact stabilization process using artificial neural networks," Journal of Computing in Civil Engineering, vol. 18, no. 4, pp. 341–349, 2004. View at Publisher · View at Google Scholar · View at Scopus

17. M. N. Kashani and S. Shahhosseini, "A methodology for modeling batch reactors using generalized dynamic neural networks," Chemical Engineering Journal, vol. 159, no. 1-3, pp. 195–202, 2010. View at Publisher · View at Google Scholar · View at Scopus

18. L. Luccarini, G. L. Bragadin, G. Colombini et al., "Formal verification of wastewater treatment processes using events detected from continuous signals by means of artificial neural networks. Case study: SBR plant," Environmental Modelling and Software, vol. 25, no. 5, pp. 648–660, 2010. View at Publisher · View at Google Scholar · View at Scopus

19. American Public Health Association, American Water Works Association, Water Pollution Control Federation, Standard Methods for the Examination of Water and Wastewater, Washington, DC, USA, 20th edition, 1998.

20. A. Tremblay, R. D. Tyagi, and R. Y. Surampalli, "Effect of SRT on nutrient removal in SBR system," Practice Periodical of Hazardous, Toxic, and Radioactive Waste Management, vol. 3, no. 4, pp. 183–190, 1999. View at Publisher · View at Google Scholar · View at Scopus

21. H. Zhao, O. J. Hao, T. J. McAvoy, and C.-H. Chang, "Modeling nutrient dynamics in sequencing batch reactor," Journal of Environmental Engineering, vol. 123, no. 4, pp. 311–318, 1997. View at Scopus

22. M. Cote, B. P. A. Grandjean, P. Lessard, and J. Thibault, "Dynamic modelling of the activated sludge process: improving prediction using neural networks,"

Water Research, vol. 29, no. 4, pp. 995–1004, 1995. View at Publisher · View at Google Scholar · View at Scopus

23. R. M. Aghav, S. Kumar, and S. N. Mukherjee, "Artificial neural network modeling in competitive adsorption of phenol and resorcinol from water environment using some carbonaceous adsorbents," Journal of Hazardous Materials, vol. 188, no. 1-3, pp. 67–77, 2011. View at Publisher · View at Google Scholar · View at Scopus
24. B. B. Ekici and U. T. Aksoy, "Prediction of building energy consumption by using artificial neural networks," Advances in Engineering Software, vol. 40, no. 5, pp. 356–362, 2009. View at Publisher · View at Google Scholar · View at Scopus
25. G. N. Smith, Probability and Statistics in Civil Engineering: An Introduction, Collins, London, UK, 1986..

Chapter 7

A NOVEL LEARNING SCHEME FOR CHEBYSHEV FUNCTIONAL LINK NEURAL NETWORKS

Satchidananda Dehuri

Department of Information and Communication Technology, Fakir Mohan University, Vyasa Vihar, Balasore, Orissa 756019, India

ABSTRACT

A hybrid learning scheme (ePSO-BP) to train Chebyshev Functional Link Neural Network (CFLNN) for classification is presented. The proposed method is referred as hybrid CFLNN (HCFLNN). The HCFLNN is a type of feed-forward neural networks which have the ability to transform the nonlinear input space into higher dimensional-space where linear separability is possible. Moreover, the proposed HCFLNN combines the best attribute of particle swarm optimization (PSO), back propagation learning (BP learning), and functional link neural networks (FLNNs). The proposed method eliminates the need of hidden layer by expanding the input patterns using Chebyshev orthogonal polynomials. We have shown its effectiveness of classifying the unknown pattern using the publicly available datasets obtained from UCI repository. The computational results are then compared with functional link neural network (FLNN) with a generic basis functions, PSO-based FLNN, and EFLN. From the comparative study, we observed that the performance of the HCFLNN outperforms FLNN, PSO-based FLNN, and EFLN in terms of classification accuracy.

INTRODUCTION

In recent years, higher-order neural networks [1], particularly FLNN, have been widely used to classify nonlinearly separable patterns and can be viewed as a problem of approximating an arbitrary decision boundary. Broadly, artificial neural networks have become one of the most acceptable soft computing tools for approximating the decision boundaries of a classification problem [2, 3]. In fact, a multilayer perceptron (MLP) with a suitable architecture is capable of approximating virtually any function of interest [4]. This does not mean that finding such a network is easy. On the contrary, problems, such as local minima trapping, saturation, weight interference, initial weight dependence, and overfitting, make neural network training difficult.

An easy way to avoid these problems consists in removing the hidden layers. This may sound a little inconsiderate at first, since it is due to them that nonlinear input-output relationships can be captured. Encouragingly enough, the removing procedure can be executed without giving up nonlinearity, provided that the input layer is endowed with additional higher-order units [5, 6]. This is the idea behind higher-order neural networks (HONNs) [7] like functional link neural networks (FLNNs) [8], ridge polynomial neural networks (RPNNs) [1, 7], and so on. HONNs are simple in their architectures and require fewer number of weights to learn the underlying approximating polynomials. This potentially reduces the number of required training parameters. As a result, they can learn faster since each iteration of the training procedure takes less time. This makes them suitable for complex problem solving where the ability to retrain or adopt new data in real time is critical. Currently, there have been many algorithms used to train the functional link neural networks, such as back-propagation learning algorithm [2], genetic algorithm [9], particle swarm optimization [10], and so on. Back-propagation learning algorithms have their own limitations. However, we can advocate that if the search for the BP learning algorithms starts from the near optimum with a small tuning of the learning parameters, the searching results can be improved.

Genetic algorithms and particle swarm optimization can be used for training the FLNN to reduce the local optimality and speed up the convergence. But training using genetic algorithm is discouraging because of the following limitations: in the training process, it requires encoding and decoding operator which is commonly treated as a long-standing barrier of neural networks researchers. The important problem of applying genetic algorithms to train neural networks may be unsatisfactory because recombination operators incur several problems, such as competing conventions [11] and the epistasis effect [12]. For better performance, real coded genetic algorithms [13, 14] have been introduced. However, they generally employ random mutations, and, hence, still require lengthy local searches near a local optima. On the other hand, PSO has some attractive properties. It retains previous useful information, whereas GAs destroy the previous knowledge of the problems once the population changes. PSO encourages constructive cooperation and information sharing among particles, which enhances the search for a global optimal solution. Successful applications of PSO to some optimization problems such as function minimization [15, 16] and neural networks design [17, 18] have demonstrated its potential. It is considered to be capable to reduce the ill effect of the BP learning algorithm of neural networks, because it does not require gradient and differentiable information.

Unlike the GA, the PSO algorithm has no complicated operators such as cross-over and mutation. In the PSO algorithm, the potential solutions, called as particles, are obtained by flowing through the problem space by following the current optimum particles. Generally speaking, the PSO algorithm has a strong ability to find the most optimistic result, but it has a disadvantage of easily getting into a local optimum. After suitably modulating the parameters for the PSO algorithm, the rate of convergence can be speeded up, and the ability to find the global optimistic result can be enhanced. The PSO algorithm search is based on the orientation by tracing *pbest*, that is, each particle's best position in its history, and tracing *gbest* that is all particles best position in their history, it can rapidly arrive around the global optimum. However, because the PSO algorithm has several parameters to be adjusted by empirical approach, if these parameters are not appropriately set, search will proceed very slow near the global optimum. Hence, to cope up with this problem, we suggested a novel evolvable PSO (ePSO) and back propagation (BP) algorithm as a learning method of Chebyshev functional link neural network (CFLNN) for fine tuning of the connection weights.

Outline

The remainder of this paper is organized as follows. Some the recently proposed functional link neural networks (FLNNs) are reviewed in Section 2. Section 3 provides the detailed algorithm of HCFLNN for classification. In Section 4, we have presented experimental results with a comparative study. Section 5 concludes the article with a future research scope.

FUNCTIONAL LINK NEURAL NETWORKS

FLNNs are higher order neural networks without hidden units introduced by Klassen et al. [19] in 1988. Despite their linear nature, FLNNs can capture nonlinearly input-output relationships, provided that they are fed with an adequate set of polynomial inputs, or the functions might be a subset of a complete set of orthonormal basis functions spanning an n-dimensional representation space, which are constructed out of the original input attributes [20].

In contrast to the linear weights of the input patterns produced by the linear links of artificial neural network, the functional link acts on an element of a pattern or on the entire pattern itself by generating a set of linearly independent functions, then evaluating these functions with the pattern as an argument. Thus, class separability is possible in the enhanced feature space. For a D-dimensional classification problem, there are $((D + r)!/D! \cdots r!)$ possible polynomials up to degree r that can be constructed. For most of the real life problems, this is too big number, even for degree 2, which obviously discourages us from achieving our goal. However, we can still resort to constructive and pruning algorithms in order to address this problem. In fact,

Sierra et al. [21] have proposed a new algorithm for the evolution of functional link networks which makes use of a standard GAs [9] to evolve near minimal linear architectures. Moreover, the complexity of the algorithm still needs to be investigated.

However, the dimensionality of many problems is itself very high and further increasing the dimensionality to a very large extent that may not be an appropriate choice. So, it is advisable and also a new research direction to choose a small set of alternative functions, which can map the function to the desired extent with an output of significant improvement. FLNN with a trigonometric basis functions for classification, as proposed in [8], is obviously an example. Chebyshev FLNN is also another improvement in this direction, the detailed is discussed in Section 3. Some of the potential contributions in FLNNs and their success for application in variety of problems are given below.

Haring and Kok [22], has proposed an algorithm that uses evolutionary computation (specifically genetic algorithm and genetic programming) for the determination of functional links (one based on polynomials and another based on expression tree) in neural network. Patra and Pal [23] have proposed a FLNN and applied to the problem of channel equalization in a digital communication channel. It relies on BP-learning algorithm. Haring et al. [24] were presenting a different ways to select and transform features using evolutionary computation and show that this kind of selection of features is a special case of so-called functional links.

Dash et al. [25] have proposed a FLNN with trigonometric basis functions to forecast the short-term electric load. Panagiotopoulos et al. [26] have reported better results by applying FLNN for planning in an interactive environment between two systems: the challenger and the responder. Patra et al. [27] have proposed a FLNN with back-propagation learning for the identification of nonlinearly dynamic systems.

With the encouraging performance of FLNN [23, 27], Patra and van den Bos [28] further motivated and came up with another FLNN with three sets of basis functions such as Chebyshev, Legendre, and power series to develop an intelligent model of the CPS involving less computational complexity. In the sequel, its implementation can be economical and robust.

In [21], a genetic algorithm for selecting an appropriate number of polynomials as a functional input to the network has been proposed by Sierra et al. and applied to the classification problem. However, their main concern was the selection of optimal set of functional links to construct the classifier. In contrast, the proposed method gives much emphasis on how to develop the learning skill of the classifier.

A Chebyshev functional link artificial neural networks have been proposed by Patra and Kot [29] for nonlinearly dynamic system identification. This is obviously another improvement in this direction and also a source of inspiration to further validate this method in other application domain. The proposed method is clearly an example. Singh and Srivastava [30] have estimated the degree of insecurity in a power system with a set of orthonormal trigonometric basis functions.

In [31], an evolutionary search of genetic type and multiobjective optimization such as accuracy and complexity of the FLNN in the Pareto sense is used to design a generalized FLNN with internal dynamics and applied to system identification.

Majhi and Shalabi [32] have applied FLNN for digital watermarking, their results show that FLNN has better performance than other algorithms in this line. In [33], a comparative performance of three artificial neural networks has been given for the detection and classification of gear faults. Authors reported that FLNN is comparatively better than others.

Misra and Dehuri [8] have used a FLNN for classification problem in data mining with a hope to get a compact classifier with less computational complexity and faster learning. Purwar et al. [34] have proposed a Chebyshev functional link neural network for system identification of unknown dynamic nonlinearly discrete-time systems. Weng et al. [35] have proposed a reduced decision feedback Chebyshev functional link artificial neural networks (RDF-CFLANN) for channel equalization.

Two simple modified FLANNs are proposed by Krishnaiah et al. [36] for estimation of carrageenan concentration. In the first model, a hidden layer is introduced and trained by EBP. In the second model, functional links are introduced to the neurons in the hidden layer, and it is trained by EBP. In [37], a FLANN with trigonometric polynomial functions is used in intelligent sensors for harsh environment that effectively linearizes the response characteristics, compensates for nonidealities, and calibrates automatically. Dehuri et al. [38] have proposed a novel strategy for feature selection using genetic algorithm and then used as the input in FLANN for classification.

With this discussion, we can conclude that a very few applications of HONNs have so far been made in classification task. Although theoretically this area is rich, but application specifically in classification is poor. Therefore, the proposed contribution can be another improvement in this direction.

HYBRID CHEBYSHEV FLNN

Chebyshev Functional Link Neural Network

It is well known that the nonlinearly approximation of the Chebyshev orthogonal polynomial is very powerful by the approximation theory. Combining the characteristics of the FLNN and Chebyshev orthogonal polynomial the Chebyshev functional link neural network what we named as CFLNN is resulted. The proposed method utilizes the FLNN input-output pattern, the nonlinearly approximation capabilities of Chebyshev orthogonal polynomial, and the evolvable particle swarm optimization(ePSO)-BP learning scheme for classification.

The Chebyshev FLNN used in this paper is a single-layer neural network. The architecture consists of two parts, namely transformation part (i.e., from a low-dimensional feature space to high-dimensional feature space) and learning part. The transformation deals with the input feature vector to the hidden layer by approximate transformable method. The transformation is the functional expansion (FE) of the input pattern comprising of a finite set of Chebyshev polynomial. As a result, the Chebyshev polynomial basis can be viewed as a new input vector. The learning part uses the newly proposed ePSO-BP learning.

Alternatively, we can approximate a function by a polynomial of truncated power series. The power series expansion represents the function with a very small error near the point of expansion, but the error increases rapidly as we employ it at points farther away.

The computational economy to be gained by Chebyshev series increases when the power series is slowly convergent. Therefore, Chebyshev series are frequently used for approximations to functions and are much more efficient than other power series of the same degree. Among orthogonal polynomials, the Chebyshev polynomials converge rapidly than expansion in other set of polynomials [8]. Moreover, Chebyshev polynomials are easier to compute than trigonometric polynomials. These interesting properties of Chebyshev polynomial motivated us to use CFLNN for approximation of decision boundaries in the feature space.

Evolvable Particle Swarm Optimization (ePSO)

Evolvable particle swarm optimization (ePSO) is an improvement over the PSO [10]. PSO is a kind of stochastic algorithm to search for the best solution by simulating the movement and flocking of birds. The algorithm works by initializing a flock of birds randomly over the searching space, where every bird is called as a particle. These particles fly with a certain velocity and find the global best position after some iteration. At each iteration *k*, the *i*th particle is represented by a vector x^k_i in multidimensional space to characterize its position. The velocity is used to characterize its velocity. Thus, PSO maintains a set of positions:

$$S = \{x_1^k, x_2^k, \ldots, x_N^k\} \tag{1}$$

and a set of corresponding velocities

$$V = \{v_1^k, v_2^k, \ldots, v_N^k\}. \tag{2}$$

Initially, the iteration counter k = 0, and the positions x_i^0 and their corresponding velocities v_i^0 (i = 1, 2, . . . ,N) are generated randomly from the search space Ω.. Each particle changes its position per iteration. The new position x_i^{k+1}. of the *i*th particle (i = 1, 2, . . . ,N) is biased towards its best position p_i^k with minimized functional value *f*(.) referred to as personal best or *pbest*, found by the particle so far, and the very best position p^k_g, referred to as the global best or *gbest*, found by its companions. The *gbest* is the best position in the set

$$P = \{p_1^k, p_2^k, \ldots, p_N^k\}, \quad \text{where } p_i^0 = x_i^0, \forall i. \tag{3}$$

We can say a particle in *P* as good or bad depending on its personal best being a good or bad point in P. Consequently, we call the ith particle (jth particle) in P the worst (the best) if p^k_i (p^k_j) is the least (best) fitted, with respect to function value in P. The pbest and gbest is denoted as p^k_i and p^k_g ,respectively.

At each iteration k, the position x^k_i of the ith particle is updated by a velocity v^{k+1}_i which depends on three components: its current velocity v^k_i , the cognition term (i.e., the weighted difference vectors $(p^k_i - x^k_i)$), and the social term (i.e., the weighted difference vector $(p^k_g - x^k_i)$).

Specifically, the set P is updated for the next iteration using

$$x_i^{k+1} = x_i^k + v_i^{k+1}, \tag{4}$$

$$\text{where } v_i^{k+1} = v_i^k + r_1 \cdot c_1 \cdot (p_i^k - x_i^k) + r_2 \cdot c_2 \cdot (p_g^k - x_i^k).$$

The parameters r_1 and r_2 are uniformly distributed in random numbers in [0, 1] and c_1 and c_2, known as the cognitive and social parameters, respectively, and are popularly chosen to be $c_1 = c_2 = 2.0$ [40]. Thus, the values $r_1 \cdot c_1$ and $r_2 \cdot c_2$ introduce some stochastic weighting in the difference vectors $(p^k_i - x^k_i)$ and $(p^k_g - x^k_i)$, respectively. The set P is updated as the new positions x^{k+1}_i that are created using the following rules with a minimization of the cost function:

$$p_i^{k+1} = x_i^{k+1} \quad \text{if } f\left(x_i^{k+1}\right) < f\left(p_i^k\right), \text{ otherwise } p_i^{k+1} = p_i^k. \tag{5}$$

This process of updating the velocities v^k_i, positions x^k_i, , and the is repeated until a user-defined stopping condition is met.

We now briefly present a number of improved versions of PSO and then show where our modified PSO can stand.

Shi and Eberhart [39] have done the first modification by introducing a constant inertia ω, which controls how much a particle tends to follow its current directions compared to the memorized *pbest* p^k_i and the *gbest* p^k_g. Hence, the velocity update is given by

$$v_i^{k+1} = \omega \cdot v_i^k + r_1 \cdot c_1 \cdot \left(p_i^k - x_i^k\right) + r_2 \cdot c_2 \cdot \left(p_g^k - x_i^k\right), \tag{6}$$

where the values of and are realized component wise.

Again Shi and Eberhart [40] proposed a linearly varying inertia weight during the search. The inertia weight is linearly reduced during the search. This entails a more globally search during the initial stages and a more locally search during the final stages. They also proposed a limitation of each particle's velocity to a specified maximum velocity v^{max}. The maximum velocity was calculated as a fraction τ $(0 < \tau \leq 1)$ of the distance between the bounds of the search space, that is, $v^{max} = \tau \cdot (x^u - x^l)$.

Fourie and Groenwold [41] suggested a dynamic inertia weight and maximum velocity reduction. In this modification, an inertia weight and maximum velocity are then reduced by fractions α and β, respectively, if no improvement in p^k_g occur after a prespecified number of iterations *h*, that is,

$$\text{if } f\left(p_g^k\right) = f\left(p_g^{k-1}\right) \text{ then } w_{k+1} = \alpha w_k \text{ and } v_k^{max} = \beta v_k^{max}, \tag{7}$$

where α and β are such that 0 < α, β < 1.

Clerc and Kennedy [42] introduced another interesting modification to PSO in the form of a constriction coefficient *x*, which controls all the three components in velocity update rule. This has an effect of reducing the velocity as the search progress. In this modification, the velocity update is given by

$$v_i^{k+1} = \chi\left(v_i^k + r_1 c_1\left(p_i^k\right) + r_2 c_2\left(p_g^k - x_i^k\right)\right),$$
$$\text{where } \chi = \frac{2}{\left|2 - \phi - \sqrt{\phi^2 - 4\phi}\right|}, \quad \phi = c_1 + c_2 > 4. \tag{8}$$

Da and Ge [18] also modified PSO by introducing a temperature like control parameter as in the simulated annealing algorithm. Zhang et al. [43] have modified the PSO by introducing a new inertia weight during the velocity update. Generally in the beginning stages of their algorithm, the inertial weight ω should be reduced rapidly, when around optimum, the inertial weight ω should be reduced slowly. They adopted the following rule:

$$\omega = \omega_0 - \left(\frac{\omega_1}{\text{MAXITER1}}\right) * t, \quad \text{if } 1 \le t \le \text{MAXITER1},$$
$$\omega = (\omega_0 - \omega_1) * \exp\left(\frac{(\text{MAXITER1} - k)}{\nu}\right), \tag{9}$$
$$\text{if MAXITER1} < k \le \text{MAXITER},$$

where ω_0 is the initial inertia weight, ω_1 is the inertial weight of linear section ending, MAXITER is the total searching generations, MAXITER1 is the used generations that inertia weight is reduced linearly, and k is a variable whose range is [1,MAXITER]. By adjusting k, they are getting different ending values of inertial weight. In this work, the inertial weight is evolved as a part of searching the optimal sets of weights. However, the evolution of inertial weight is restricted between an upper limit (ω_u) and lower limit ω_l. If it exceeds the boundary during the course of training the network, then the following rule is adopted for restricting the value of ω:

$$\omega = \omega^{l} + \frac{c\_value}{3\omega^{u}}\left(\omega^{u} - \omega^{l}\right), \tag{10}$$

where c_ value is the exceeded value.

In addition, the proposed method also uses the adaptive cognitive acceleration coefficient (c_1) and the social acceleration coefficients (c_2). c_1 has been allowed to decrease from its initial value of c_{1i} to c_{1f} while c_2 has been increased from c_{2i} to c_{2f} using the following equations as in [44]:

$$\begin{aligned} c_1^k &= \left(c_{1f} - c_{1i}\right)\frac{k}{\text{MAXITER}} + c_{1i}, \\ c_2^k &= \left(c_{2f} - c_{2i}\right)\frac{k}{\text{MAXITER}} + c_{2i}. \end{aligned} \tag{11}$$

ePSO-BP Learning Algorithm

The ePSO-BP is an learning algorithm which combines the ePSO global searching capability with the BP algorithm local searching capability. Similar to the GA [9], the ePSO algorithm is a global algorithm, which has a strong ability to find global optimistic result, and this ePSO algorithm, however, has a disadvantage that the search around global optimum is very slow. The BP algorithm, on the contrary, has a strong ability to find local optimistic result, but its ability to find the global optimistic result is weak. By combining the ePSO with the BP, a new algorithm referred to as ePSO BP hybrid learning algorithm is formulated in this paper. The fundamental idea for this hybrid algorithm is that at the beginning stage of searching for the optimum, the PSO is employed to accelerate the training speed. When the fitness function value has not changed for some generations, or value changed is smaller than a predefined number, the searching process is switched to gradient descending searching according to this heuristic knowledge. Similar to the ePSO algorithm, the ePSO BP algorithm's searching process is also started from initializing a group of random particles. First, all the particles are updated according to (4), until a new generation set of particles are generated, and then those new particles are used to search the global best (gbest) position in the solution space. Finally, the BP algorithm is used to search around the global optimum. In this way, this hybrid algorithm may find an optimum more quickly. The procedure for this ePSO BP algorithm can be summarized by the following computational steps.

(1) Initialize the positions and velocities of a group of particles randomly in the range of [0, 1]. Initialize the cognitive and social acceleration initial and final coefficients (i.e., c_{1i}, c_{1f} , c_{2i}, and c_{2f}).

(2) Evaluate each initialized particle's fitness value, and pi is set as the positions of the current particles, while pg is set as the best position of the initialized particles.

(3) If the maximal iterative generations are arrived, go to Step 10, else, go to Step 4.

(4) The best particle of the current particles is stored. The positions and velocities of all the particles are updated according to (4) and (6), then a group of new particles are generated.

(5) Adjust the value of c_1 and c_2 by using (11).

(6) Adjust the inertia weights ω according to equation (10) if it flies beyond the boundary of ω.

(7) Evaluate each new particle's fitness value, and the worst particle is replaced with the stored best particle. If the ith particle's new position is better than pi, pi is set as the new position of the ith particle. If the best position of all new particles is better than p_g , then p_g is updated.

(8) If the current p_g is unchanged for 15 consecutive generations, then go to Step 9; else, go to Step 3.

(9) Use the BP algorithm to search around p_g for some epochs, if the search result is better than p_g, output the current search result, or else, output p_g.

(10) Output the global optimum p_g.

The parameter ω, in the above ePSO BP algorithm, evolves simultaneously with the weights of the CFLANN during the course of training. The parameter MAXITER1 is generally adjusted to an appropriate value by many repeated experiments, then an adaptive gradient descending method is used to search around the global optimum pg. The BP algorithm based on gradient descending has parameter called learning rate which controls the convergence of the algorithm to an optimal local solution. In practical applications, users usually employed theoretical, empirical, or heuristicmethods to set a good value for this learning rate.

In this paper, we adopted the following strategy for learning rate:

$$\mu = k * \exp\left(-v * \text{epoch}\right), \tag{12}$$

where μ is learning rate, k and v are constants, epoch is a variable that represents iterative times, through adjusting k and v and we can control the reducing speed of learning rate.

ePSO-BP Learning Algorithm for CFLNN

Learning of a CFLNN may be considered as approximating or interpolating a continuous multivariate function φ(X) by an approximating function φW(X). In CFLNN architecture, a set of basis functions φ and a fixed number of weight parameters W are used to represent φW(X). With a specific choice of a set of basis functions ψ, the problem is then to find the weight parameters W that provide the best possible approximation of φ on the set of input-output samples. This can be achieved by iteratively updating W. The interested reader about the detailed theory of FLNN can refer to [21].

Let k training patterns be applied to the FLNN and can be denoted by X_i,Y_i, i = 1, 2, . . . , k and let the weight matrix be W. At the ith instant i = 1, 2, . . . , k, the Ddimensional input pattern and the CFLNN output are given by $X_i = x_{i1}, x_{i2}, \ldots, x_{iD}$, i = 1, 2, . . . , k, and $Y_i = [y_i]$, respectively. Its corresponding target pattern is represented by $Y_i = [y_i]$, i = 1, 2, . . . , k. Hence $\forall i$, $X = [X_1,X_2, \ldots ,X_k]T$.

The augmented matrix of D-dimensional input pattern and the CFLNN output are given by

$$\langle X : \hat{Y} \rangle = \begin{pmatrix} x_{11} & x_{12} & . & x_{1D} & : & \widehat{y_1} \\ x_{21} & x_{22} & . & x_{2D} & : & \widehat{y_2} \\ . & . & . & . & : & . \\ . & . & . & . & : & . \\ x_{k1} & x_{k2} & . & x_{kD} & : & \widehat{y_k} \end{pmatrix}. \tag{13}$$

As the dimension of the input pattern is increased from D to D by a set of basis functions φ, given by φ (Xi) = [Ch1(xi1),Ch2(xi1),. . . ,$Ch_1(xi_2)$,$Ch_2(xi_2)$ . . . ,$Ch_1(xi_D)$,Ch_2 (xi_D) ,. . .]. The k × D dimensional weight matrix is given by W = [W_1,W_2, . . . ,W_k]T, where W_i is the weight vector associated with the ith output and is given by W_i = [wi_1,wi_2,wi_3, . . . ,wi_D]. The ith output of the CFLNN is given by yi(t) = ρ(ΣD j=1ψj(xi j) · wi j) φ i. The error associated with the ith output is given by ei(t) = yi(t)− yi(t). Using the ePSO back-propagation (BP) learning, the weights of the CFLNN can be optimized. The high-level algorithms then can be summarized as follows.

(1) Input the set of given k training patterns.
(2) Choose the set of orthonormal basis functions.
(3) For i = 1 : k
(4) Expand the feature values using the chosen basis functions.
(5) Calculated the weighted sum and then fed to the output node.
(6) error = error + e(k)
(7) End for
(8) If the error is tolerable then stop otherwise go to (9).
(9) Update the weights using ePSO BP learning rules and go to step (3).

EMPIRICAL STUDY

This section is divided into five subsections. Section 4.1 describes the datasets taken from UCI [45] repository of machine learning databases. The parameters required for the proposed method are given in Section 4.2. The performance of the hybrid CFLNN using some of the datasets especially considered by Sierra et al. [21] compared with the model proposed by Sierra et al. in Section 4.3. In Section 4.4, the classification accuracy of hybrid CFLNN is compared with FLNN [8]. In Section 4.5, we compared the performance of hybrid CFLNN with FLNN proposed in [8] using the cost matrix analysis and then compared with the results obtained by StatLog project [46].

Description of the Datasets

The availability of results, with previous evolutionary and constructive algorithms (e.g., Sierra et al. [21], Preshelt [47]) has guided us the selection of the following varied datasets taken from the UCI repository of machine learning databases for the addressed neural network learning. Table 1 presents a summary of the main features of each database that has been used in this study.

Table 1. Summary of the datasets

Dataset	Patterns	Attrib.	Clas.	Patterns in class 1	Patterns in class 2	Patterns in class 3
IRIS	150	4	3	50	50	50
WINE	178	13	3	71	59	48
PIMA	768	8	2	500	268	–
BUPA	345	6	2	145	200	–
HEART	270	13	2	150	120	–
CANCER	699	9	2	458	241	–

Parameters

All the algorithms have some parameters that have to be provided by the user. The parameters for the proposed hybrid CFLNN are listed in Table 2. However, the parameters for other algorithms are set based on the suggestion. The parameters for EFLN were adopted as suggested in [21]. Similarly, the parameters for FLNN were set as suggested in [8].

Table 2. Description of the parameters

Symbol	Purpose of the symbol
N	Size of the swarm
ω	Inertia weight
ω^u	Upper limit of the inertia
ω^l	Lower limit of the inertia
c_1	Cognitive parameter
c_{1i}	Left boundary value of cognitive parameter
c_{1f}	Right boundary value of cognitive parameter
c_2	Social parameter
c_{2i}	Left boundary value of social parameter
c_{2f}	Right boundary value of social parameter
MAXITER	Maximum iterations for stopping an algorithm

The values of the parameters used in this paper are as follows. We set N = 20 *d, where d is the dimension of the problem under consideration. The upper limit (ωu) and lower limit (ωl) of the inertia are set to [0.2, 1.8]. Similarly, the initial and final value of cognitive acceleration coefficients are set to $c1_i = 2.5$ and $c1_f = 0.5$. The initial and final value of social acceleration coefficients are set to $c2_i = 0.5$ and $c2_f = 2.5$. the maximum number of iteration is fixed to MAXITER = 500.

In the case of BP learning, the learning parameter μ and the momentum factor v in hybrid CFLNN was chosen after a several runs to obtain the best results. In the similar manner, the functional expansion of the hybrid CFLNN was carried out.

Hybrid CFLNN versus EFLN

In this subsection, we will compare the results of hybrid CFLNN with the results of EFLN with polynomial basis functions of degree 1, 2, and 3. The choice of the polynomial degree is obviously a key question in FLNN with polynomial basis functions.

However, Sierra et al. [21] have given some guidance to optimize the polynomial degree that can best suit to the architecture. Considering degrees of the polynomial 1, 2, and 3, the possible number of expanded inputs of the above datasets are given in Table 3.

Table 3. Possible number of expanded inputs of degrees ONE, TWO, and THREE

Dataset	Attributes	Degree 1	Degree 2	Degree 3
IRIS	4	5	15	35
WINE	13	14	105	560
PIMA	8	9	45	165
BUPA	6	7	28	84
HEART	13	14	105	560
CANCER	9	10	55	220

For the sake of convenience, we report the results of the experiments conducted on CANCER and BUPA and then compared with the methods EFLN [21]. We partitioned both datasets into three sets: training, validation, and test sets. Both the networks are trained for 1500 epochs (it should be carefully examined) on the training set, and the error on the validation set was measured after every 10 epochs. Training was stopped when a maximum of 1500 epochs had been trained. The test set performance was then computed for that state of the network which had minimum validation set error during the training process. This method called early stopping is a good way to avoid overfitting of the network to the particular training examples used, which would reduce the generalization performance. The average error rate corresponding to HCFLNN, and EFLN w.r.t. training, validation, and testing of CANCER, and BUPA datasets are shown in Table .

Table 4. Comparative results of HCFLNN with EFLN for the cancer and PIMA dataset by considering the average training error (MTre), average validation error (MVe), and average test error (MTe)

Dataset	HCFLNN			EFLN		
	MTre	MVe	MTe	MTre	MVe	MTe
Cancer 1	4.01	2.76	2.57	4.27	1.89	2.09
Cancer 2	3.95	3.97	4.66	4.37	2.96	3.96
cancer 3	4.13	3.51	4.43	3.29	3.01	4.65
BUPA 1	16.26	21.98	22.62	19.07	22.44	23.29
BUPA 2	17.90	24.12	22.35	19.84	18.63	20.37
BUPA 3	15.34	19.92	21.96	16.68	17.81	24.44

Hybrid CFLNN versus FLNN

Here, we will discuss the comparative performance of hybrid CFLNN with FLNN using three datasets IRIS, WINE, and PIMA. In this case, the total set of samples are randomly divided into two equal folds. Each of these two folds are alternatively used either as a training set or as a test set. As the proposed learning method ePSO BP learning is a stochastic algorithm, so 10 independent runs were performed for every single fold. The training results obtained in the case of HCFLNN, averaged over 10 runs, are compared with the single run of FLNN. Similarly, the performance of both classifiers in test set is illustrated herein.

The plotted results clearly indicate that the performance of HCFLNN is competitive with FLNN, whereas in other classification problems like WINE and PIMA, the HCFLNN is showing a clear boundary.

The comparative performance of HCFLNN with FLNN [8] is given in Tables 5 and 6 w.r.t to the different confidence level () of 95% and 98%, respectively.

Table 5. Comparative average performance ofHCFLNN and FLNN [21] based on the confidence level (α = 95%).

Dataset	HCFLNN	FLNN
IRIS train	0.9964 ± 0.0136	0.9866 ± 0.0260
Test set	0.9864 ± 0.0262	0.9866 ± 0.0260
WINE train	0.9842 ± 0.0259	0.9605 ± 0.0405
Test set	0.9708 ± 0.0350	0.9550 ± 0.0431
PIMA train	0.8064 ± 0.0395	0.7877 ± 0.0409
Test set	0.7928 ± 0.0405	0.7812 ± 0.0414

Table 6. Comparative Average Performance of HCFLNN and FLNN [8] based on the Confidence Level (α = 98%).

Dataset	HCFLNN	FLNN
IRIS Train	0.9964 ± 0.0161	0.9866 ± 0.0309
Test set	0.9864 ± 0.0312	0.9866 ± 0.0309
WINE Train	0.9842 ± 0.0308	0.9605 ± 0.0481
Test set	0.9708 ± 0.0416	0.9550 ± 0.0512
PIMA Train	0.8064 ± 0.0470	0.7877 ± 0.0486
Test set	0.7928 ± 0.0482	0.7812 ± 0.0492

Performance of Hybrid CFLNN versus FLNN Based on Heart Data

In this subsection, we will explicitly examine the performance of the HCFLNN model by considering the heart dataset with the use of the 9-fold cross validation methodology. The reason for using 9-fold cross validation is that to compare the performance with the performance of few of the representative algorithms considered in StatLog Project [46]. In 9-fold cross validation, we partition the database into nine subsets (heart1.dat, heart2.dat,…, heart9.dat), where eight subsets are used for training, and the remaining one is used for testing. The process is repeated nine times in such a way that each time a different subset of data is used for testing. Thus, the dataset was randomly segmented into nine subsets with 30 elements each. Each subset contains about 56% of samples from class 1 (without heart disease) and 44% of samples from class 2 (with heart disease).

The procedure makes use of a weight matrix, which is described in Table 7.

Table 7. Weight Matrix of classes to Penalize

Real Classification	Model Classification	
	Class 1	Class 2
Class 1	0	ω_2
Class 2	ω_1	0

The purpose of such a matrix is to penalize wrongly classified samples based on the weight of the penalty of the class. In general, the weight of the penalty for class 2 samples that are classified as class 1 samples is ω_1, while the weight of the penalty for class 1 records that are classified as class 2 samples is ω_2. Therefore, the metric used for measuring the cost of the wrongly classifying patterns in the training and test dataset is given by (14).

$$C_{train} = \frac{(S_1 \times \omega_1 + S_2 \times \omega_2)}{S_{train}},$$
$$C_{test} = \frac{(S_1 \times \omega_1 + S_2 \times \omega_2)}{S_{test}}, \qquad (14)$$

where C_{train} is the cost of the training set; C_{test} is the cost of test set; S_1 and S_2 denote the patterns that are wrongly classified as belong to class 1 and 2, respectively; Strain and Stest are the total number of training and test patterns, respectively.

Table 8 presents the errors and costs of the training and test sets for the FLANN model with a weight value of $\omega_1 = 5$ and $\omega_2 = 1$.

Table 8. Heart disease classification performance of FLANN models

Data subset	Error in training set		Error in test set		C_{train}	C_{test}
	Class 1	Class 2	Class 1	Class 2		
Heart1	13/133	14/107	1/17	1/13	0.35	0.2
Heart2	14/133	12/107	2/17	1/13	0.31	0.23
Heart3	13/134	15/106	4/16	2/14	0.37	0.47
Heart4	13/133	10/107	1/17	4/13	0.26	0.7
Heart5	13/133	16/107	3/17	2/13	0.39	0.43
Heart6	13/134	14/106	6/16	0/14	0.35	0.2
Heart7	15/133	13/107	0/17	3/13	0.33	0.5
Heart8	18/133	17/107	1/17	0/13	0.43	0.03
Heart9	20/134	9/106	2/16	1/14	0.27	0.23
Mean					0.34	0.33

Table 9 illustrates the performance of HCFLANN based on the above definition of cost matrix. The errors in training and test set are explicitly given.

Table 9. Heart disease classification performance of HCFLANN models

Data subset	Error in training set		Error in test set		C_{train}	C_{test}
	Class 1	Class 2	Class 1	Class 2		
Heart1	13/133	14/107	1/17	1/13	0.35	0.2
Heart2	13/133	12/107	1/17	2/13	0.30	0.36
Heart3	12/134	13/106	5/16	1/14	0.32	0.33
Heart4	13/133	10/107	4/17	1/13	0.26	0.30
Heart5	13/133	15/107	3/17	2/13	0.37	0.43
Heart6	13/134	12/106	5/16	1/14	0.30	0.30
Heart7	14/133	13/107	1/17	2/13	0.33	0.37
Heart8	16/133	16/107	0/17	2/13	0.40	0.33
Heart9	18/134	10/106	2/16	1/14	0.28	0.23
Mean					0.32	0.31

The classification results found by the HCFLNN for the heart disease dataset were compared with the results found in the StatLog project [46]. According to [46], comparison consists of calculating the average cost produced by the nine data subsets used for validation. Table 10 presents the average cost for the nine training and test subsets. The result of the HCFLNN is highlighted in bold.

Table 10. Comparative classification performance of HCFLNN, FLNN with the algorithms considered in [46] using the heart disease bench mark datset

Methods	C_{test}	C_{train}
HCFLNN	0.31	0.32
FLNN	0.33	0.34
$HNFB^{-1}$	0.37	0.59
Bayes	0.37	0.35

CONCLUSIONS AND RESEARCH DIRECTIONS

In this paper, we developed a new hybrid Chebyshev functional link neural network (HCFLNN). The hybrid model is constructed using the newly proposed ePSO- back propagation learning algorithm and functional link artificial neural network with the orthogonal Chebyshev polynomials.

The model was designed for the task of classification in data mining. The method was experimentally tested on various benchmark datasets obtained from publicly available UCI repository. The performance of the proposed method demonstrated that the classification task is quite well in WINE and PIMA whereas showing a competitive performance with FLNN in IRIS. Further, we compared this model with EFLN and FLNN, respectively. The comparative results of the developed model is showing a clear edge over FLNN. Compared with EFLN, the proposed method has been shown to yield state-of-the-art recognition error rate for the classification problems such as CANCER and BUPA.

With this encouraging results of HCFLNN, our future research includes: (i) testing the proposed method on a more number of real life bench mark classification problems with highly nonlinearly boundaries, (ii) mapping the input features with other polynomials such as Legendre, Gaussian, Sigmoid, power series, and so forth, for better approximation of the decision boundaries, (iii) the stability and convergence analysis of the proposed method, and (iv) the evolution of optimal FLNN using particle swarm optimization.

The HCFLNN architecture, because of its simple architecture and computational efficiency, may be conveniently employed in other tasks of data mining and knowledge discovery in databases [4, 8] such as clustering, feature selection, feature extraction, association rule mining, regression, and so on. The extra calculation generated by the higher-order units can be eliminated, provided that these polynomial terms are stored in memory instead of being recalculated each time the HCFLNN trained.

REFERENCES

1. J. Ghosh and Y. Shin, "Efficient higher-order neural networks for classification and function approximation," International Journal of Neural Systems, vol. 3, pp. 323–350, 1992.
2. S. Haykin, Neural Networks: A Comprehensive Foundation, Prentice Hall, Englewood Cliffs, NJ, USA, 1999.
3. O. L. Mangasarian and E. W. Wild, "Nonlinear knowledge-based classification," IEEE Transactions on Neural Networks, vol. 19, no. 10, pp. 1826–1832, 2008. View at Publisher · View at Google Scholar · View at PubMed
4. K. Hornik, "Approximation capabilities of multilayer feedforward networks," Neural Networks, vol. 4, no. 2, pp. 251–257, 1991.
5. C. L. Giles and T. Maxwell, "Learning, invariance, and generalization in high-order neural networks," Applied Optics, vol. 26, no. 23, pp. 4972–4978, 1987.
6. Y. H. Pao, Adaptive Pattern Recognition and Neural Network, Addison-Wesley, Reading, Mass, USA, 1989.
7. E. Artyomov and O. Yadid-Pecht, "Modified high-order neural network for invariant pattern recognition," Pattern Recognition Letters, vol. 26, no. 6, pp. 843–851, 2005. View at Publisher · View at Google Scholar
8. B. B. Misra and S. Dehuri, "Functional link neural network for classification task in data mining," Journal of Computer Science, vol. 3, no. 12, pp. 948–955, 2007.
9. D. E. Goldberg, Genetic Algorithms in Search, Optimization and Machine Learning, Morgan Kaufmann, 1989.
10. J. Kennedy and R. Eberhart, "Particle swarm optimization," in Proceedings

of the IEEE International Conference on Neural Networks, pp. 1942–1948, Pisacataway, NJ, USA, December 1995.

11. J. D. Schaffer, D. Whitley, and L. J. Eshelman, "Combinations of genetic algorithms and neural networks: a survey of the state of the art," in Proceedings of International Workshop on Combinations of Genetic Algorithms and Neural Networks, pp. 1–37, 1992.
12. Y. Davidor, "Epistasis variance: suitability of a representation to genetic algorithms," Complex Systems, vol. 4, pp. 368–383, 1990.
13. L. J. Eshelman and J. D. Schaffer, "Real coded genetic algorithms and interval schemata," in Foundation of Genetic Algorithms, L. D. Whitley, Ed., pp. 187–202, Morgan Kaufmann, 1993.
14. H. Muhlenbein and D. Schlierkamp-Voosen, "Predictive models for the breeder genetic algorithm I. Continuous parameters optimization," Evolutionary Computation, vol. 1, no. 1, pp. 24–49, 1993.
15. J. F. Schutte and A. A. Groenwold, "A study of global optimization using particle swarms," Journal of Global Optimization, vol. 31, no. 1, pp. 93–108, 2005. View at Publisher · View at Google Scholar · View at MathSciNet
16. M. M. Ali and P. Kaelo, "Improved particle swarm algorithms for global optimization," Applied Mathematics and Computation, vol. 196, no. 2, pp. 578–593, 2008. View at Publisher · View at Google Scholar
17. J. Yu, S. Wang, and L. Xi, "Evolving artificial neural networks using an improved PSO and DPSO," Neurocomputing, vol. 71, no. 4–6, pp. 1054–1060, 2008. View at Publisher · View at Google Scholar
18. Y. Da and X. R. Ge, "An improved PSO-based ANN with simulated annealing technique," Neurocomputing, vol. 63, pp. 527–533, 2005. View at Publisher · View at Google Scholar
19. M. S. Klassen, Y. H. Pao, and V. Chen, "Characteristics of the functional link net: a higher order delta rule net," in Proceedings of the 2nd Annual International Conference on Neural Networks, vol. 1, pp. 507–513, San Diago, Calif, USA, 1988.
20. Y. H. Pao and Y. Takefuji, "Functional-link net computing: theory, system architecture, and functionalities," Computer, vol. 25, no. 5, pp. 76–79, 1992. View at Publisher · View at Google Scholar
21. A. Sierra, J. A. Macías, and F. Corbacho, "Evolution of functional link networks," IEEE Transactions on Evolutionary Computation, vol. 5, no. 1, pp. 54–65, 2001. View at Publisher · View at Google Scholar
22. B. Haring and J. N. Kok, "Finding functional links for neural networks by evolutionary computation," in Proceedings of the 5th Belgian-Dutch Conference on Machine Learning (BENELEARN '95), T. Van de Merckt, et al., Ed., pp. 71–78, Brussels, Belgium, 1995.
23. J. C. Patra and R. N. Pal, "A functional link artificial neural network for adaptive channel equalization," Signal Processing, vol. 43, no. 2, pp. 181–195, 1995.

24. S. Haring, J. N. Kok, and M. C. van Wezel, "Feature selection for neural networks through functional links found by evolutionary computation," in Proceedings of the 2nd International Symposium on Advances in Intelligent Data Analysis, Reasoning about Data, X. Liu, et al., Ed., vol. 1280 of Lecture Notes in Computer Science, pp. 199–210, 1997.

25. P. K. Dash, A. C. Liew, and H. P. Satpathy, "A functional-link-neural network for short-term electric load forecasting," Journal of Intelligent and Fuzzy Systems, vol. 7, no. 3, pp. 209–221, 1999.

26. D. A. Panagiotopoulos, R. W. Newcomb, and S. K. Singh, "Planning with a functional neural-network architecture," IEEE Transactions on Neural Networks, vol. 10, no. 1, pp. 115–127, 1999.

27. J. C. Patra, R. N. Pal, B. N. Chatterji, and G. Panda, "Identification of nonlinear dynamic systems using functional link artificial neural networks," IEEE Transactions on Systems, Man, and Cybernetics, Part B, vol. 29, no. 2, pp. 254–262, 1999. View at Publisher · View at Google Scholar · View at PubMed

28. J. C. Patra and A. van den Bos, "Modeling of an intelligent pressure sensor using functional link artificial neural networks," ISA Transactions, vol. 39, no. 1, pp. 15–27, 2000.

29. J. C. Patra and A. C. Kot, "Nonlinear dynamic system identification using Chebyshev functional link artificial neural networks," IEEE Transactions on Systems, Man, and Cybernetics, Part B, vol. 32, no. 4, pp. 505–511, 2002. View at Publisher · View at Google Scholar · View at PubMed

30. S. N. Singh and K. N. Srivastava, "Degree of insecurity estimation in a power system using functional link neural network," European Transactions on Electrical Power, vol. 12, no. 5, pp. 353–358, 2002. View at Publisher · View at Google Scholar

31. T. Marcu and B. Koppen-Seliger, "Dynamic functional link neural networks genetically evolved applied to system identification," in Proceedings of European Symposium on Artificial Neural Networks (ESANN '04), pp. 115–120, Bruges, Belgium, 2004.

32. B. Majhi and H. Shalabi, "An improved scheme for digital watermarking using functional link artificial neural network," Journal of Computer Science, vol. 1, no. 2, pp. 169–174, 2005.

33. I. A. Abu-Mahfouz, "A comparative study of three artificial neural networks for the detection and classification of gear faults," International Journal of General Systems, vol. 34, no. 3, pp. 261–277, 2005. View at Publisher · View at Google Scholar

34. S. Purwar, I. N. Kar, and A. N. Jha, "On-line system identification of complex systems using Chebyshev neural networks," Applied Soft Computing Journal, vol. 7, no. 1, pp. 364–372, 2007. View at Publisher · View at Google Scholar

35. W. D. Weng, C. S. Yang, and R. C. Lin, "A channel equalizer using reduced decision feedback Chebyshev functional link artificial neural networks," Information Sciences, vol. 177, no. 13, pp. 2642–2654, 2007. View at Publisher

· View at Google Scholar

36. D. Krishnaiah, D. M. R. Prasad, A. Bono, P. M. Pandiyan, and R. Sarbatly, "Application of ultrasonic waves coupled with functional link neural network for estimation of carrageenan concentration," International Journal of Physical Sciences, vol. 3, no. 4, pp. 90-96, 2008.
37. J. C. Patra, G. Chakraborty, and S. Mukhopadhyay, "Functional link neural network-based intelligent sensors for harsh environments," Sensors & Transducers Journal, vol. 90, pp. 209-220, 2008.
38. S. Dehuri, B. B. Mishra, and S.-B. Cho, "Genetic feature selection for optimal functional link artificial neural network in classification," in Proceedings of the 9th International Conference on Intelligent Data Engineering and Automated Learning (IDEAL '08), C. Fyfe, et al., Ed., vol. 5326 of Lecture Notes in Computer Science, pp. 156-163, 2008. View at Publisher · View at Google Scholar
39. Y. Shi and R. Eberhart, "A modified particle swarm optimizer," in Proceedings of the IEEE International Conference on Evolutionary Computation (ICEC '98), pp. 69-73, IEEE Press, Pisacataway, NJ, USA, May 1998.
40. Y. Shi and R. C. Eberhart, "Parameter selection in particle swarm optimization," in Evolutionary Programming VII, vol. 1447 of Lecture Notes in Computer Science, pp. 591-600, Springer, Berlin, Germany, 1998.
41. P. C. Fourie and A. A. Groenwold, "The particle swarm optimization algorithm in size and shape optimization," Structural and Multidisciplinary Optimization, vol. 23, no. 4, pp. 259-267, 2002. View at Publisher · View at Google Scholar
42. M. Clerc and J. Kennedy, "The particle swarm-explosion, stability, and convergence in a multidimensional complex space," IEEE Transactions on Evolutionary Computation, vol. 6, no. 1, pp. 58-73, 2002. View at Publisher · View at Google Scholar
43. J. R. Zhang, J. Zhang, T. M. Lok, and M. R. Lyu, "A hybrid particle swarm optimization-back-propagation algorithm for feedforward neural network training," Applied Mathematics and Computation, vol. 185, no. 2, pp. 1026-1037, 2007. View at Publisher · View at Google Scholar
44. A. Ratnaweera, S. K. Halgamuge, and H. C. Watson, "Self-organizing hierarchical particle swarm optimizer with time-varying acceleration coefficients," IEEE Transactions on Evolutionary Computation, vol. 8, no. 3, pp. 240-255, 2004. View at Publisher · View at Google Scholar
45. C. L. Blake and C. J. Merz, "UCI repository of machine learning databases," http://www.ics.uci.edu/ mlearn/MLRepository.html.
46. R. P. Lippmann, "An introduction to computing with neural networks," IEEE ASSP Magazine, vol. 4, no. 2, pp. 4-22, 1987.
47. L. Preshelt, "Proben1-a set of neural network benchmark problems and benchmarking rules," Tech. Rep. 21/94, Universitat Karlsruhe, Karlsruhe, Germany, 1994.

Chapter 8

ACTIVATION DETECTION ON FMRI TIME SERIES USING HIDDEN MARKOV MODEL

Rong Duan[1] and Hong Man[2]

[1] AT&T Labs, Florham Park, NJ 07932, USA

[2] Department of Electrical and Computer Engineering, Stevens Institute of Technology, Hoboken, NJ 07030, USA

ABSTRACT

This paper introduces two unsupervised learning methods for analyzing functional magnetic resonance imaging (fMRI) data based on hidden Markov model (HMM). HMM approach is focused on capturing the first-order statistical evolution among the samples of a voxel time series, and it can provide a complimentary perspective of the BOLD signals. Two-state HMM is created for each voxel, and the model parameters are estimated from the voxel time series and the stimulus paradigm. Two different activation detection methods are presented in this paper. The first method is based on the likelihood and likelihood-ratio test, in which an additional Gaussian model is used to enhance the contrast of the HMM likelihood map. The second method is based on certain distance measures between the two state distributions, in which the most likely HMM state sequence is estimated through the Viterbi algorithm. The distance between the on-state and off-state distributions is measured either through a t-test, or using the Kullback-Leibler distance (KLD). Experimental results on both normal subject and brain tumor subject are presented. HMM approach appears to be more robust in detecting the supplemental active voxels comparing with SPM, especially for brain tumor subject.

INTRODUCTION

Functional magnetic resonance imaging (fMRI) is a well-established technique to monitor brain activities in the field of cognitive neuroscience. The temporal behavior of each fMRI voxel reflects the variations in the concentration of oxyhemoglobin and deoxyhemoglobin, measured through blood oxygen level-dependent (BOLD) contrast. BOLD signal is generally considered as an indirect indicator for brain activities, because neural activations may increase blood flow in certain regions of the brain.

Characteristics of fMRI Data

fMRI data are collected as a time series of 3 D images. Each point in the 3 D image volume is called a voxel. fMRI data have four important characteristics: (1) large data volume; (2) relatively low SNR; (3) hemodynamic delay and dispersion; (4) fractal properties. Typically, one fMRI data set includes over 1 0 0 -K voxels from a whole brain scan and therefore has 1 0 0 -K time series. The observed time sequences are combinations of different types of signals, such as task-related, function-related, and transiently task-related (different kinds of transiently task-related signals coming from different regions of brain). These are the signals that convey brain activation information. There are also many types of noises, which can be physiology-related, motion-related, and scanning-related. The signal to noise ratio (SNR) in typical fMRI time series can be quite low, for example, around 0 . 2 to 0 . 5 . For different regions and different trails, the SNR level also varies significantly. Such noise nature causes major difficulty in signal analysis. Hemodynamic delay and dispersion further increase the complexity of fMRI signal structure. Special efforts have been made to construct flexible hemodynamic response function (HRF) which can model the hemodynamic delay and dispersion through various regions and different subjects [1, 2]. fMRI data also have fractal properties, which means that a class of objects may have certain interesting properties in common. In other words, fMRI data are approximately scale invariant or scale free.

Methodology of Analyzing fMRI Data

Two areas of fMRI-based neural systems study have attracted lots of attention over the past two decades: functional activity detection and functional connectivity detection. Functional activity detection aims to locate the spatial areas that are associated with certain psychological tasks, commonly specified by a predefined paradigm. Functional connectivity detection focuses on finding spatially separated areas that have high temporal correlations [3]. Generally, functional connectivity detection is conducted under the resting-state condition. The differences in biophysical motivations and experiment designs of these two studies are reflected in their methodologies. Functional activity detection compares the temporal series of each voxel with the excitation paradigm and functional connectivity detection compares the voxel timeseries with other series in a predefined spatial region, that is, Region of Interesting (ROI), or "seed" region. Functional activity detection is more on the temporal correlation and functional connectivity detection is more on spatial correlation. Even though the two areas have some differences, they share many common statistical modelling strategies. Both of them attempt to build models to abstract the spatial and temporal relations from the observed fMRI data. To choose a model that can capture the properties of the time series accurately and efficiently is essential in both study areas.

A large number of methods have been proposed to analyze fMRI data. Most of them can be characterized into one of these two categories: modelling based approach and data driven approach. Reference [4] provided a detailed review. Even though the authors claimed the methodologies as functional connectivity detection, certain amount of the reviewed methods were commonly used in functional activity detection study too. This paper focuses on constructing a model to extract voxel temporal characteristics and test the voxel activities using functional activity detection as example. All the models referred following are for this task if no further clarification.

An established software called statistical parametric map (SPM) is a typical functional activity detection modelling package based on general linear model (GLM) [5], general linear model transforms a voxel time series into a space spanned by a set of basis vectors defined in the design matrix. These basis vectors include a set of paradigm waveforms convolved with hemodynamic response function (HRF), as well as several low-frequency DCT bases. The residual errors of this linear transform is modelled as Gaussian pdf. The key component of this method is how to constitute the design-matrix which can accurately model the brain activation effects and separate noises. Using GLM to analyze fMRI data has following intrinsic assumptions:

- the activation patterns are spatially distributed in the same way for all subjects,
- the response between input stimulation and brain response is linear,
- the HRF function is the same for every voxel,
- the time series observation has a known Gaussian distribution,
- the variance and covariance between repeated measurements are invariant,
- the time courses of different factors affecting the variance of fMRI signals can be reliably estimated in advance,
- the signals at different voxels are independent, and
- the intensity distribution of background (nonnative areas) is known whereas the distribution of active areas is not known.

Reference [6] substituted paradigm with the average temporal series of ROI as seed and applied SPM on functional connectivity detection. And the most recent release of SPM incorporates dynamic causal modeling to infer the interregional coupling, but it is designed more on EEG and MEG data [7].

There are some other methods which can be considered as special cases of GLM. For example, direct subtraction method subtracts the average of "off" period from the average of "on" period. Voxels with significant difference will then be identified as active. Students't-test can be used to measure the difference in the means by the standard deviations in "off" and "on" periods. The larger the t-value is, the larger the "on-off" difference is, and the more active the voxel is. Correlation coefficient is another special case of GLM. It measures the correlation coefficient between a reference function waveform and each voxel temporal signal waveform. Voxels with large correlation coefficient are considered to be connected. If the reference function waveform is defined by paradigm [8], it is functional activity detection, and if the reference function waveform is defined by some seed time course, it is functional connectivity detection [9].

There exist some problems in GLM-based methods. For example, GLM assumes one HRF function for all voxels. The BOLD signal is only an indirect indicator of neural activity, and many no neural changes in the body could also influence the BOLD signal. Different brain areas may have different hemodynamic responses, which would not be accurately reflected by the general linear model. Also, GLM method typically requires grouping or averaging data over several task/control blocks, which reduces sensitivity for detecting transient task-related changes, and make it insensitive to significant changes not consistently time-synched to the task block design. Low SNR makes it possible for no task-relevant components overshadow task-relevant components and further reduces the sensitivity and specificity. GLM only considers the time series and ignores relationships between voxels, hindering the detection of brain regions acting as functional units during the experiment. Another problem is that the GLM method does not extract the intrinsic structure of the data, which may significantly weaken its effectiveness when the a priori of fMRI signal in response to the experimental events is not known or may not be constant across all voxels.

Besides GLM-based methods, a few methods have been proposed to improve the accuracy of modeling fMRI temporal signals. Reference [10] introduced a Bayesian modeling method which used a two-state HMM to infer an optimal state sequence through Markov Chain Monte Carlo sampling. The method assumed the observation is a linear combination of a two-state HMM, which infer hidden psychological states, plus constant and trend. The model is designed as the combination of offset, linear trend and a set of two-state

HMMs state sequences start at different time points. MCMC is used to estimate the optimal state sequence for each voxel. This method is good in interpreting the dynamics in each voxel, but the computing complexity is big concern as mentioned by the authors, and also the totally paradigm-free approach might introduce noise that irrelevant with the experiment design. Reference [11] applied state-space model and Kalman filter to model the baseline and stimulus effect without any parametric constrain. Reference [12] employed multiple reference functions with 100 ms shift to find the highest correlation coefficient reference function for specific voxels, which avoids the common practice of using a single-reference function for all voxels. Reference [13] proposed Gaussian mixture models to describe the mutually exclusive fMRI time sequence. Reference [14] introduced an unsupervised learning method based on hidden semi-Markov event sequence models (HSMESMs) method which had the advantage of explicitly modeling the state occupancy duration. The method decomposed an observation into true positive events, false positive events, and missing observations. The "off-on" paradigm transitions were modeled as left to right HMM true positive states, and the other periods were considered as semi-Markov false positive states. The likelihood of HSMESM was calculated iteratively to detect activity base on predefined threshold. Reference [15] used first-order Markov chain to estimate the time series, t-test, and mutual information to detect the actions. All these methods are essentially two-stage approach. The temporal property is modeled at each voxel independently and then spatial modeling is performed based on the summarized statistics from temporal analysis. Fully Bayesian spatiotemporal modeling [16] considered spatial and temporal information together. This method decomposed the observation data into spatiotemporal signal and noise, and space-time simultaneously specified autoregressive model (STSAR) was employed to construct noise model. Half-cosine HRF model and activation height model were used to construct fMRI signal models.

Granger causality analysis [17] and dynamic causal modeling [18] are two popular methods in functional connectivity detection in recent years. A series comments and controversies [19–22] have been dedicated to comparing these two methods on model selection, causality, and deconvolution from biophysiological view. Reference [23] criticized dynamic causal modeling from computation complexity and model validation from mathematical perspective. The advantage of these two methods are that they consider the spatial and temporal information at the same time, but the disadvantage is the model complexity.

All the modelling-based approaches mentioned above are either too simple to capture the temporal or spatial dynamics for different voxels and subjects, or too complicated to estimate parameters accurately and inference easily.

In addition to these modeling-based methods, there are also data driven methods in analyzing fMRI data. One popular example of this approach is independent component analysis (ICA). ICA decomposes a 4D fMRI data volume (3D spatial and 1D temporal) into a set of maximum temporal or spatial independent components by minimizing the mutual information between these components. ICA does not require the knowledge of stimulus or paradigm in data decomposition, and similar voxel activation patterns will usually appear in the same component. ICA is also called blind source separation, because it does not need prior knowledge, and it is able to identify "transient task related" components that could not be easily identified by the paradigm. The first application of ICA in fMRI data was the spatial ICA (sICA) [24]. Temporal ICA (tICA) was introduced later by [25]. Reference [26] compared the sICA with tICA and reported that the beneficial of each method depends on the independence of the underlying spatial or temporal signal. sICA maximizes independence spatially and the corresponding temporal information might be highly correlated, and vice versa for tICA. To consider the mutual independence between space and time simultaneously, [27] proposed a spatiotemporal independent component analysis (stICA). Extended from entropy-based one-dimension ICA decomposition introduced in [28], the authors embedded the spatial and temporal components at the same time and also incorporated the spatial skewed probability density function to replace the kurtosis and symmetric probability density function in decomposing the independent signals. As pointed out in [29], the disadvantages of the Infomax and entropy-based stICA algorithms used in [27] are that the number of parameters needed to be estimated is large, the local minima and sensitive to noise characteristics of the gradient descent optimization methods. To improve the stability, robustness, and simplify the computing complexity, [29] adopted the generalized eigenvalue decomposition and joint diagonalization on both spatial and temporal autocorrelation to achieve spatial and temporal independent signals simultaneously. ICA methods have showed promising results in fMRI analysis, but similar as all other data-driven methods, it is hard to interpret the output and it usually requires special knowledge and human intervention. Also, ICA does not specify which component, among many output components, is the activation component, and there is no statistical confidence level of each components extracted.

Clustering is another well-developed data driven approach in brain activity and connectivity detection. It has been used to identify regions with similar patterns of activations. Common clustering algorithms include hierarchical clustering, crisp clustering, K-means, self-organizing maps (SOM), and fussy clustering. The major drawback of most clustering methods is that they make assumptions about cluster shapes and sizes, which may deviate in observed data structures. The optimization techniques used in clustering may also result in local maxima and instable results. In addition, the number of clusters is frequently determined heuristically and randomly initialized, which makes the output inconsistent with each trial.

In this paper, we propose a simple dynamic state space model, which attempts to model the voxel time series as a random process driven by the experimental paradigm or some ROI area seed series. For a given voxel, its behavior is described by a two-state hidden Markov model with certain state distributions and state transitions. The HMM parameters are estimated from the prior statistics of the paradigm as well as from the testing time series. Two methods are introduced to detect the voxel activation based on the estimated HMM. The first method calculates the likelihood of each time series, given its HMM, and forms a likelihood map for all the voxels reside in a fMRI slice. A simple Gaussian model is also used to improve the contrast of this likelihood map. The second method uses the t-test or the Kullback-Leibler distance (KLD) to measure the distance between the on-state distribution and the off-state distribution. These distributions are estimated based on the most likely HMM state sequence, which is calculated through a Viterbi algorithm. The contribution of the method is that it unifies the robustness, stability, and reliability under the same framework in estimating paradigm driven fMRI study. First, it incorporates the dynamic characteristics of fMRI time series by adapting 2 -state HMM model, which is robust in detecting active voxels with different delay and dispersion behaviors. Second, the proposed method utilizes paradigm prior knowledge in parameter estimation, which is not only to simplify the computing compared with the approach in [10], but also to improve the stability and reliability of the output due to the stability of paradigm.

The rest of this paper is organized as follows. In Section 2, we introduce the two-state hidden Markov model approach for fMRI data. In Section 3, we discuss activation detection methods base on the estimated HMM. In Section 4, we present the experimental results on two sets of fMRI data, one is normal subject and the other is brain tumor subject, and compare the results with GLM-based statistical parametric mapping package (SPM) [5].

HIDDEN MARKOV MODEL FOR FMRI TIME SERIES

Hidden Markov Model

HMM is a very efficient stochastic method in modeling sequential data of which the distribution patterns tend to cluster and alternate among different clusters [30]. A hidden Markov model consists of a finite set of states. In a traditional Markov chain, the state is directly visible to the observer, and the state transition probabilities are the only parameters. In an HMM, only the observations influenced by the state are visible. Each of the hidden state is associated with a probability distribution. Transitions among the states are measured by transition probabilities. The most common first-order HMM implies that the state at any given time depends only on the state at the previous time step.

An HMM can be described by the following elements [31]: (1) a set of observations $O\{T\}$, where T is the number of time samples; (2) a set of states $Q\{N\}$, where N is the number of states; (3) a state-transition probability distribution $A = \{a_{ij}\}$, where $a_{ij} = P[q_t + 1 = S_j | q_t = S_i]$, $1 \le i, j \le N$; (4) observation probability distribution for each state $B = \{ b j (x) \}$, where $b j (x) = P [o t = x \mid q t = S j] , 1 \leq j \leq N$, $x \in \Re$ is a possible observation value; (5) an initial state distribution $\pi = \{ \pi j \}$, where $\pi j = P [q 1 = S j] , 1 \leq j \leq N$.

An HMM is therefore denoted by $\lambda = \{ \ , B , \pi \}$. We further model each state distribution as a Gaussian pdf:

$$P\left[O_t = x \mid q_t = S_j\right] = \frac{1}{\sigma_j\sqrt{2\pi}} e^{-(x-\mu_j)^2/(2\sigma_j^2)}, \quad j \in \{0,1\}. \tag{1}$$

Let $Q = q_1, q_2, \ldots, q_T$ be a possible state sequence and assume that the observation samples are independent, the likelihood of an observed sequence given this HMM can be calculated as:

$$\begin{aligned} P(O \mid \lambda) &= \sum_Q P(O \mid Q, \lambda) P(Q \mid \lambda) \\ &= \sum_Q \pi_{q_1} b_{q_1}(o_1) a_{q_1 q_2} b_{q_2}(o_2) \cdots a_{q_{T-1} q_T} b_{q_T}(o_T). \end{aligned} \tag{2}$$

Given the observation O and the HMM, the most likely state sequence $Q = \{ q_1, q_2, \ldots, q_T \}$, which maximizes the likelihood $P(Q \mid O, \lambda)$, can be calculated through the Viterbi algorithm [36]. The Viterbi path score function is defined as:

$$\delta_t(i) = \max_{q_1, q_2, \ldots, q_{t-1}} P[q_1 q_2 \cdots q_t = i, o_1 o_2 \cdots o_t \mid \lambda], \tag{3}$$

where $\delta t (i)$ is the highest probable path ending in state i at time t. The induction can be expressed as:

$$\delta_{t+1}(j) = \max_{1 \leq i \leq N} \left[\delta_t(i) a_{ij}\right] b_j(o_{t+1}). \tag{4}$$

In an application of HMM, multiple HMMs are trained by different groups of labeled data. The HMM parameters are estimated based on these training data. The test data will be assigned to the one which has the maximum likelihood.

Brain Activation Detection

HMM Likelihood Methods

In our unsupervised learning methods, HMM parameters are estimated directly from the experimental paradigm or the voxel time series under examination. This is different from conventional HMM applications where HMM parameters are usually estimated from some training data. The attempt of avoiding training process is motivated by the fact that the true activation behavior varies from voxel to voxel and from patient to patient. Therefore, it is not advisable to use the parameters from certain set of voxels to characterize other voxels.

Since the simple block paradigm has only two levels, "on, off," in this work we let the number of state $N = 2$, that is, on-state S_1 and off-state S_0.

Because of the first-order Markov assumption, that is, $P(q_t = j \mid q_{t-1} = i, q_{t-2} = k, \ldots) = P(q_t = j \mid q_{t-1} = i)$, the distribution of a state duration is exponential, and the expected value of a state duration can be expressed as:

$$\bar{d}_i = \frac{1}{1 - a_{ii}}. \qquad (5)$$

Given an experimental paradigm, let the length (i.e., time samples) of the ON period be L_{on}, and the length of off period be L_{off}, the transition matrix A can be estimated as $a_{00} = 1/(1 - L_{off})$, $a_{01} = 1 - a_{00}$, $a_{11} = 1/(1 - L_{on})$, $a_{10} = 1 - a_{11}$.

The parameters in B can be estimated from the voxel time series . Assuming that the time samples are normalized, let p_{on} denote the paradigm ON periods, and *p o f f* denote the paradigm off periods, the off-state *S* 0 Gaussian parameters are

$$\mu_0 = \frac{1}{|p_{\text{off}}|} \sum_{t \in p_{\text{off}}} o_t, \qquad \sigma_0 = \sqrt{\frac{1}{|p_{\text{off}}|} \sum_{t \in p_{\text{off}}} (o_t - \mu_0)^2}, \quad (6)$$

and the on-state *S* 1 Gaussian parameters are

$$\mu_1 = \frac{1}{|p_{\text{on}}|} \sum_{t \in p_{\text{on}}} o_t, \qquad \sigma_1 = \sqrt{\frac{1}{|p_{\text{on}}|} \sum_{t \in p_{\text{on}}} (o_t - \mu_1)^2}, \quad (7)$$

where |poff | is the total number of time samples in the off periods, and |pon| is the total number of time samples in the ON periods.

Because the paradigm always starts at the off state, the parameters in π are set as π 0 = 1 and π 1 = 0 .

Given a 2-state HMM as specified, if an observation sequence does have two distinguishable states in consistence with the paradigm states, the resulting { 0 , σ 0 } will be clearly different from { μ 1 , σ 1 } , and the likelihood of such sequence given this model will be relatively high. If an observation sequence does not have such clear 2-state characteristic, the corresponding state transition will be somehow random and will not fit well with the specified *A* matrix. In such situation, the likelihood of this sequence will be relatively low. Therefore, the value of voxel sequence likelihood can provide an indication about the activation of this voxel. A likelihood test on an fMRI slice will be able to produce a likelihood map with each point representing the likelihood of a voxel on this slice.

[1]The Delphi technique consists in reaching consensus of experts by requesting ideas about relevant project risks anonymously using questionnaires. The results are summarized and recirculated to the experts for further analysis. This approach reduces bias in the data and restricts a person from having excessive weight on the outcome.

[2]Other techniques for risk assessment can be consulted in [29, p. 41-46]

To enhance the contrast of this likelihood map, we introduce a simple Gaussian model for the $p\ o\ f\ f$ samples. This model is consistent with the $S\ 0$ state distribution in the 2-state HMM. The likelihood of the entire sequence is calculated based on this model. The expectation is that if a voxel is non-active, its distribution in $p\ o\ f\ f$ periods and $p\ o\ n$ periods should be similar, and therefore the likelihood to this model should be relatively high; on the other hand, if the voxel is active, its distribution in $p\ o\ n$ periods will be quite different from the distribution in $p\ o\ f\ f$ periods, and therefore the likelihood of the whole sequence on this model will be relatively low. The substraction of the HMM log likelihood map and the Gaussian log likelihood map is equivalent to a general likelihood ratio test, and it provides an activation map with enhanced contrast.

State Distribution Distance Methods

If a voxel is active, its fMRI time series can be partitioned into segments associated with two states, and each state can be described by a distribution. The assumption is that if the on-state distribution is significantly different from the off-state distribution, we have high confidence to declare a voxel as active, and vice versa. Therefore, the second method we are investigating attempts to measure the distance between the presumed on-state and off-state distributions.

There are many techniques available for measuring the distance of two distributions. We study two of such measures in this work, one is the t-test, and the other is the Kullback-Leibler divergence. Both on-state and off-state distributions are models as simple Gaussian pdfs.

Given the Gaussian parameters, $\{\ 0\ ,\ \sigma\ 0\ \}$ and $\{\ \mu\ 1\ ,\ \sigma\ 1\ \}$, the t-test calculates the difference of two mean values corrected by their variance values

$$t = \frac{\mu_1 - \mu_0}{\sqrt{(\sigma_{\text{on}}^2/|p_{\text{on}}|) + \left(\sigma_{\text{off}}^2/|p_{\text{off}}|\right)}}. \tag{8}$$

A t-map is produced after the t-test is applied to all the voxles on an fMRI slice. High t values in the map usually indicate active voxles.

The Kullback-Leibler divergence [37] is frequently used as a distance measure for two probability densities, although in theory it is not a true distance measure because it is not symmetric. In general it is defined in the form of "relative entropy,"

$$D\left(p_i(x) \| p_j(x)\right) = -\int p_i(x) \log \frac{p_j(x)}{p_i(x)} dx. \tag{9}$$

For two Gaussian pdfs, a close form expression for KLD is available:

$$D\left(p_i(\cdot;\mu_i,\sigma_i) \| p_j\left(\cdot;\mu_j,\sigma_j\right)\right) = \frac{1}{2}\left[\log\left(\frac{\sigma_j^2}{\sigma_i^2}\right) - 1 + \frac{\sigma_i^2}{\sigma_j^2} + \frac{\left(\mu_i - \mu_j\right)^2}{\sigma_j^2}\right]. \tag{10}$$

These are well-established methods. However a critical issue in fMRI analysis is how to estimate the correct on-state and off-state distributions. A simple assumption is to let all time samples in the paradigm ON periods be the on-state samples and let all samples in the paradigm off periods be the off-state samples. We refer to this approach as the "paradigm state" approach. The SPM takes a similar approach, except that the block paradigm is convolved with an HRF, which is normally a low-pass filter characterizing the nature voxel response to a stimulus. The μ 0 and μ 1 are obtained by projecting the time series to the HRF convolved paradigm waveform, and the σ 0 and σ 1 are set to be the same to model the residual error between the voxel time series and the weighted paradigm waveform.

We take a different approach by applying the 2-state HMM on each voxel series and calculate the most likely state sequence using the Viterbi algorithm. We refer to this approach as the "Viterbi path" approach. Then the on-state and off-state statistics are calculated according to the optimal state assignment for each time sample. The

$\{0, \sigma 0\}$ are obtained from all samples belonging to the off-state, and $\{\mu 1, \sigma 1\}$ are obtained from all samples belonging to the on-state.

EXPERIMENTAL RESULTS

Normal Subject

The data set is collected from a test with self-paced bilateral sequential thumb-to-digits opposition task. The task paradigm consists of a 32 sec baseline followed by 4 cycles of 30 sec ON and 30 sec OFF. The time series is sampled at 0.25 Hz, which produces 68 time samples for each voxel. The first four samples are ignored during analysis because of initial unstable measurement. The BOLD image is acquired in a 1.5 T GE echo speed horizon scanner with the following parameters: TR/TE = 4000/60, FOV = 24 cm, 64×64 matrix, slice thickness 5 mm without gap, and 28 slices to cover the entire brain. Following acquisition of the functional data (with a resolution of $3.75 \times 3.75 \times 5\ mm^3$), a set of 3 mm slice thickness, high resolution (256×256 matrix size), gadolinium-enhanced images are also obtained according to clinical imaging protocol. The data is aligned to remove the limited motion between data sets then smoothed with a Gaussian kernel before further processing [5]. We further normalize each time series with the mean and variance of its paradigm off period. In order to compensate DC drifting in many voxels, each time series is partitioned into four equal-length segments, and normalization is performed separately on each of these segments. In the reported results, only one fMRI transverse slice is shown.

We first compare three methods based on two different distribution distance measures. These include the SPM with a t-test or an f-test, and our HMM Viterbi path method with a t-test or a KLD measure. The results are shown in Figure 1. From these results we can see that the primary motor and secondary motor areas are effectively highlighted by all these methods. We also have the following observations: (1) the HMM Viterbi path methods produce more compact and clearly highlighted regions, which indicates that Viterbi path estimation is more accurate than paradigm state estimation; (2) the HMM Viterbi path t-test method performs similarly to SPM t-test with some minor differences, mostly along the outer frontal regions; (3) the KLD methods have resemblance to SPM F-test in the sense that their results are pure positive, while t-test results are signed.

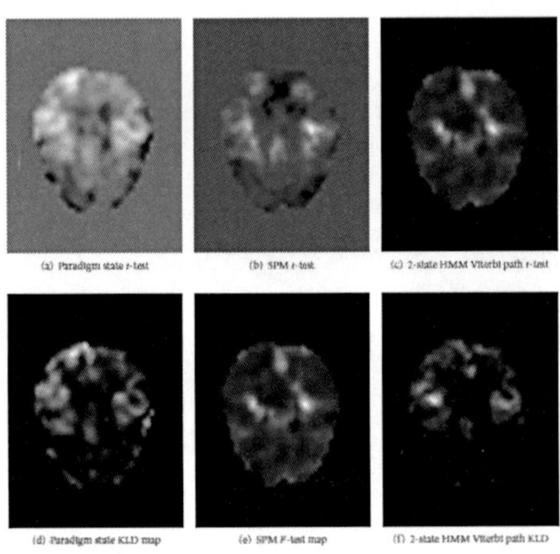

Figure 1: (a), (b), and (c) are t-test map for paradigm-defined state, SPM method, and 2-state HMM Viterbi path map respectively; (d), (e), and (f) are KLD map for paradigm defined state, SPM F-test, and 2-state HMM Viterbi path KLD map, respectively. The HMM Viterbi path methods (c) and (f) produce more compact and clearly highlighted regions than paradigm state estimation (a) and (d); HMM Viterbi path methods perform similarly to SPM with some minor differences.

To test the effectiveness of our HMM likelihood ratio method, we compare its result with an SPM t-test result. In Figure 2, (a) shows the two-state HMM log-likelihood map; (b) shows the Gaussian log-likelihood map of the same slice; (c) shows the log-likelihood ratio test map. It can be seen that HMM log-likelihood map is almost the reverse of Gaussian log-likelihood map, which validates our expectation in Section 2.2.1. (c) is similar to (a), yet with enhanced contrast. This result resembles the SPM t-test result, although their magnitude scales are quite different.

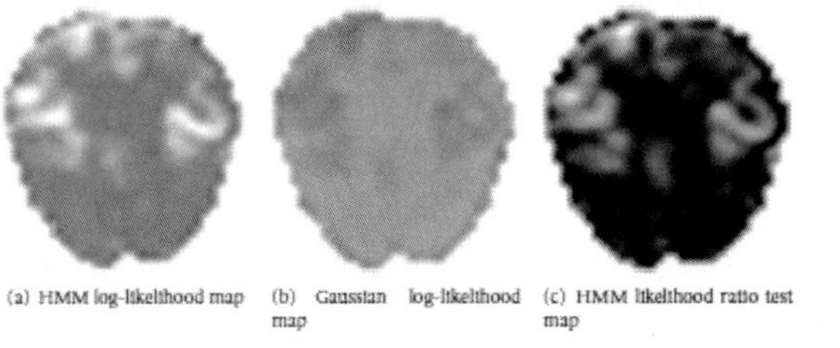

(a) HMM log-likelihood map (b) Gaussian log-likelihood map (c) HMM likelihood ratio test map

Figure 2: (a) HMM log-likelihood map—2-state HMM model is applied to all voxels. The active voxels with obvious 2-state on/off patterns will have relative high likelihood given this model; (b) Gaussian log-likelihood map—"off"-state Gaussian model is applied to all voxels. The nonactive voxels with obvious 2-state on/off patterns will have relative high likelihood given this model; (c) HMM likelihood ratio test map—subtraction of HMM log-likelihood map and Gaussian log-likelihood map equivalent to general likelihood ration test, and it enhances the contrast for activation map.

We examine several active voxels detected by SPM and by HMM likelihood ratio test. In Figure 3, the SPM t-map and the HMM log likelihood ratio map are thresholded at certain level to yield similar number of active voxels. The corresponding voxel time series marked with "A," "B," "C," and "D" are shown in Figure 4. The voxels "A" and "B" can be detected by both SPM and HMM likelihood ratio test. The voxels "C" and "D" are only highlighted by the HMM likelihood ratio test.

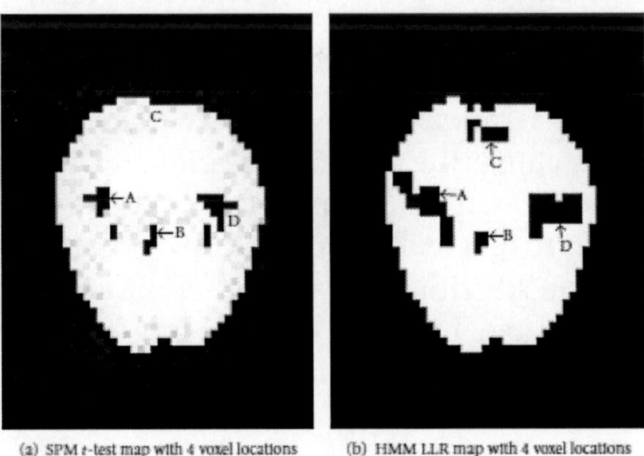

(a) SPM t-test map with 4 voxel locations (b) HMM LLR map with 4 voxel locations

Figure 3: Glass map for SPM t-test and HMM likelihood ratio and 4 voxel time series. "A" and "B" are detected by both SPM and HMM methods, while "C" and "D" are only detected by the HMM log-likelihood ratio method.

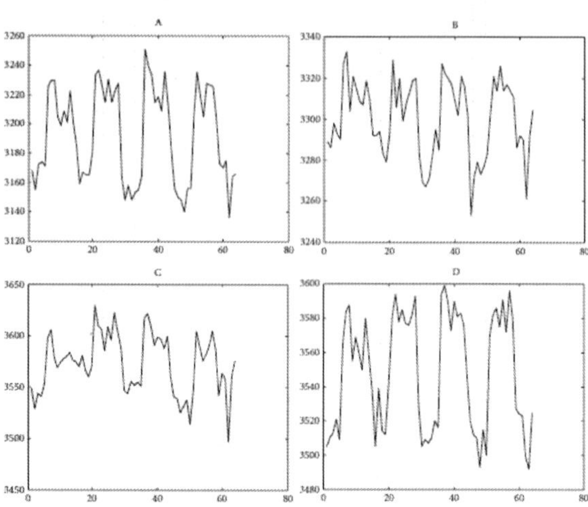

Figure 4: The time series of four active voxels. "A" and "B" are detected by both SPM and HMM methods, while "C" and "D" are only detected by the HMM log-likelihood ratio method.

Brain Tumor Subject

Functional MRI is not only used for normal brain function mapping, it is also widely used for neurosurgical planning and neurologic risk assessment in the treatment of brain tumors. The growth of a tumor can cause functional areas to shift from their original locations. Large tumors can cause these critical regions to shift dramatically. Localizing the motor strip and coregistering the results to a surgical scan prior to a neurosurgical intervention can help guide the direct cortical stimulation during an awake craniotomy and possibly shorten operation time. In some cases, using fMRI to confirm the expected location of the motor strip may avoid awake neurosurgery altogether.

The HRF for brain tumor patient is more complicated than that for normal healthy subjects. We compare our unsupervised 2 -state HMM model with GLM-based SPM on brain tumor patient and found 2 -state HMM model is more robust to HRF and it is more sensitive in detecting supplemental motor activation.

The machine specification and the functional data acquisition for a tumor patient is the same as for the normal subject described above. The experiment design is different. The test is self-paced bilateral sequential thumb-to-digits opposition task. The task paradigm consists of a 2 0 sec baseline followed by 4 cycles of 2 0 sec ON and 2 0 sec off. Each point is 2 sec for a total of 3 min. The time series is totally 9 0 time samples for each voxel. The first 3 samples are ignored during analysis because of initial unstable measurement. The patient has a tumor on his left frontal lobe. As seen in the high resolution fMRI image in Figure 5(a).

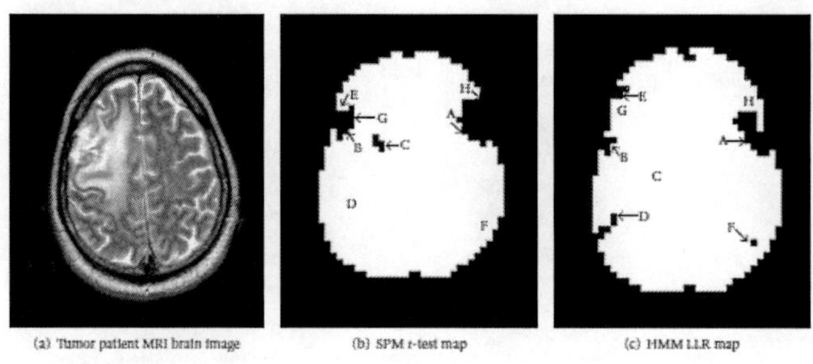

Figure 5: Tumor patient high-resolution image and glass maps for SPM test and 2-state HMM likelihood ratio test. The patient has a tumor on his left frontal lobe from (a). No supplemental voxels from SPM t-test (b). "D" and "F" are supplemental voxels detected from HMM LLR map in (c).

Figure 5(b) is a thresholded SPM t-test map, both left and right motor areas are detected by SPM and there is no supplemental voxels. SPM t-test shows that the tumor does not impact the patient's motor area. Thresholded HMM likelihood ratio test result shown in Figure 5(c) indicates some weak motor activation in the left side motor area. In addition, there are some supplemental motor activation detected on surrounding areas. We further study several active voxels from Figures 5(b) and 5(c). The locations of selected active voxels are marked as "A," "B," "C," "D," "E." "F," "G," and "H" in each figures, respectively. The corresponding voxel time series are shown from Figure 6. From these results, we can see that there are three types of voxels. The voxels "A" and "B" are detected by both SPM and

HMM likelihood ratio test, which exhibit strong activation patterns. Voxels "C", "G," and "H" are detected only by SPM, and in fact they are either very weak activations or false positives. Voxels "D," "E," and "F" are detected only in HMM likelihood ratio test and their time series have strong activation patterns related to the paradigm but with different delay and dispersion. These results reaffirmed our understanding that SPM has difficulty in locating active voxels with unexpected delay and dispersion behaviors.

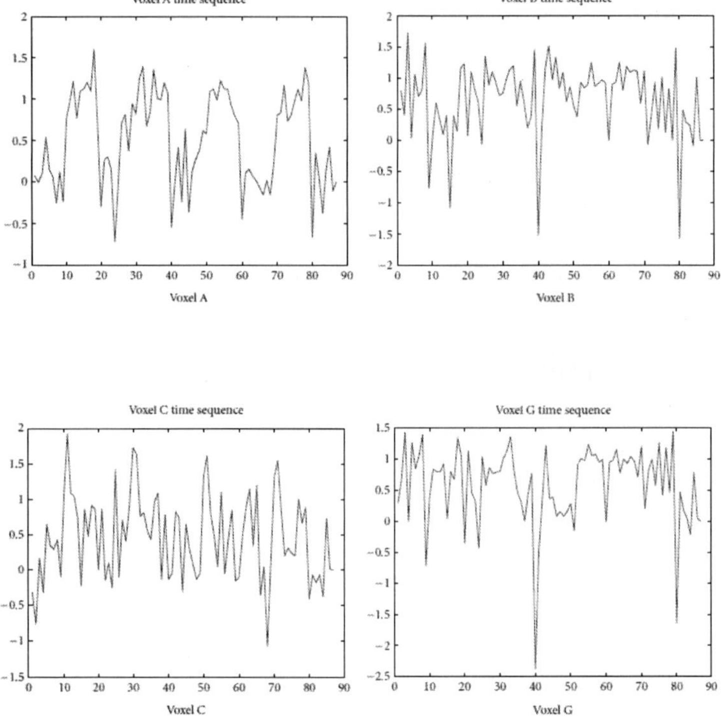

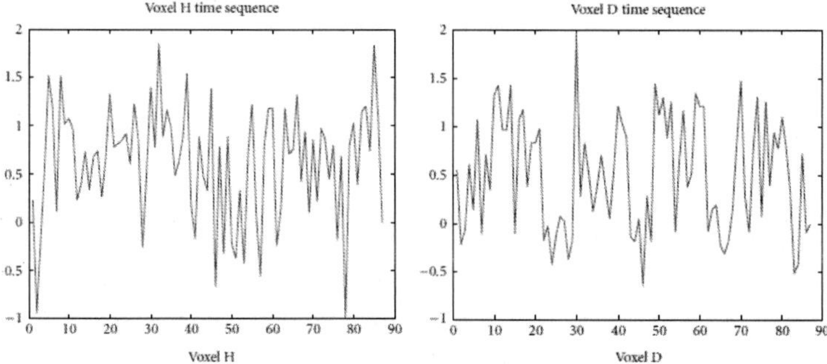

Figure 6: Voxel time series, voxels "A" and "B" are detected by both SPM t-test and 2-state HMM likelihood ratio test; voxels "C," "G," and "H" are detected by SPM t-test only. "D," "E," and "F" are detected by 2-state HMM likelihood ratio test only.

CONCLUSION REMARKS AND FUTURE WORKS

In this paper we have presented HMM-based method to detect active voxels in fMRI data. A 2 -state HMM model is built based on paradigm on/off periods, and a 1-state HMM model is built based on paradigm off period. A log-likelihood ratio map is generated using the two log-likelihoods. Viterbi path is obtained for the 2 -state HMM model. According to the Viterbi path, t-test map and KLD map are generated. From experiments we see that HMM methods are as effective as SPM method, and sometime HMM methods can detect supplemental active voxels that SPM may miss, especially in complicated cases with such as tumor patients. Overall we consider that the HMM methods are complementary to the SPM method, because SPM focuses on capturing fMRI signal waveform characteristics while HMM method attempts to describe fMRI signal stochastic behaviors. In other words, the HMM methods can provide a second opinion to the SPM test results, which can be very helpful in practical situations.

REFERENCES

1. M. W. Woolrich, T. E. J. Behrens, and S. M. Smith, "Constrained linear basis sets for HRF modelling using Variational Bayes," NeuroImage, vol. 21, no. 4,

pp. 1748–1761, 2004.

2. P. Ciuciu, J. B. Poline, G. Marrelec, J. Idier, C. Pallier, and H. Benali, "Unsupervised robust nonparametric estimation of the hemodynamic response function for any fMRI experiment," IEEE Transactions on Medical Imaging, vol. 22, no. 10, pp. 1235–1251, 2003.
3. L. Lee, L. M. Harrison, and A. Mechelli, "A report of the functional connectivity workshop, Dusseldorf 2002," NeuroImage, vol. 19, no. 2, pp. 457–465, 2003.
4. K. Li, L. Guo, J. Nie, G. Li, and T. Liu, "Review of methods for functional brain connectivity detection using fMRI," Computerized Medical Imaging and Graphics, vol. 33, no. 2, pp. 131–139, 2009.
5. K. J. Friston, A. P. Holmes, K. J. Worsley, J. P. Poline, C. D. Frith, and R. S. J. Frackowiak, "Statistical parametric maps in functional imaging: a general linear approach," Human Brain Mapping, vol. 2, no. 4, pp. 189–210, 1994.
6. M. D. Greicius, B. Krasnow, A. L. Reiss, and V. Menon, "Functional connectivity in the resting brain: a network analysis of the default mode hypothesis," Proceedings of the National Academy of Sciences of the United States of America, vol. 100, no. 1, pp. 253–258, 2003.
7. J. Ashburner, "Spm:a history," NeuroImage, vol. 62, no. 2, pp. 791–800, 2012.
8. G. K. Wood, "Visualization of subtle contrast-related intensity changes using temporal correlation," Magnetic Resonance Imaging, vol. 12, no. 7, pp. 1013–1020, 1994.
9. J. Cao and K. Worsley, "The geometry of correlation fields with an application to functional connectivity of the brain," Annals of Applied Probability, vol. 9, no. 4, pp. 1021–1057, 1999.
10. P. Hojen-Sorensen, L. Hansen, and C. Rasmussen, "Baysian modelling of fmri time series," in Proceedings of the 13th Annual Conference on Advances in Neural Information Processing Systems (NIPS '99), pp. 754–760, 2000.
11. C. Gossl, D. Auer, and L. Fahtmeir, "Dynamic models in fmri," Magnetic Resonance in Medicine, vol. 43, no. 1, pp. 72–81, 2000.
12. M. Singh, W. Sungkarat, J. W. Jeong, and Y. Zhou, "Extraction of temporal information in functional MRI," IEEE Transactions on Nuclear Science, vol. 49, no. 5, pp. 2284–2290, 2002.
13. V. Sanguineti, C. Parodi, S. Perissinotto et al., "Analysis of fMRI time series with mixtures of Gaussians," in Proceedings of the International Joint Conference on Neural Networks (IJCNN '2000), vol. 1, pp. 331–335, July 2000.
14. S. Faisan, L. Thoraval, J. P. Armspach, and F. Heitz, "Unsupervised learning and mapping of brain fMRI signals based on hidden semi-Markov event sequence models," in Proceedings of the 6th International Conference on Medical Image Computing and Computer-Assisted Intervention (MICCAI '03), pp. 75–82, November 2003.
15. B. Thirion and O. Faugeras, "Revisiting non-parametric activation detection on fMRI time series," in Proceedings of the IEEE Workshop on Mathematical Methods in Biomedical Image Analysis, vol. 1, pp. 121–128, December 2001.

16. M. W. Woolrich, M. Jenkinson, J. M. Brady, and S. M. Smith, "Fully bayesian spatio-temporal modeling of FMRI data," IEEE Transactions on Medical Imaging, vol. 23, no. 2, pp. 213–231, 2004.
17. Roebroeck, E. Formisano, and R. Goebel, "Mapping directed influence over the brain using Granger causality and fMRI," NeuroImage, vol. 25, no. 1, pp. 230–242, 2005.
18. K. J. Friston, L. Harrison, and W. Penny, "Dynamic causal modelling," NeuroImage, vol. 19, no. 4, pp. 1273–1302, 2003.
19. K. Friston, "Dynamic causal modeling and Granger causality comments on: the identification of interacting networks in the brain using fMRI: model selection, causality and deconvolution," NeuroImage, vol. 58, pp. 303–305, 2011. View at Publisher · View at Google Scholar · View at Scopus
20. O. David, "fMRI connectivity, meaning and empiricism. Comments on: Roebroeck et al. The identification of interacting networks in the brain using fMRI: model selection, causality and deconvolution," NeuroImage, vol. 58, pp. 306–309, 2011.
21. Roebroeck, E. Formisano, and R. Goebel, "Reply to Friston and David. After comments on: the identification of interacting networks in the brain using fMRI: model selection, causality and deconvolution," NeuroImage, vol. 58, pp. 296–302, 2011.
22. Roebroeck, E. Formisano, and R. Goebel, "Reply to Friston and David. After comments on: the identification of interacting networks in the brain using fMRI: model selection, causality and deconvolution," NeuroImage, vol. 58, pp. 310–311, 2011.
23. G. Lohmann, K. Erfurth, K. Mller, and R. Turner, "Critical comments on dynamic causal modelling," NeuroImage, vol. 59, pp. 2322–2329, 2012.
24. M. Mckeown, S. Makeig, G. Brown et al., "Analysis of fmri data by blind seperation into independent spatial components," Human Brain Mapping, vol. 6, pp. 160–188, 1998.
25. B. Biswal and J. L. Ulmer, "Blind source separation of multiple signal sources of fMRI data sets using independent component analysis," Journal of Computer Assisted Tomography, vol. 23, no. 2, pp. 265–271, 1999.
26. V. D. Calhoun, T. Adali, G. D. Pearlson, and J. J. Pekar, "Spatial and temporal independent component analysis of functional MRI data containing a pair of task-related waveforms," Human Brain Mapping, vol. 13, no. 1, pp. 43–53, 2001.
27. J. V. Stone, J. Porrill, N. R. Porter, and I. D. Wilkinson, "Spatiotemporal independent component analysis of event-related fMRI data using skewed probability density functions," NeuroImage, vol. 15, no. 2, pp. 407–421, 2002.
28. J. Bell and T. J. Sejnowski, "An information-maximization approach to blind separation and blind deconvolution," Neural Computation, vol. 7, no. 6, pp. 1129–1159, 1995.
29. F. J. Theis, P. Gruber, I. R. Keck, and E. W. Lang, "A robust model for spatiotemporal dependencies," Neurocomputing, vol. 71, no. 10–12, pp.

2209–2216, 2008.

30. G. McLachlan and D. Peel, Finite Mixture Models, John Wiley & Sons, New York, NY, USA, 2000.
31. L. R. Rabiner, "Tutorial on hidden Markov models and selected applications in speech recognition," Proceedings of the IEEE, vol. 77, no. 2, pp. 257–286, 1989.
32. G. Xu, Y. F. Ma, H. J. Zhang, and S. Q. Yang, "An HMM-based framework for video semantic analysis," IEEE Transactions on Circuits and Systems for Video Technology, vol. 15, no. 11, pp. 1422–1433, 2005.
33. Krogh, M. Brown, I. S. Mian, K. Sjolander, and D. Haussler, "Hidden Markov Models in computational biology applications to protein modeling," Journal of Molecular Biology, vol. 235, no. 5, pp. 1501–1531, 1994.
34. R. Durbin, S. Eddy, A. Krogh, and G. Mitchison, Biological Sequence Analysis: Probabilistic Models of Proteins and Nucleic Acids, Cambridge University Press, 1999.
35. Miller, T. Leek, and R. Schwartz, "A hidden markov model information retrieval system," in Proceedings of the 22nd Annual International ACM SIGIR Conference on Research and Development in Information Retrieval, pp. 214–221, ACM, 1999.
36. G. D. Forney, "The viterbi algorithm," Proceedings of the IEEE, vol. 61, no. 3, pp. 268–278, 1973.
37. S. Kullback and R. Leibler, "On information and sufficiency," Annals of Mathematical Statistics, vol. 22, no. 1, pp. 79–86, 1951.

Citations

CHAPTER 1

Shingo Noguchi and Osana Yuko, Improved Kohonen Feature Map Probabilistic Associative Memory Based on Weights Distribution, DOI: 10.5772/51581

CHAPTER 2

Vladimir M. Krasnopolsky, Michael S. Fox-Rabinovitz, and Alexei A. Belochitski, "Using Ensemble of Neural Networks to Learn Stochastic Convection Parameterizations for Climate and Numerical Weather Prediction Models from Data Simulated by a Cloud Resolving Model," Advances in Artificial Neural Systems, vol. 2013, Article ID 485913, 13 pages, 2013. doi:10.1155/2013/485913

CHAPTER 3

Quoc-Huy Phan, Su-Lim Tan, Ian McLoughlin, and Duc-Lung Vu, "A Unified Framework for GPS Code and Carrier-Phase Multipath Mitigation Using Support Vector Regression," Advances in Artificial Neural Systems, vol. 2013, Article ID 240564, 14 pages, 2013. doi:10.1155/2013/240564

CHAPTER 4

Deepti Moyi Sahoo and S. Chakraverty, "Fuzzified Data Based Neural Network Modeling for Health Assessment of Multistorey Shear Buildings," Advances in Artificial Neural Systems, vol. 2013, Article ID 962734, 12 pages, 2013. doi:10.1155/2013/962734

CHAPTER 5

Susmita Mall and S. Chakraverty, "Comparison of Artificial Neural Network Architecture in Solving Ordinary Differential Equations," Advances in Artificial Neural Systems, vol. 2013, Article ID 181895, 12 pages, 2013. doi:10.1155/2013/181895.

CHAPTER 6

Pradyut Kundu, Anupam Debsarkar, and Somnath Mukherjee, "Artificial Neural Network Modeling for Biological Removal of Organic Carbon and Nitrogen from Slaughterhouse Wastewater in a Sequencing Batch Reactor," Advances in Artificial Neural Systems, vol. 2013, Article ID 268064, 15 pages, 2013. doi:10.1155/2013/268064

CHAPTER 7

Satchidananda Dehuri, "A Novel Learning Scheme for Chebyshev Functional Link Neural Networks," Advances in Artificial Neural Systems, vol. 2011, Article ID 107498, 10 pages, 2011. doi:10.1155/2011/107498.

CHAPTER 8

Rong Duan and Hong Man, "Activation Detection on fMRI Time Series Using Hidden Markov Model," Advances in Artificial Neural Systems, vol. 2012, Article ID 190359, 12 pages, 2012. doi:10.1155/2012/190359

INDEX

D

E

F

G

H

K

L

V

W